POSTCARD HISTORY SERIES

Knoxville

TENNESSEE

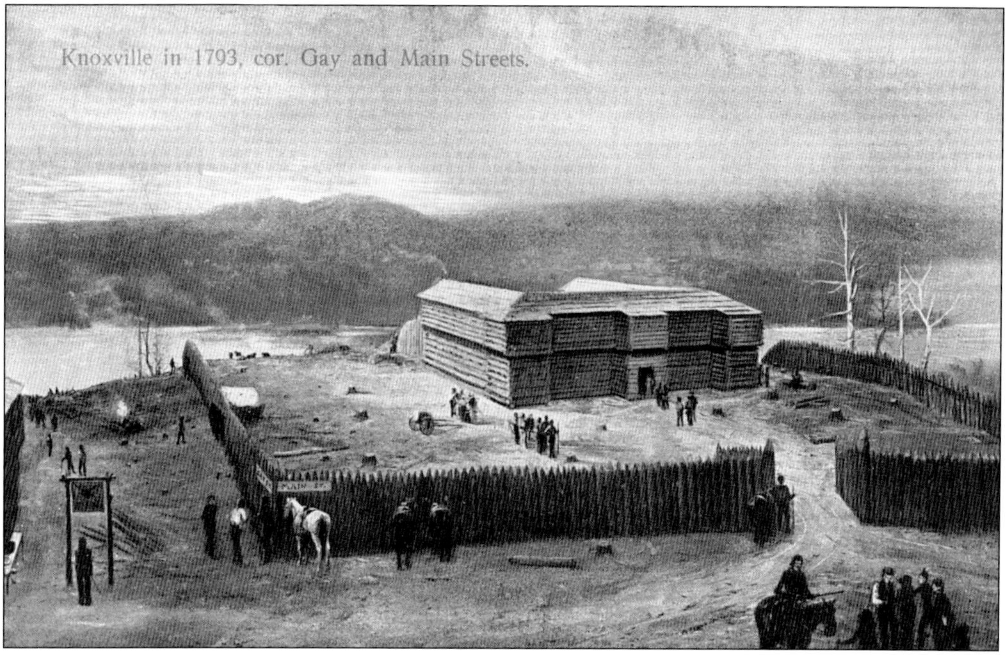

KNOXVILLE IN 1793, CORNER OF GAY AND MAIN STREETS. (Published by International Post Card Co., New York; card sent 1915.) In 1792 the U.S. Army built a large blockhouse fort, located where the Knox County Courthouse now stands, to protect Knoxville from the Creek and Cherokee Indians. The painting on the postcard is by Lloyd Branson (1854–1925), who painted it in 1901. The original now hangs in the East Tennessee Historical Center in Knoxville.

POSTCARD HISTORY SERIES

Knoxville
TENNESSEE

Elena Irish Zimmerman

ARCADIA
PUBLISHING

ISBN 978-0-7385-8987-9

Published by Arcadia Publishing
Charleston, South Carolina

Printed in the United States of America

Library of Congress Catalog Card Number: 98-85882

For all general information contact Arcadia Publishing at:
Telephone 843-853-2070
Fax 843-853-0044
E-mail sales@arcadiapublishing.com
For customer service and orders:
Toll-Free 1-888-313-2665

Visit us on the Internet at www.arcadiapublishing.com

This book is for my long-esteemed friends and fellow postcard collectors Les Lebo and Milton Hinshilwood.

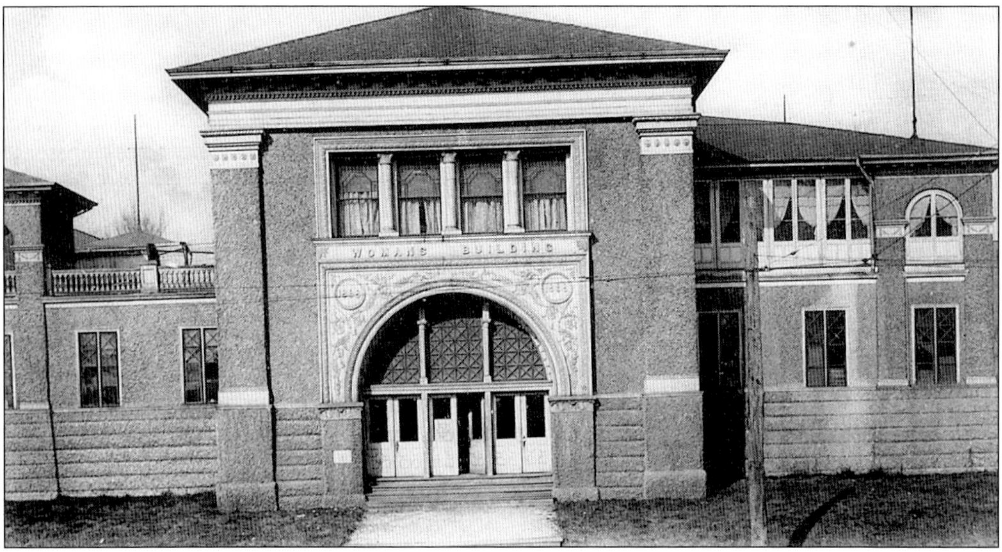

THE KNOXVILLE WOMAN'S BUILDING. (Published by Rotograph Company, New York; photograph taken pre-1906.) Originally the Knoxville Building in the Tennessee Centennial in Nashville (1897), it was moved in 1898, at the instigation of several Knox County women's organizations, from the Nashville Exposition grounds to Knoxville's Main Avenue just opposite the courthouse. Its life there was short; it burned in 1906.

Contents

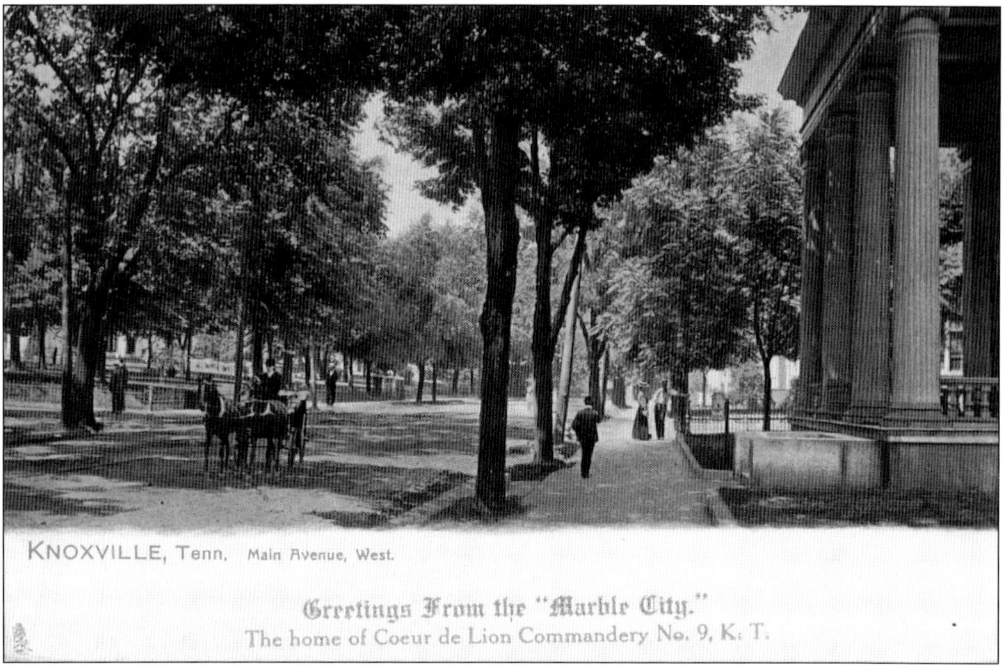

MAIN AVENUE, WEST. (Published by Raphael Tuck and Sons, London; series 2465.) This early view of one of Knoxville's fine residential areas is overprinted with a "greeting" from a local organization. Before 1933, when their block was cleared for the new post office, the McTeer, Lewis, Ault, and Nash homes stood on the north side of Main. At this end of the street the stately columns of Col. J.Y. Johnston's residence can be seen at right.

Acknowledgments

I am grateful to the people who have helped me assemble these postcards, and to those who have supplied me with elusive information. Especially I want to thank Les Lebo and Milton Hinshilwood, who have generously allowed me to use a number of cards from their collections and whose fund of knowledge about historic Knoxville was invaluable. I also want to thank Betty Curtis, for the loan of cards and her helpful input whenever needed; Marty and Larry Acuff, for their willingness to share their cards and their expertise; Rodney Snow, for his time spent on my behalf; Dr. J.C. Tumblin, for information about S.B. Luttrell; and Robert Booker, whose knowledge of Knoxville's black community was enormously helpful.

Elena Irish Zimmerman
June 1998

Introduction

This book is a glance backward into the history of Knoxville, Tennessee, as it was pictured on postcards between 1900 and 1940. It is meant to be more atmospheric than chronological, though the presentation of history is of prime importance.

Postcards came into use in the United States in 1893, providing an endless variety of images which, in the early years, cost a penny and could be mailed for a penny. Millions upon millions have been sent. In spite of escalating postage prices through the years, the postcard is still a convenience less expensive than a letter, conveying a picture along with its message.

The postcard has always been a special mail messenger which says to someone at a distance, "I was here; wish you could be here, too." The unique or picturesque aspects of a given city have always been photographed or drawn by postcard artists for out-of-town distribution; therefore, most cards show public buildings and beautiful vistas rather than individuals.

Postcards, then, are valuable as visual records of the decade in which they were printed. Senders of cards have usually thought of them as souvenirs of vacation experiences to be sent home to family and friends; however, cards have always fulfilled the historical role revealing life as it was at a particular spot in time. Cards have pictured, in addition to buildings and streets, political campaigns, wars, expositions, disasters, and famous people. They offer implicit comment on the social, ethical, and aesthetic values of the age, and they illustrate business conditions and attitudes of people toward all the activities of their lives—in their religion, amusements, art, fashion, and humor. Most are professionally photographed; however, some are amateur efforts which show more personal activities of a family or a group, such as a graduation, a picnic, or a reunion.

Before World War I (1914–18) the postcards printed in America and England were often sent to Germany for the coloring processes of which the

German printers were masters; the methods were different then and much hand work was involved. Some elaborate cards had additions of gold, tinsel, sequins, and other hand-applied decorations. This artistic detail was lost to us when the United States went to war with Germany, and after 1920 a new type of American postcard appeared. By the 1930s the texture of many cards looked like linen (aptly named "linens"), and the application of color was crude and many times garish. Linens, however, are now becoming valuable in their own right, and since 1939 the chromes produced by modern color photography have their own beauty.

The special antique aspects of the 1900–18 cards make them valuable collectors' items today, their value depending, of course, on their rarity and condition. Some collectors insist that unused cards in mint condition are the most collectible, while others (this writer included) prefer used cards with postmark (to validate year of mailing), stamp, and message from the sender to add qualities of historical and human interest.

The Knoxville cards pictured here come from a collection of about 1,000 owned by the author, with a few borrowed from collector friends. Most of them were sent between the years 1905 and 1940. The author obtained them over a period of about 20 years by attendance at many antique shows, searching for them at flea markets, and by auction bidding through periodicals.

Postcards illuminate for us the lives of the senders as well as those of the recipients. Each 3-by-5-inch card, used or unused, furnishes a precise dated segment of history and social life; furthermore, its illustration often reveals an example of memorable art or photography. Its message reveals the human concerns of the sender. In accumulation, postcards form a panorama of history. It is the author's hope that this collection of Knoxville images will evoke portions of the city's past life, and that the reader will enjoy the reminiscence as much as the author has in the preparation of it.

A Look at Knoxville History

Knoxville, Tennessee, a city surrounded by wondrous natural beauty, sits on the bank of the Tennessee River, which is formed 4 miles east by the junction of the Holston and the French Broad. The city extends from the river to the nearby hills, with the Great Smoky Mountains in the distance.

The city was first laid out in 1791 by Charles McClung, who surveyed the town site for his father-in-law, James White. In 1786 White had built a log cabin on a hill near the present downtown area and had become the first permanent settler of Knoxville. Later he added three more cabins and connected the four by a palisade of logs, making the frontier outpost known as White's fort.

William Blount, governor of the Territory South of the River Ohio, came to Tennessee in 1790 and established his headquarters at White's fort. At Blount's suggestion, White laid out streets, and the new town was named Knoxville in honor of Maj. Gen. Henry Knox, secretary of war. In 1796 Tennessee was admitted to the Union, with Knoxville as its first state capital. State government was moved to Nashville in 1812.

For the first ten years Knoxville was a frontier town on the south fork of the Wilderness Road, where frontiersmen stopped to buy supplies on their way west. One early visitor remarked that on County Court Day he observed "men jesting, singing, swearing . . . Negroes playing on their banjoes . . . and a promiscuous throng of Indians, woodsmen, and gamblers."

As time went by, Knoxville attracted people of every type—artisans, doctors, clergymen, merchants, and farmers. The growth was steady in population and in refinements of living. In 1810 the population was only 730; by 1850 it had grown to over 2,000. After the Civil War, growth was enormous with mercantile and industrial expansion, and by 1900 the city had grown to a population of 32,000.

By the mid-1800s the railroads had come, with rail connections to Chattanooga, Nashville, and Bristol; because of this traffic, Knoxville became a producer and distributor of products such as cotton textiles and clothing, marble, furniture, porcelain, flour, concrete and steel products, and agricultural implements.

The large suburbs of North and West Knoxville were annexed in 1898, and new developments were growing. Park City, Lonsdale, and Lincoln Park were residential areas, and Fountain City was expanding from its village beginnings. An extensive streetcar system, electrified in 1890, connected the business district with the neighborhoods.

Farmers produced important crops in the area: corn, wheat, hay, vegetables, and fruits such as peaches, apples, and strawberries. Livestock production developed and became important through the years.

In its first 100 years, Knoxville expanded into a bustling metropolis known as "Queen City of the Mountains." It was America's first territorial capital; it became the home of the University of Tennessee, chartered as Blount College in 1794 by the nation's first territorial legislature; it was the first capital of Tennessee (1796–1811); it was the only city that withstood a Civil War siege in 1863; and it was the site of the first National Conservation Exposition (1913).

By the 1920s Knoxville had 100 miles of paved streets and 600 miles of macadam streets. There were 14 streetcar lines, a curb market, public parks and playgrounds, first-class hotels, and 117 churches of all denominations. Special institutions included the Tennessee School for the Deaf, Eastern State Hospital, and Knoxville College for blacks. At this time the Lawson McGhee Library had a count of 145,000 volumes. Fifty-six passenger trains arrived and departed from Knoxville depots.

Since 1930 Knoxville has been known as "the Gateway to the Great Smoky Mountains National Park." Millions of tourists have visited this area since the park opened in 1934, and most of them travel through Knoxville to get there. In addition, the Tennessee Valley Authority was established in 1933 with objectives of navigation, flood control, power distribution, and soil conservation; it brought in thousands of new families. The results have impacted substantially on the cultural and economic life of the city.

Knoxville continues to grow. Its second 100 years have proven as prestigious as the first hundred.

One

History and Panorama

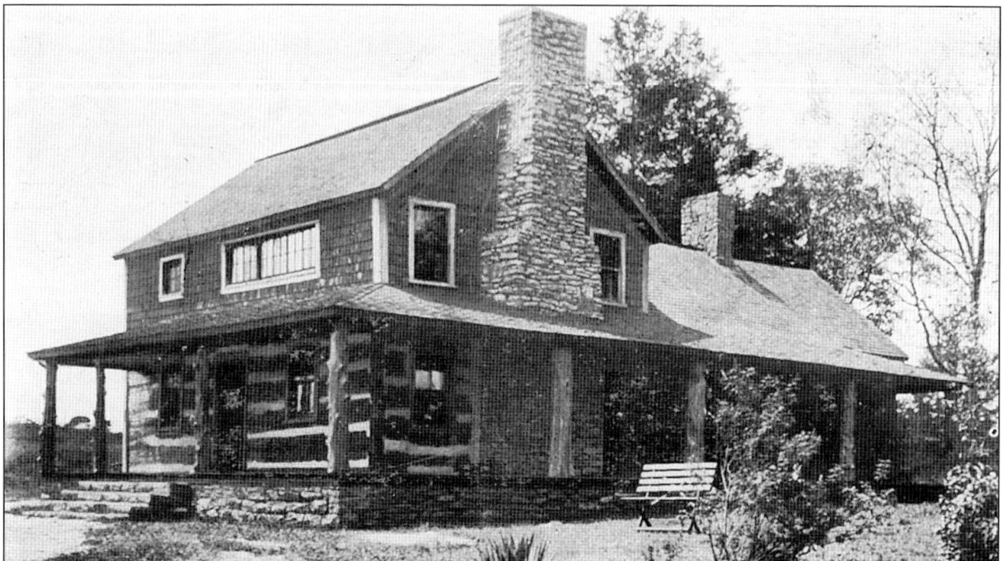

THE FIRST HOUSE IN KNOXVILLE. (No publisher or date.) The earliest building in Knoxville was the log house built in 1786 by James White. From the early 1800s until 1906 this house served as the kitchen wing of the Kennedy residence on State Street. In 1906 Isaiah Ford removed the house to Woodlawn Pike for his residence. In 1970 it was bought by the City Association of Women's Clubs and reassembled near the Coliseum.

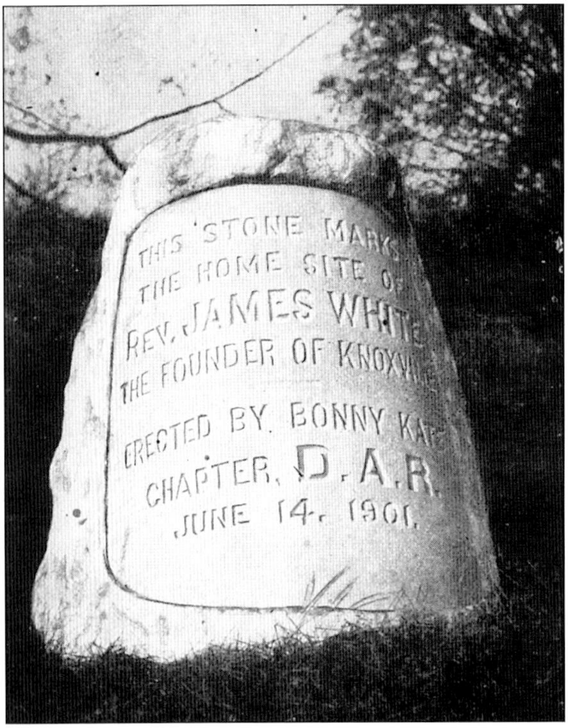

THE STONE MARKING THE HOME SITE OF THE FOUNDER OF KNOXVILLE. (Published by Reese and Reed, Knoxville; card sent 1907.) After 20 years, James White moved from his original log house to a farm east of First Creek. In 1901 the Bonny Kate Chapter of the DAR placed this marker at the site of his two-story farmhouse at 1411 Riverside Drive. This postcard identifies White as "Rev. James White." Later the inscription was changed to read "Gen. James White."

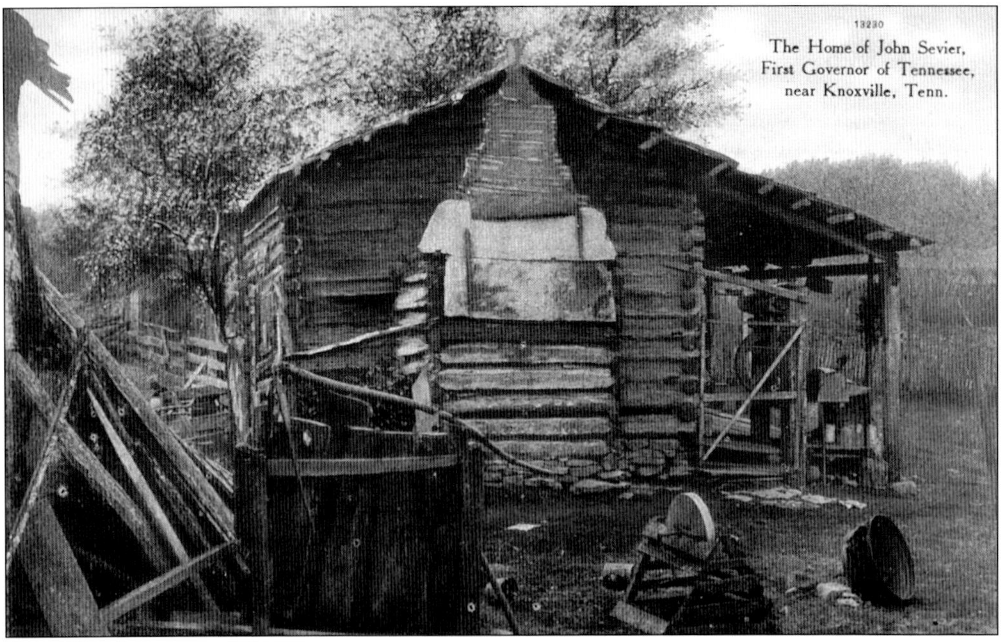

THE HOME OF JOHN SEVIER, FIRST GOVERNOR OF TENNESSEE. (No publication data.) When John Sevier became Tennessee's first governor in 1796, he chose to live in south Knox County. His "Marble Springs Plantation," located on Neubert Springs Road, is a Tennessee state shrine. Sevier died in Alabama in 1815; in 1889 his remains were interred in the Knox County Courthouse lawn. One may also see here monuments to his wives, Sarah Hawkins and Catherine "Bonny Kate" Sherrill.

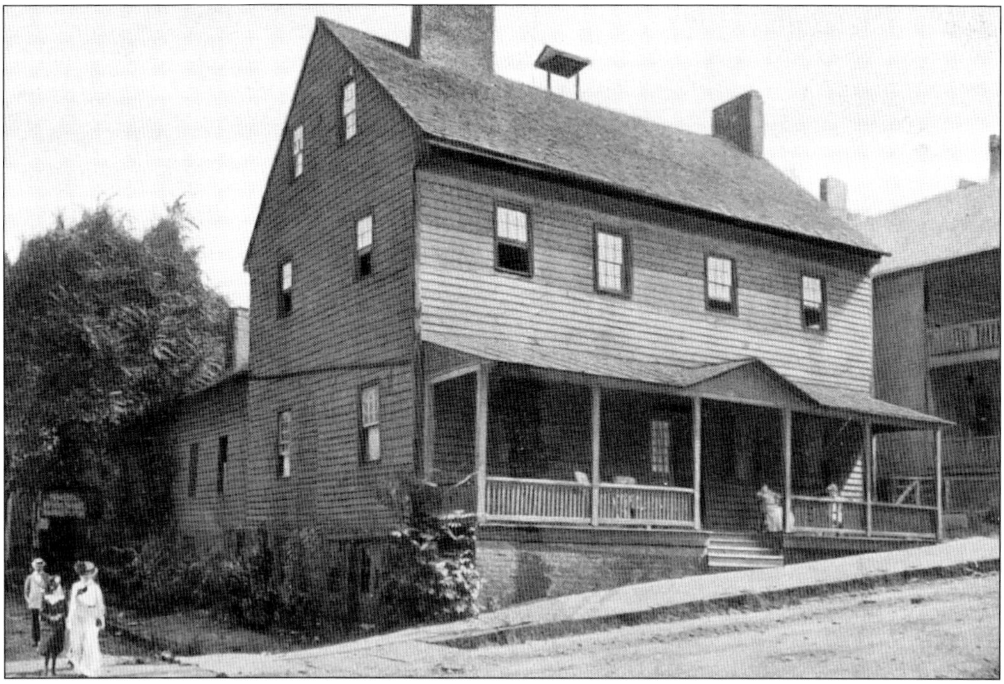

The First State Capitol. (Published by Raphael Tuck and Sons, London; series 2465; published about 1907.) John Sevier rented this house in 1797 and used it for his family as well as for transacting business of state. No capitol building was ever erected in Knoxville or was so designated; however, this dwelling did house the first state government meetings. It was located at Cumberland and Central Avenues and was torn down in 1927.

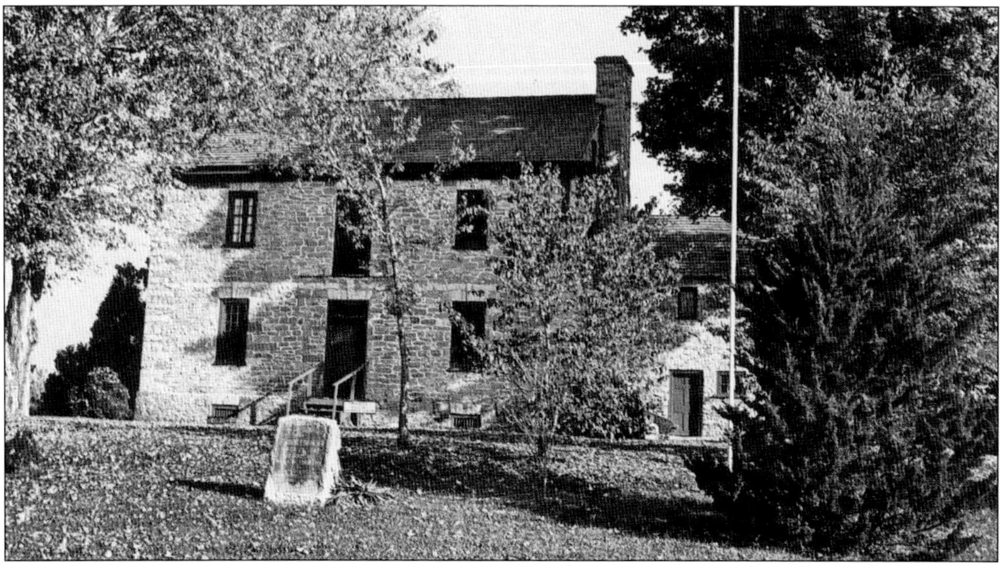

The Ramsey House. (Published by W.M. Cline Co., Gatlinburg; photo by Oscar N. Wilson.) Built in 1796 of rough cut pink marble, this house is located on Thorngrove Road. It was designed by Thomas Hope of London and built by Col. F.A. Ramsey, the surveyor who accompanied James White on his explorations here. It has been restored and is currently a historic museum.

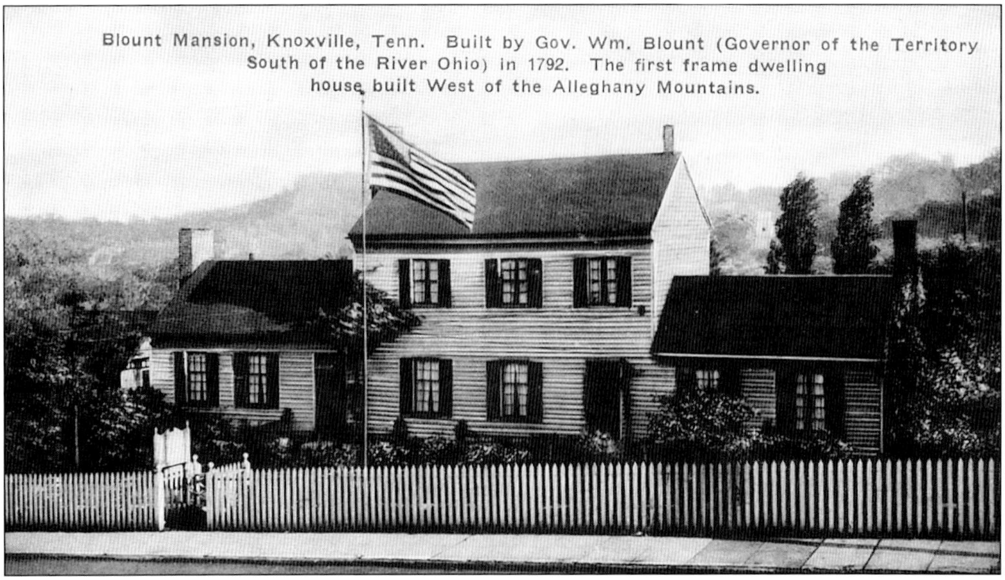

Blount Mansion. (Printed by Albertype Co., New York.) Notable as the first frame dwelling west of the Alleghenies, Blount Mansion was built in 1792, and served as the home of William Blount, governor of the Territory South of the River Ohio. All of its components were brought down the river or by pack horse from outlying districts. Located on the southwest corner of State Street and West Hill Avenue, it is of Georgian Colonial design.

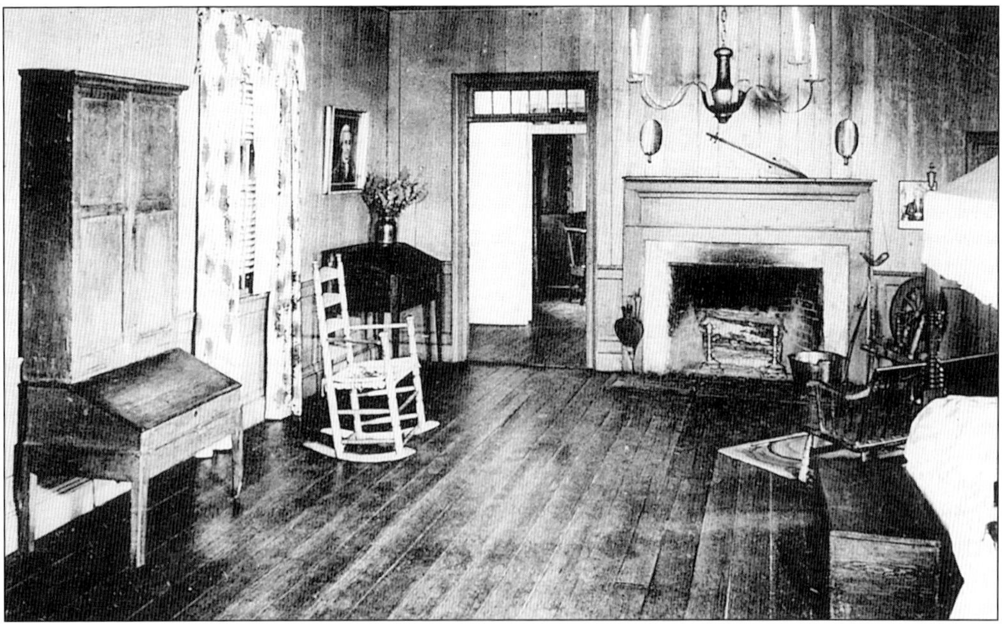

The Blount Mansion Room of State. (Published by Jim Thompson Co., Knoxville.) The walls of the mansion are of yellow pine; some boards are 16 inches deep. The mantel pieces are handmade. Several portraits occupy the walls; there is a large secretary-desk which belonged to the family of Thomas Jefferson and a dulcimer on the mantel.

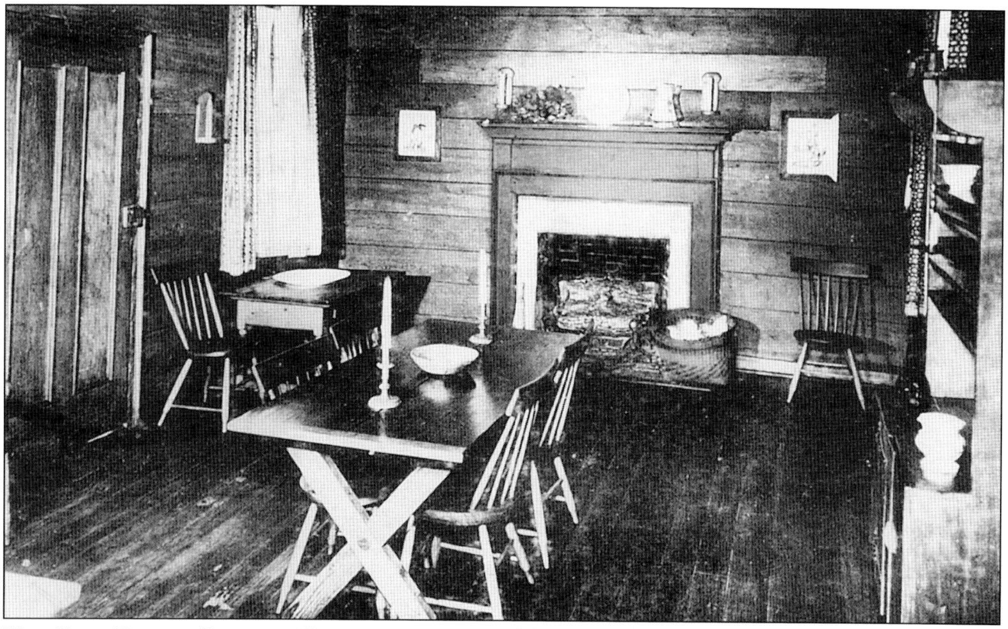

The Pine Dining Room in Blount Mansion. (Published by Jim Thompson Co., Knoxville.) The pine dining room contains a trestle table set with pewter and a hunter's board set with antique decanters and white china. A hooded cupboard contains a white porcelain soup tureen.

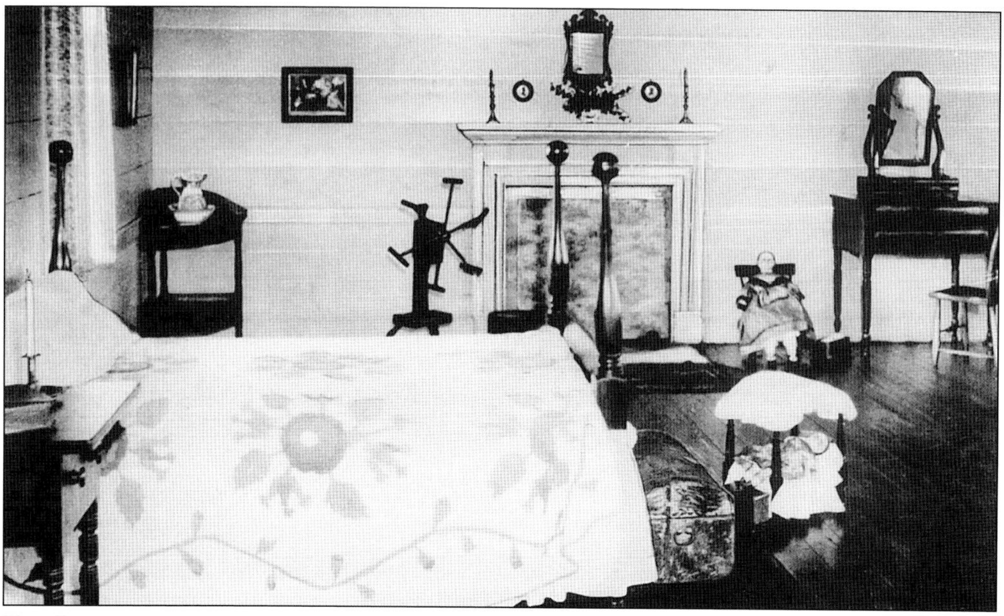

The Pioneer Bedroom in Blount Mansion. (Printed by Albertype Co., Brooklyn, NY.) The room contains a tester bed, a cradle, a chair once owned by John Adair, and two paintings by Lloyd Branson. The mansion, after decades of slow deterioration, was restored in 1925 and has been kept in repair as a historic museum.

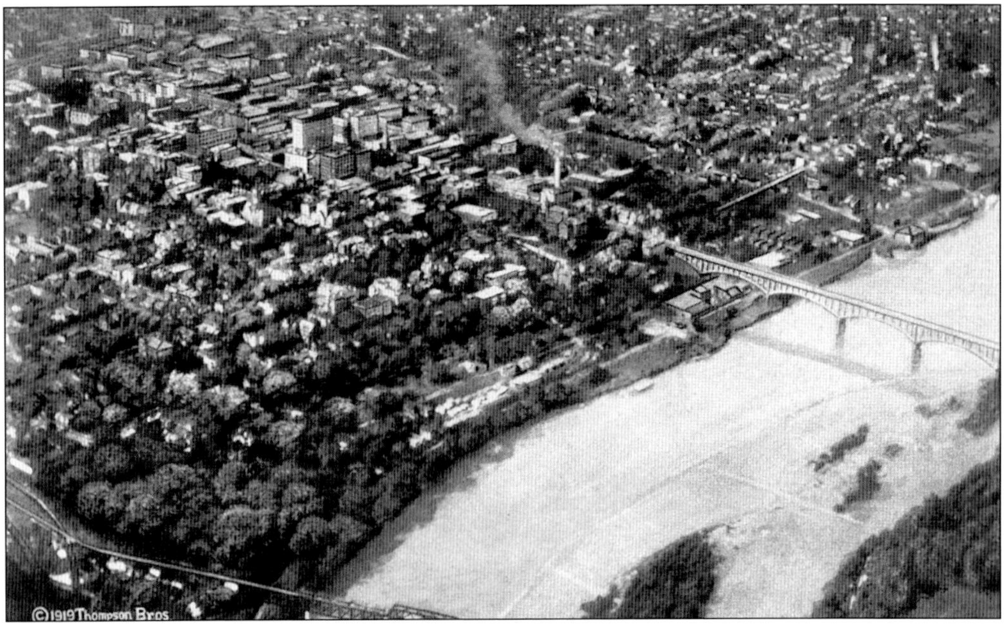

Knoxville and the Tennessee River, in a Photograph Taken by Thompson from an Aeroplane. (Published by CC&C Co. Photographed by Thompson Bros. in 1919; card sent in 1921.) This panorama of Knoxville looks northeast from the south side of the Tennessee River. The Gay Street bridge is at the right, and Holston National Bank can be seen at left center dominating the skyline.

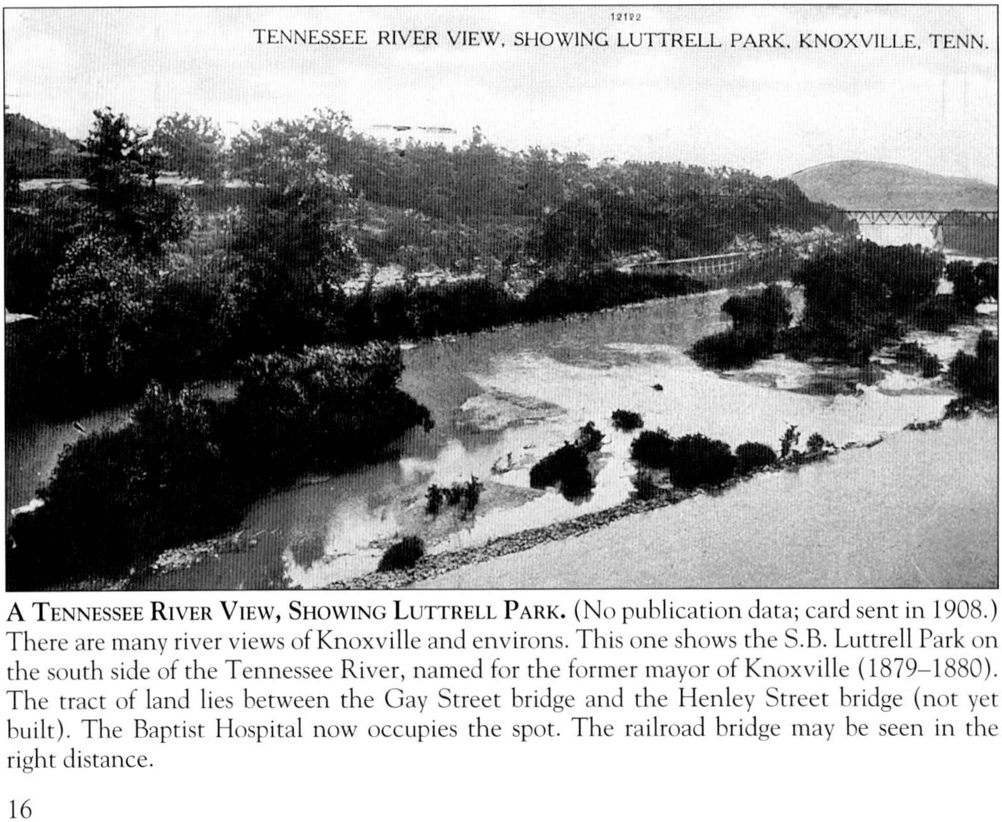

A Tennessee River View, Showing Luttrell Park. (No publication data; card sent in 1908.) There are many river views of Knoxville and environs. This one shows the S.B. Luttrell Park on the south side of the Tennessee River, named for the former mayor of Knoxville (1879–1880). The tract of land lies between the Gay Street bridge and the Henley Street bridge (not yet built). The Baptist Hospital now occupies the spot. The railroad bridge may be seen in the right distance.

Sand Barges at the Foot of Central Street. (Published by Monroe Howard Co.) Central Street runs north-south through Knoxville for many city blocks. At its south end it intersects with the Tennessee, allowing shipping to load and unload. This segment of the north side of the river also shows two houseboats (at upper center).

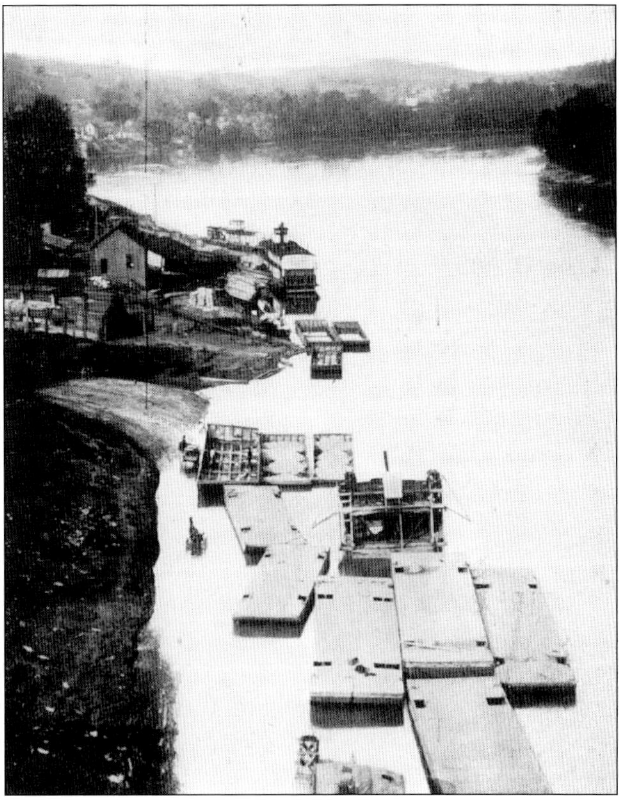

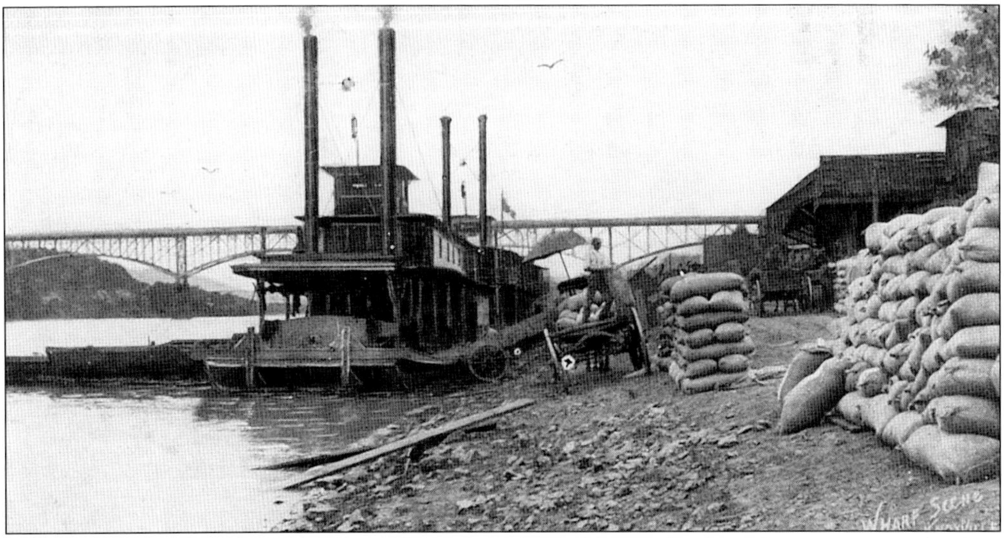

A Wharf Scene, Knoxville. (No publication data.) This early scene shows a man unloading sacks of sand or cement from his carriage with a substantial riverboat waiting for the cargo. Another carriage can be seen at right center. Riverboat traffic was always important to Knoxville's economy and recreation.

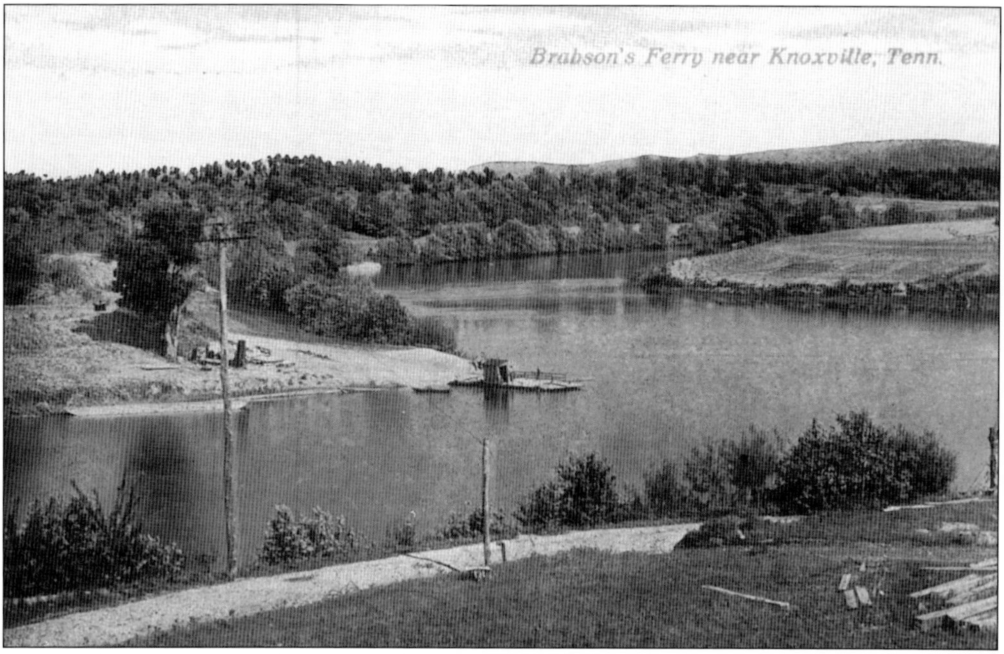

Brabson's Ferry near Knoxville. (No publication data.) Before there were bridges, there were ferryboats. The ferry at the forks of the river was the first in Knox County. This early flatbed boat provided only the most primitive accommodation.

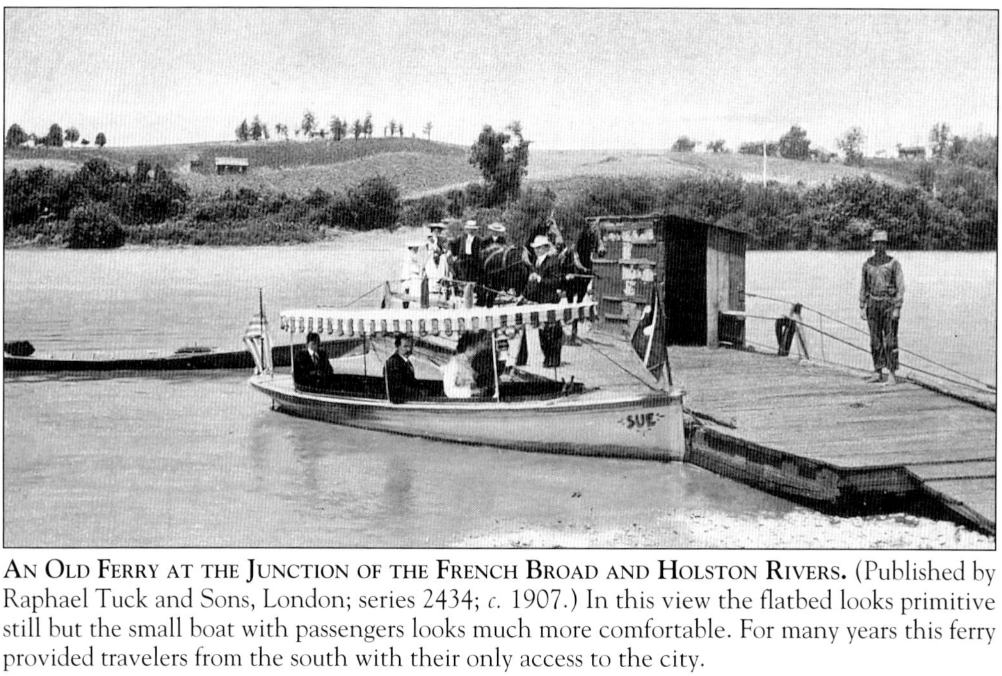

An Old Ferry at the Junction of the French Broad and Holston Rivers. (Published by Raphael Tuck and Sons, London; series 2434; *c.* 1907.) In this view the flatbed looks primitive still but the small boat with passengers looks much more comfortable. For many years this ferry provided travelers from the south with their only access to the city.

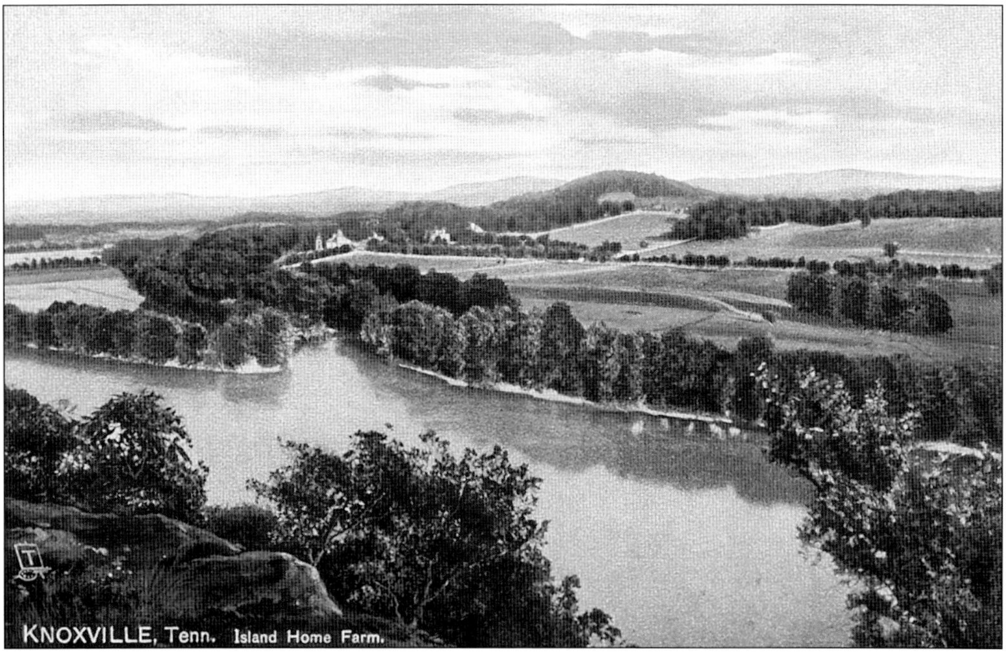

ISLAND HOME FARM. (Published by Raphael Tuck and Sons, London; series 2721; *c.* 1907.) In 1869 Perez Dickinson purchased Williams Island and began to develop the 600-acre Island Home Farm. Here he raised bumper crops and prize-winning cattle. One of Knoxville's "merchant princes," he made a fortune in the mercantile firm of Cowan and Dickinson, which later became Cowan, McClung and Co. He died in 1901 at age 88.

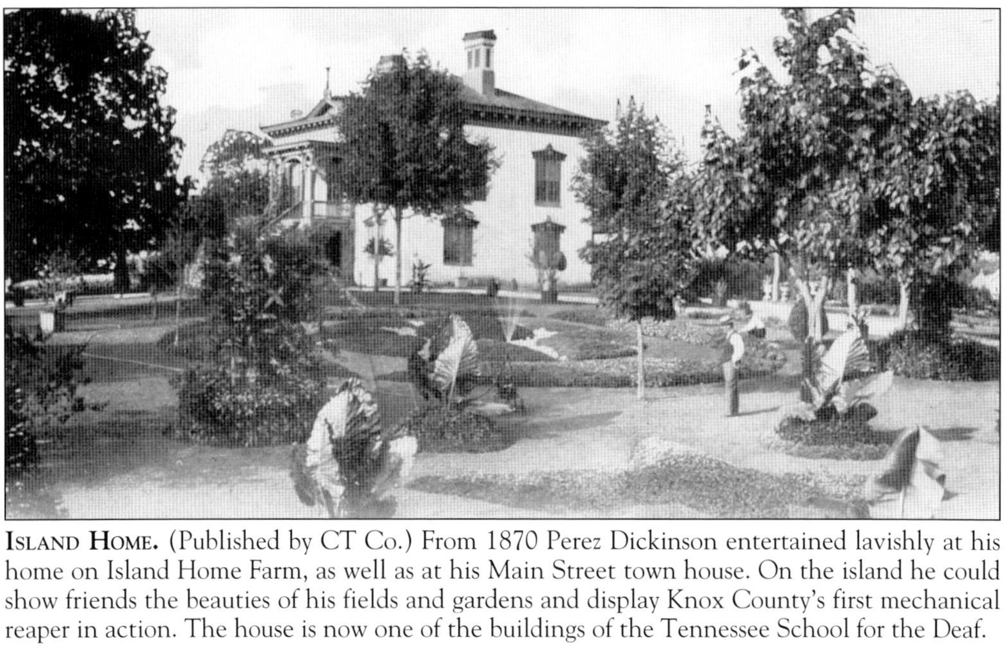

ISLAND HOME. (Published by CT Co.) From 1870 Perez Dickinson entertained lavishly at his home on Island Home Farm, as well as at his Main Street town house. On the island he could show friends the beauties of his fields and gardens and display Knox County's first mechanical reaper in action. The house is now one of the buildings of the Tennessee School for the Deaf.

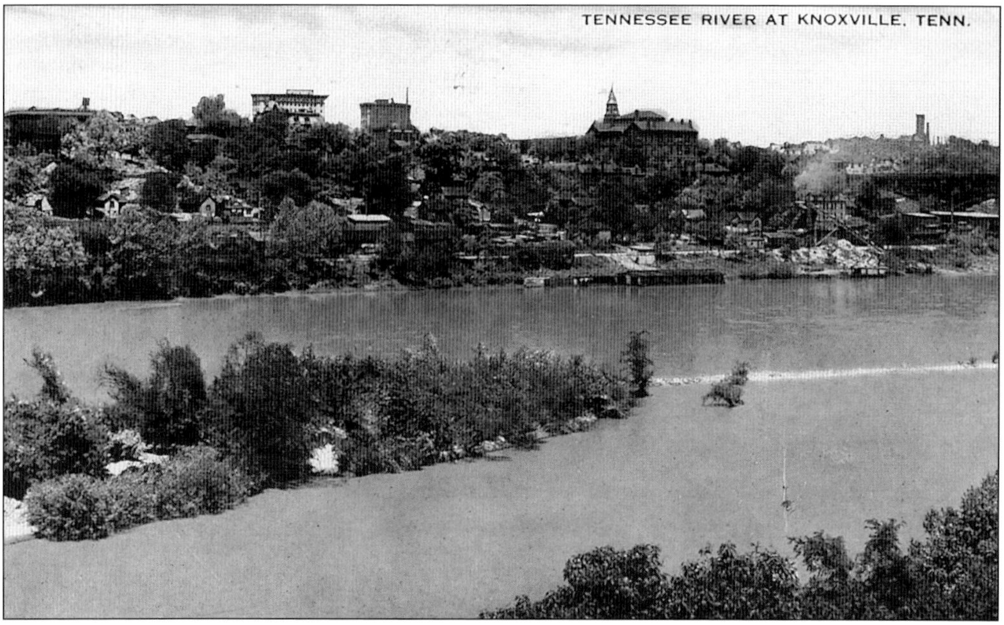

THE TENNESSEE RIVER AT KNOXVILLE. (Published by Octochrome; card sent 1916.) A river view shows Knoxville as we look north across the river just west of the Gay Street bridge, seen at the extreme right. Sand barges and river industry are at the shoreline. The County Courthouse (identified by its tower at top right) is also in view, along with the rectangular white "skyscraper" of the Holston Bank Building (at left) and the Knoxville Banking and Trust (later Burwell) Building (in the center).

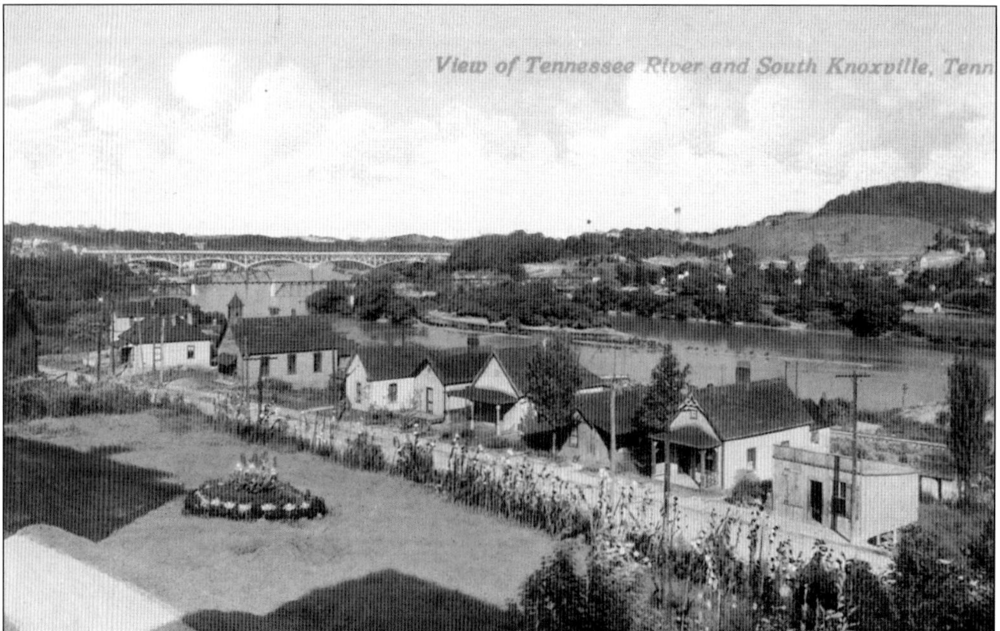

A VIEW OF THE TENNESSEE RIVER AND SOUTH KNOXVILLE. (Published by F.G. Asquith Co., Knoxville; card sent 1912.) Located somewhat east of the Gay Street bridge, a group of modest homes and a tiny church form the focus of this view south of the river.

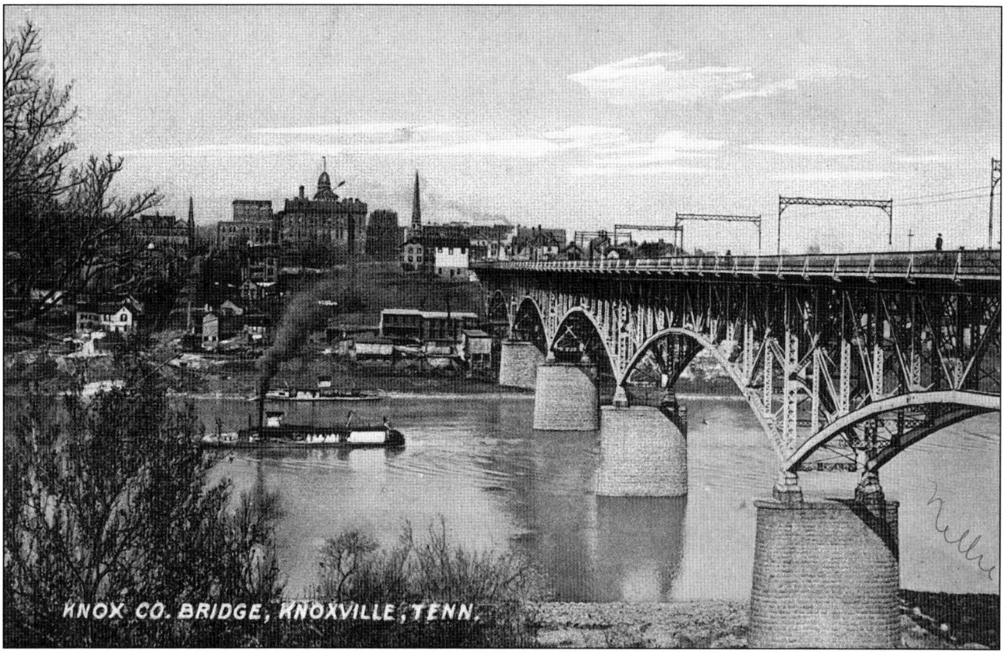

THE KNOX COUNTY BRIDGE. (Published by the Rotograph Co., 1905.) Now known as the Gay Street bridge, this structure was completed in 1898, the fourth attempt to span the river. Made of steel and concrete, it excited much admiration. It is 1,600 feet long and cost $25,000. One can see the Courthouse just across the span, as well as the spire of the First Baptist Church, then located on Gay Street.

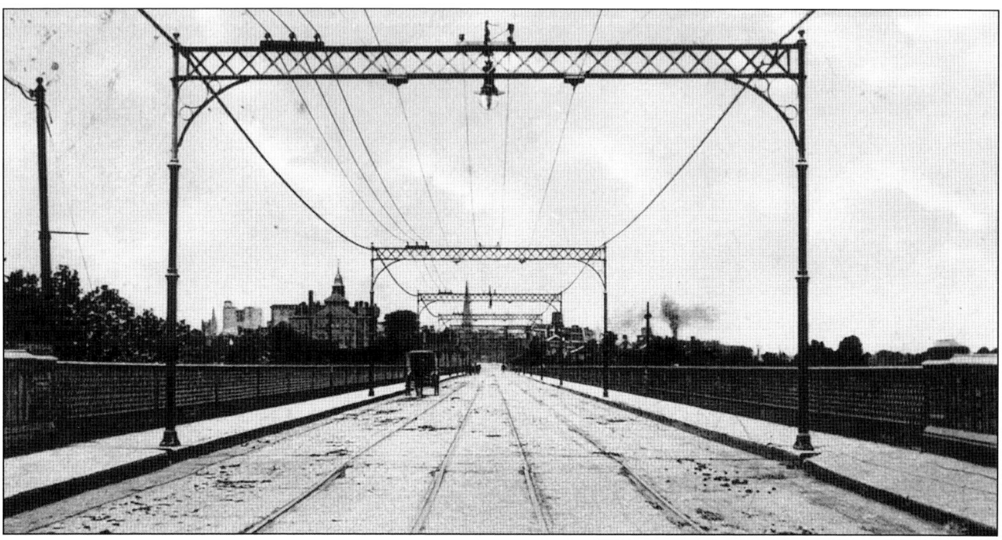

THE TENNESSEE RIVER BRIDGE. (Published by A.N.C., New York; card sent 1908.) We see here the Gay Street bridge as one saw it while crossing it in 1908. A horse and carriage are at left. There are trolley tracks and several overhead trestles to support the electric wiring. The roadbed evidently has not been cleaned for a while.

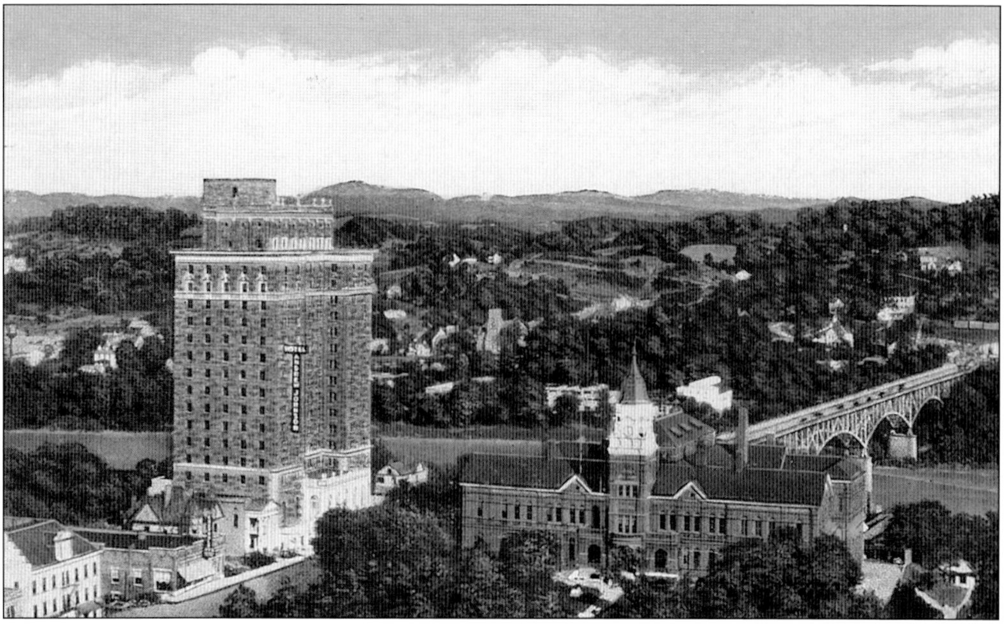

A View of the Andrew Johnson Hotel and Courthouse. (Published by Asheville Post Card Co., *c.* 1930.) From the north side of the river we see the Gay Street bridge at right and the Courthouse at near center. The Andrew Johnson Hotel towers at left center.

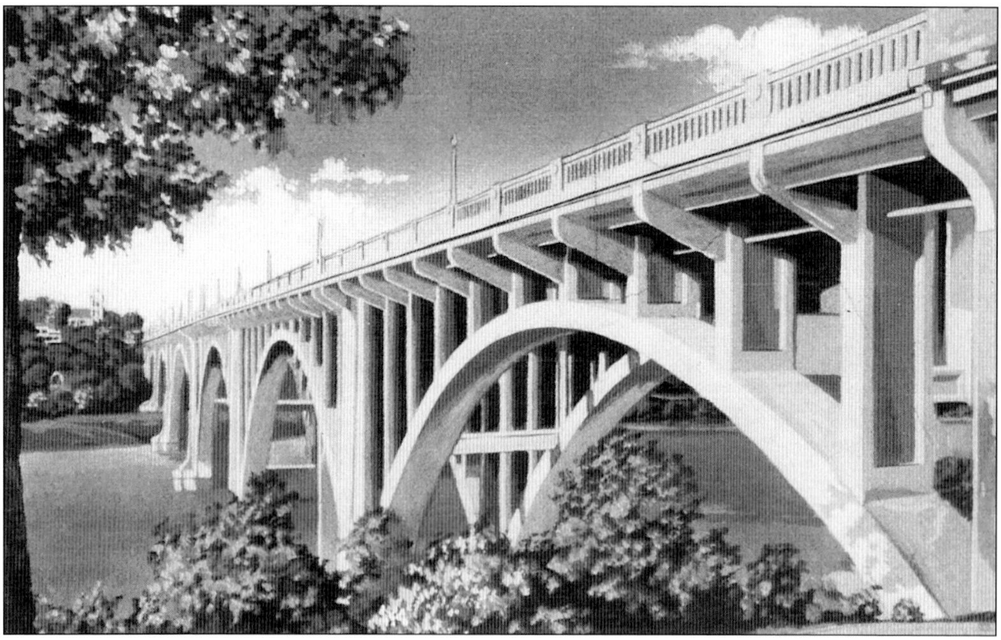

The Henley Street Bridge, a Memorial to Colonel David Henley, Revolutionary Soldier. (Published by Knoxville Paper Co., *c.* 1933.) A handsome structure of concrete with six imposing arches, the Henley Street bridge spans the Tennessee River at the south end of Broadway (Henley Street). It is 1,800 feet long and rises 300 feet above the low water mark. It cost a million dollars and was opened to traffic in 1932.

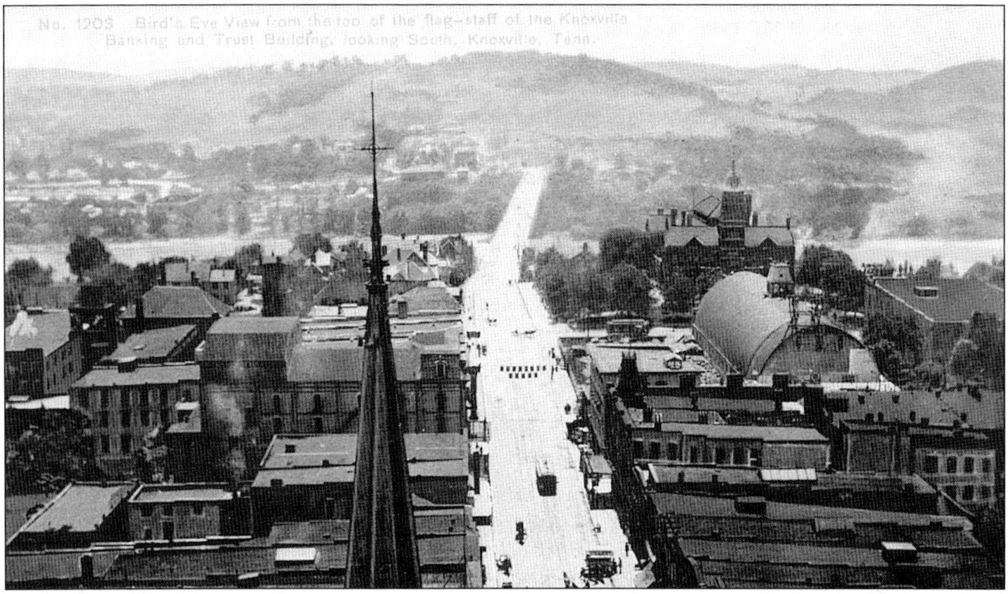

A Bird's-Eye View from the Top of the Flagstaff of the Knoxville Banking and Trust Building, Looking South. (Published by Reese and Reed, Knoxville.) This is the south end of Gay Street about 1906. The steeple in the foreground belongs to the First Baptist Church; the round-roofed building at right is the old Hippodrome Amusement Company. Across Gay Street the third building on the left is Staub's Theatre, and festooned across the street is a banner advertising Kuhlman's Drugs.

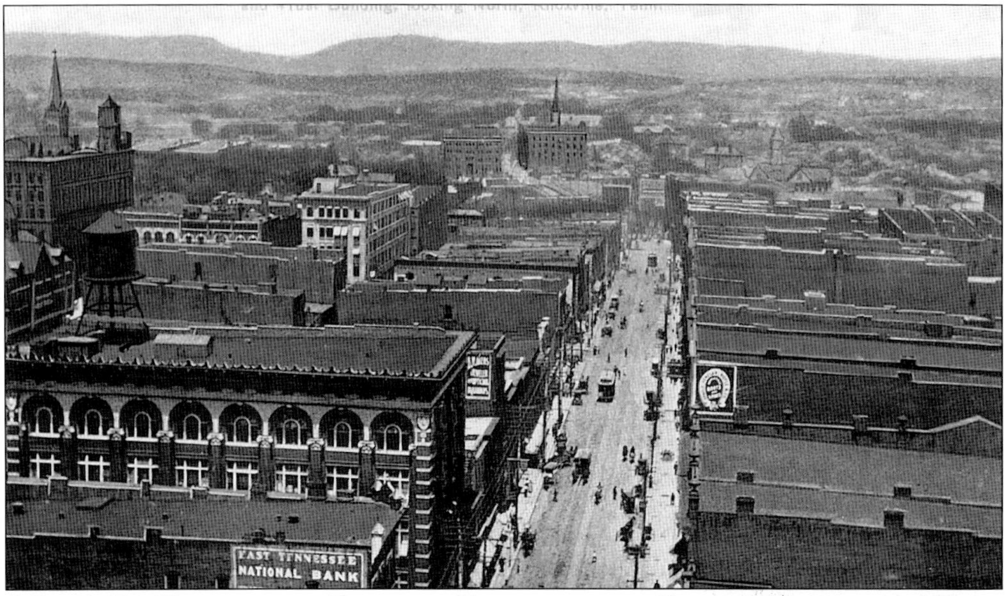

A Bird's-Eye View from the Top of the Flagstaff of the Knoxville Banking and Trust Building, Looking North. (Published by Reese and Reed, Knoxville.) Looking north along Gay Street from Union about 1906, we see the East Tennessee National Bank at left, with Miller's Department Store just across Union Street from it. Farther up the street there is a jeweler-optician, and across the street, Boyle's Boots and Shoes. The usual trolleys, carriages, and pedestrians dot the street.

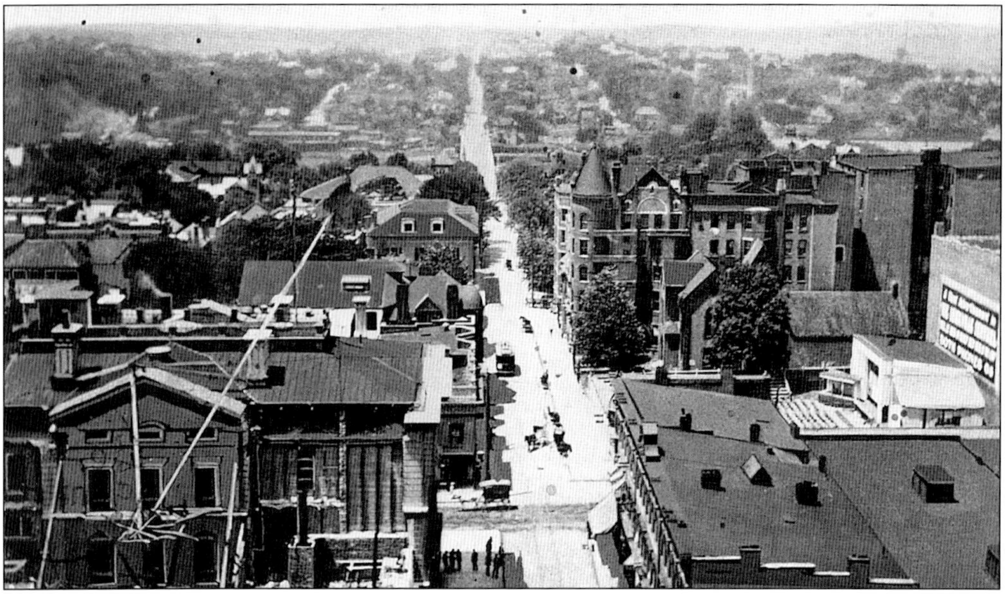

A BIRD'S-EYE VIEW FROM THE TOP OF THE FLAGSTAFF OF THE KNOXVILLE BANKING AND TRUST BUILDING, LOOKING WEST. (Published by Reese and Reed, Knoxville; card sent 1909.) Here we are looking along Clinch Avenue to the west. The construction in the foreground is the Custom House undergoing enlargement (completed in 1910). In the center distance is the Vendome Hotel, and at the right center is the Airdome Theatre.

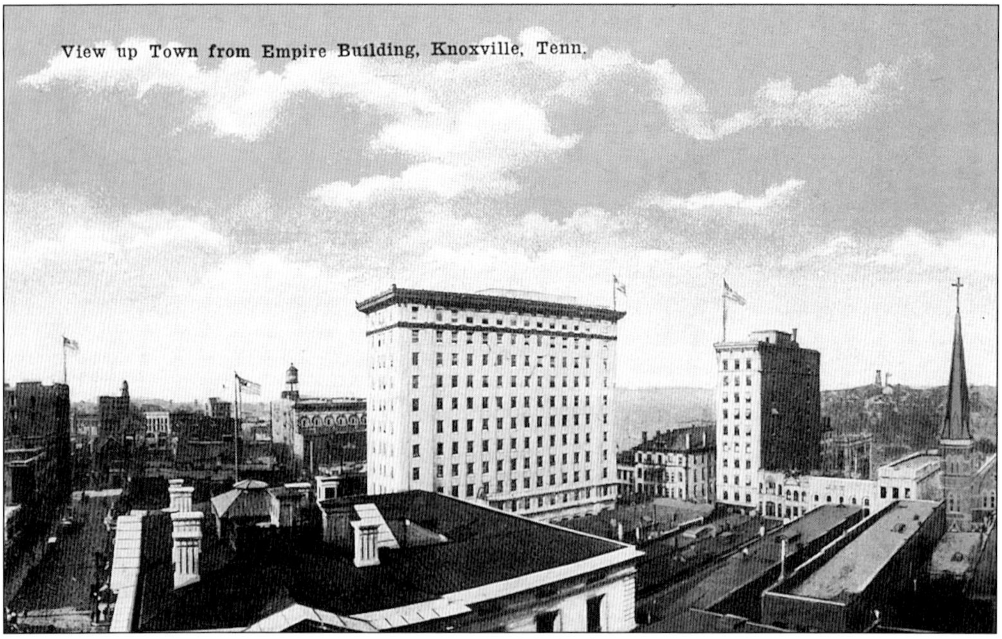

A VIEW UPTOWN FROM THE EMPIRE BUILDING. (Published by E.C. Kropp Company, Milwaukee.) Dominating the downtown landscape about 1915 is the Holston Bank at center, with the Burwell Building at right. The Hotel Imperial stands to the left of the Burwell, and at extreme right is the First Baptist Church, located here until 1924. To the immediate left of the Holston we see the water tank and rounded top windows of Miller's Store.

Two

Buildings and Businesses

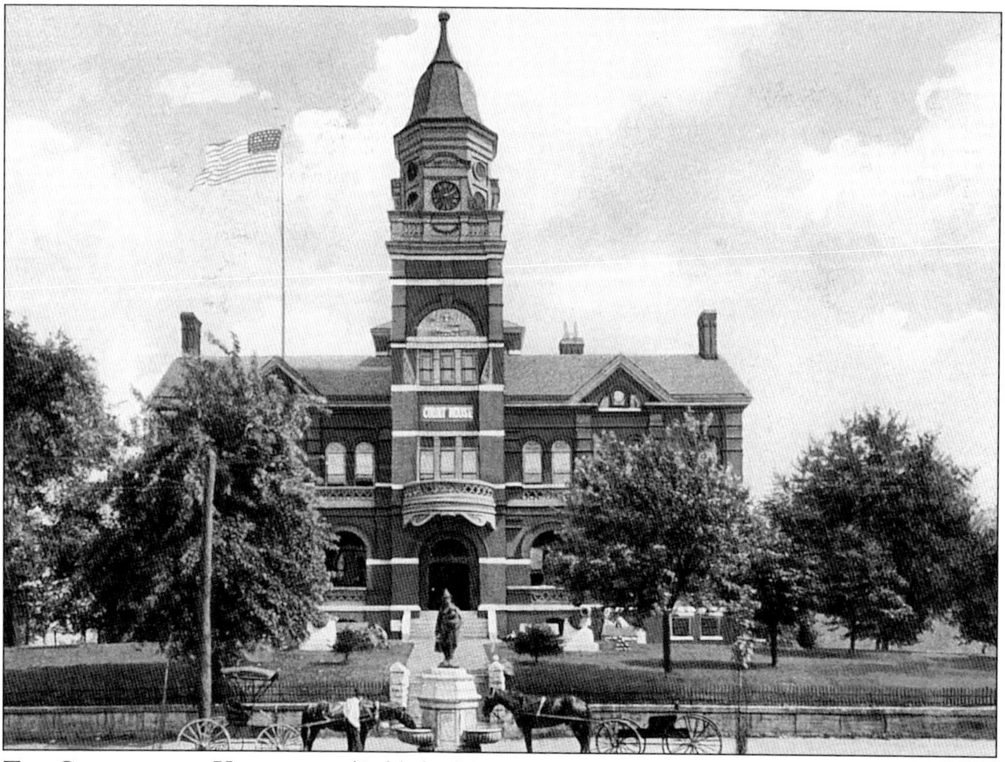

THE COURTHOUSE, KNOXVILLE. (Published by Raphael Tuck and Sons, London; series 2465; *c.* 1907.) In 1885 Knox County government moved into this imposing Queen Anne style courthouse built on the site of the early blockhouse fort, now the corner of Gay and Main Streets. A horse trough at curbside supported the statue of a fireman with a baby in his arms. The statue has since been removed to Summit Hill Drive.

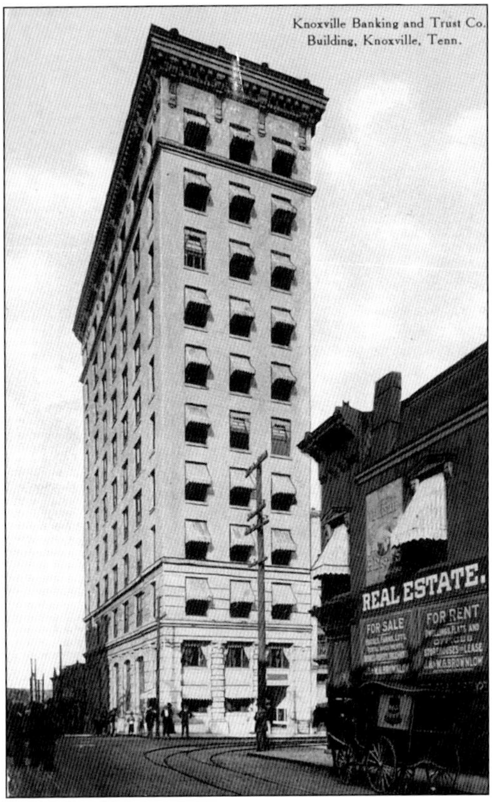

THE KNOXVILLE BANKING AND TRUST CO. (Published by S.H. Kress and Co.) Located on the corner of Gay and Clinch, Knoxville Banking and Trust was Knoxville's tallest building in 1908. Later C.B. Atkin purchased it, doubled its size, and named it in honor of his wife, Mary Burwell. In 1928 the Tennessee Theater opened in the newer section of the building.

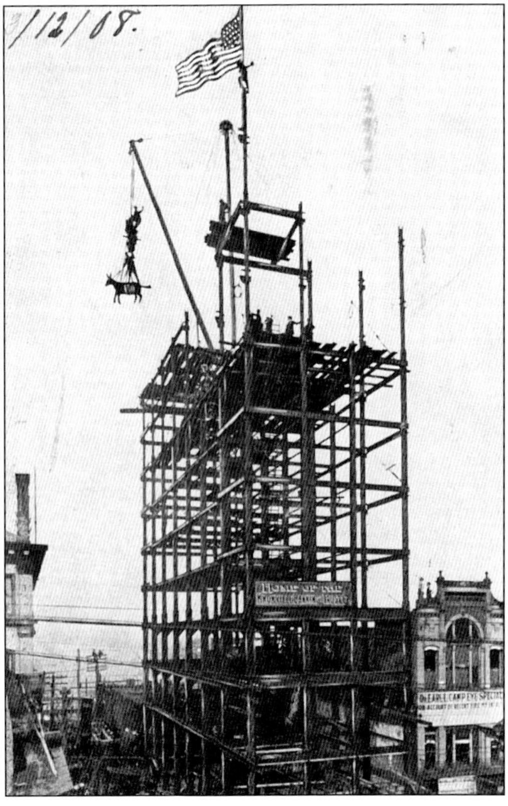

MAUD UP IN THE AIR—TEN STORIES. (No publishing data; card sent 1908.) An interesting trick—to hoist a mule up ten stories—emphasizes the height of the new Knoxville Banking and Trust Building under construction. The human "high flyers" seem to be enjoying the spectacle.

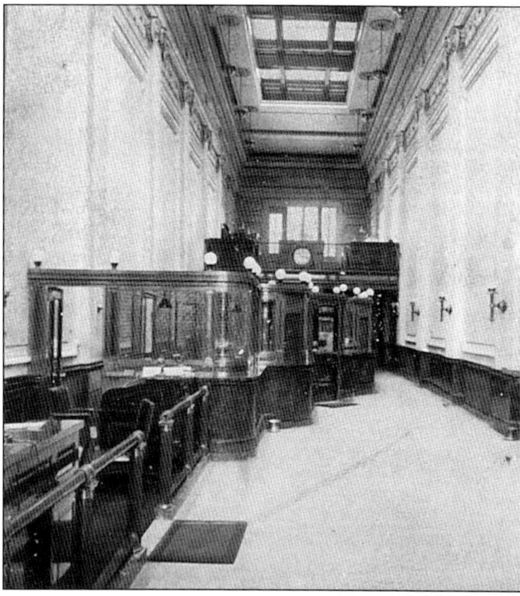

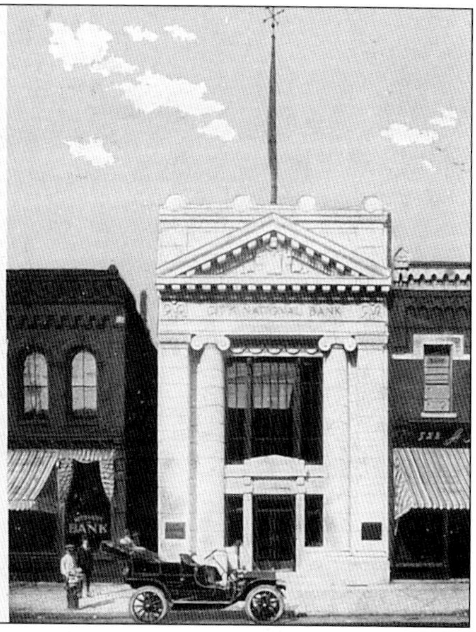

CITY NATIONAL BANK, INTERIOR AND EXTERIOR VIEWS. (Published by Charles C. Cullen, Knoxville.) City National Bank was founded by William S. Shields (1853–1933), who came to Knoxville in 1888 and advanced to its presidency in 1892. By 1913 City Bank was one of the three largest banks in Knoxville. In 1930 it was absorbed by East Tennessee National Bank.

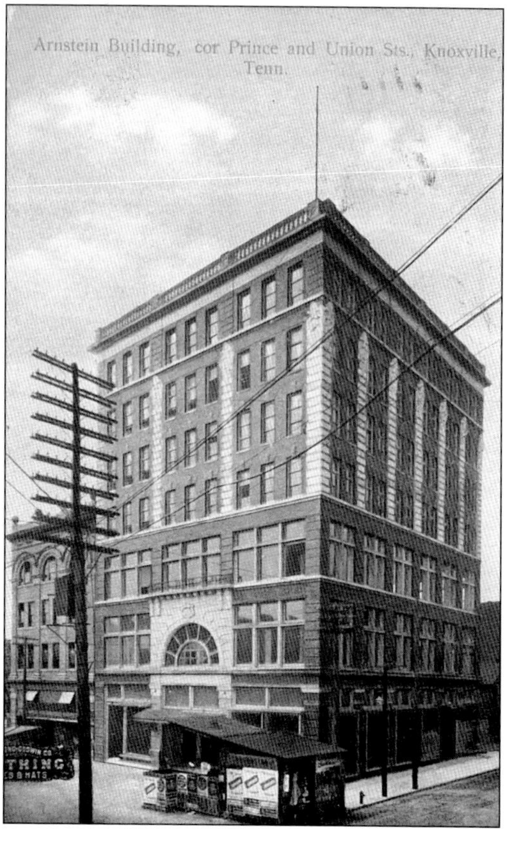

THE ARNSTEIN BUILDING. (Published by International Post Card Co., New York; card sent 1908.) In 1905 the Arnstein Department Store was built on the corner of Market and Union. A seven-story "skyscraper," it was the first steel-frame building erected in Knoxville. The architects were the Baumann brothers, who detailed it in Renaissance Revival style. A longtime quality store, it closed in 1928 and was later leased to the Tennessee Valley Authority for offices. In 1976 it was sold and renovated again.

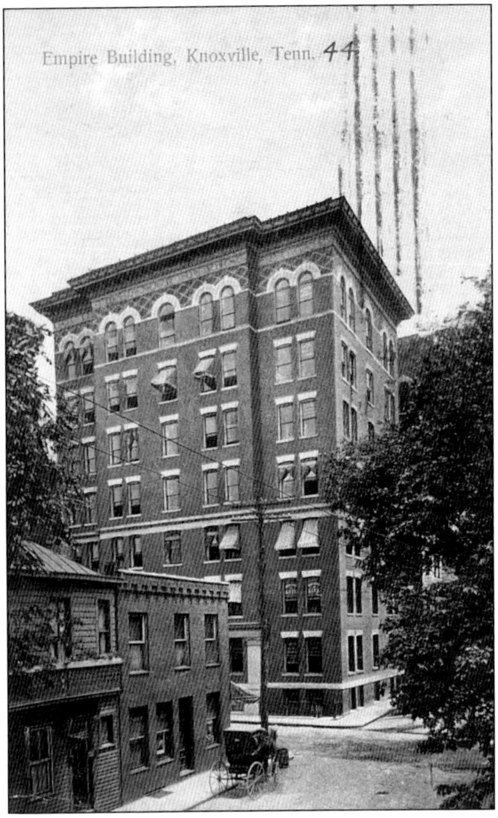

The Empire Building. (Published by International Post Card Co., New York; card sent 1905.) This seven-story building occupied the corner of Market and Church, one block south of the Custom House. It was torn down in the 1970s; Vantage Bank now occupies the space.

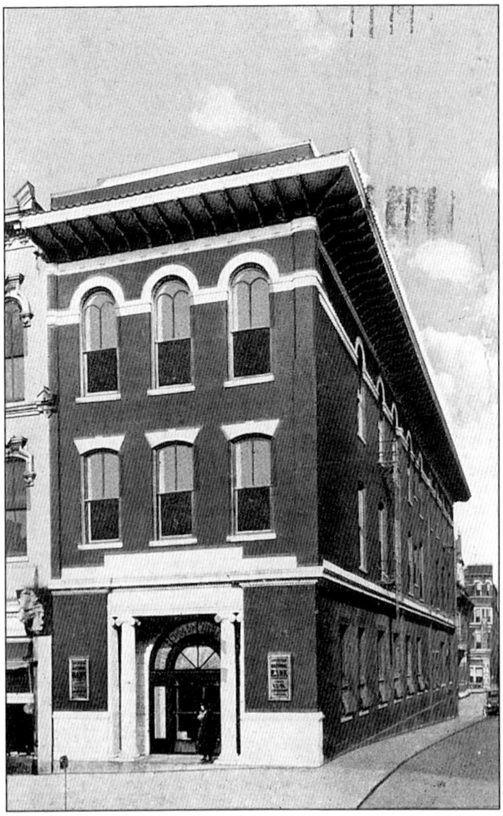

American National Bank. (Published by Curt Teich, Chicago; card sent 1928.) Another of the many banks organized in Knoxville early in the century, American National was founded in 1913. It occupied this building on the northeast corner of Gay Street and Commerce Avenue.

The Holston National Bank Building. (Published by Howard's Bookstore, Knoxville; card sent 1912.) Located at 531 South Gay at Clinch, this "skyscraper" was built in 1908. Designed by John K. Peebles of Norfolk, Virginia, the building exhibits the Classical Revival style. It was reorganized as the Hamilton National Bank in 1930, and subsequently became United American. Today it is the Charter Federal Building.

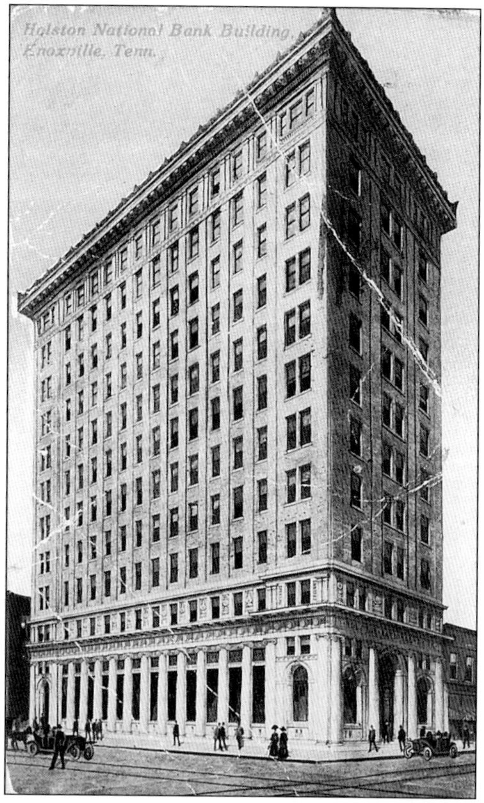

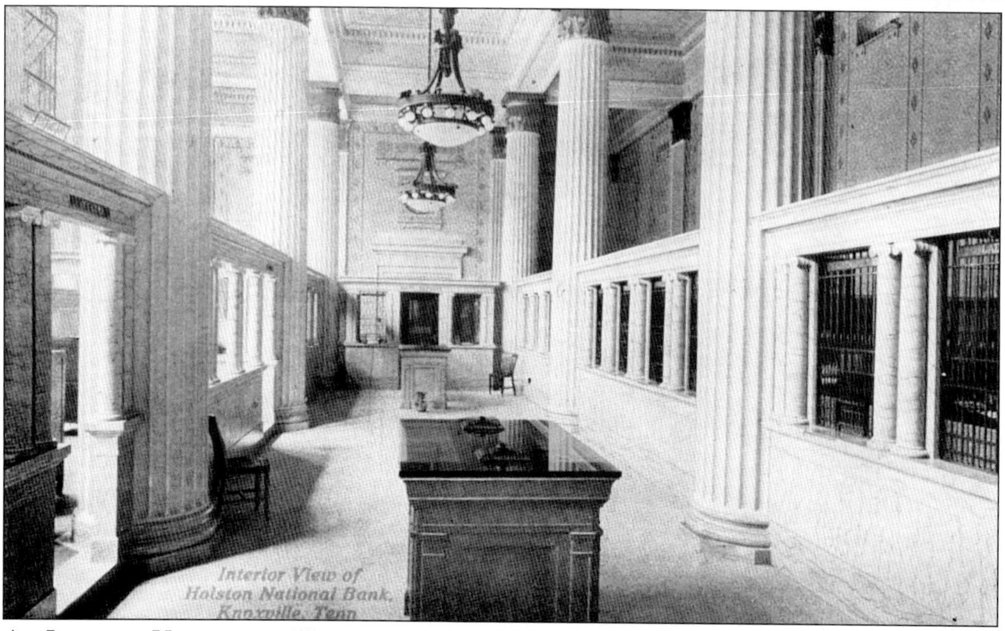

An Interior View of the Holston National Bank. (Published by Octochrome.) Carrying out the classic decor, the interior of the Holston National Bank provides a cool elegance. Note the tellers' cages secure behind bars; the window to the extreme right is reserved for "ladies." A gold spittoon resides in the distance at center.

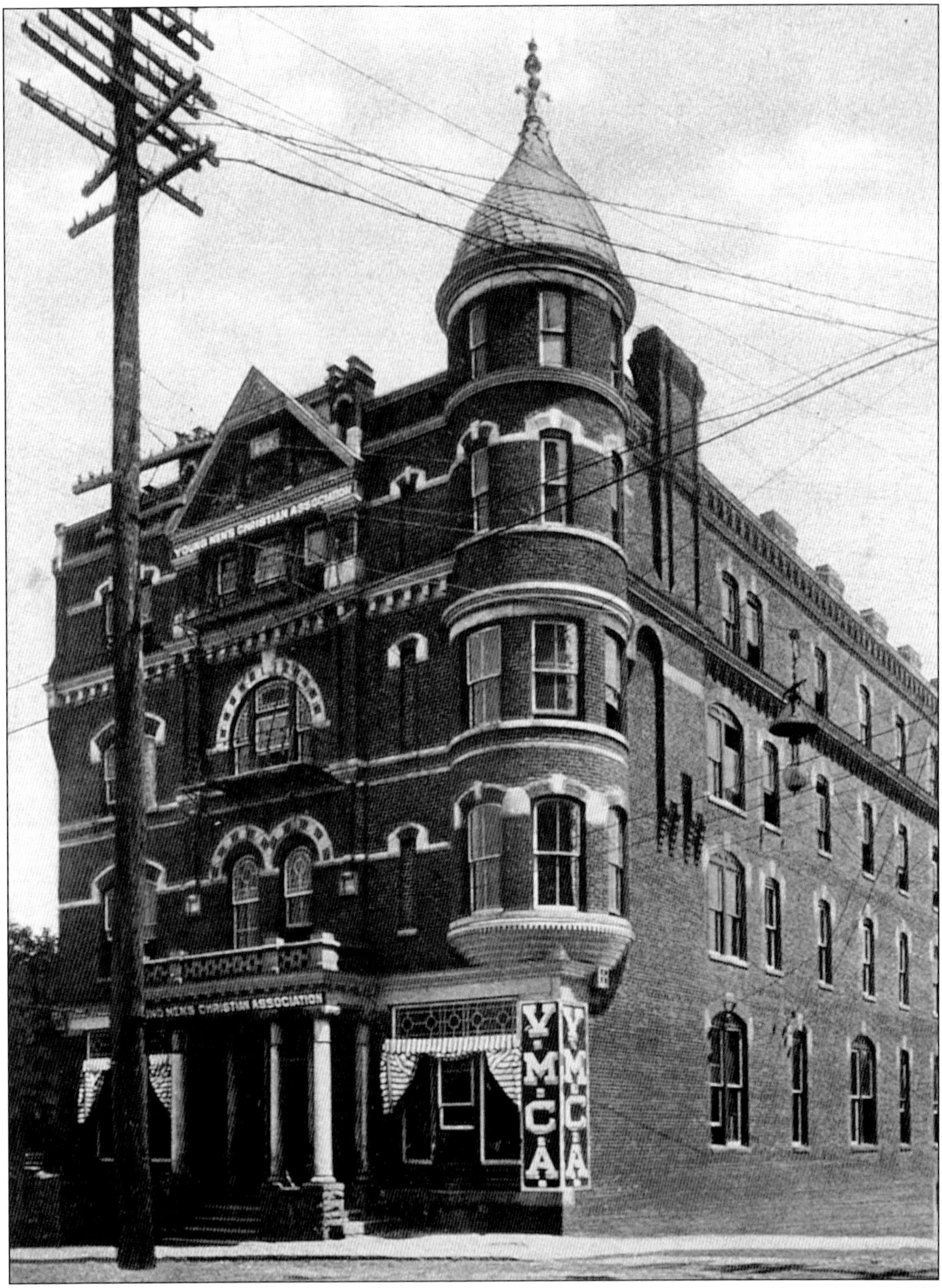

The YMCA Building. (Published by International Post Card Company, New York.) This handsome building, formerly the Palace Hotel, located at the corner of State and Commerce, was Knoxville's first building devoted to this cause, whose goal was to develop a Christian personality. Some of the advantages offered here around 1900 were sociability, gymnastics, swimming, finding employment, Bible study, and night school, which began operation in 1908. The present YMCA at Locust and Clinch dates from 1929.

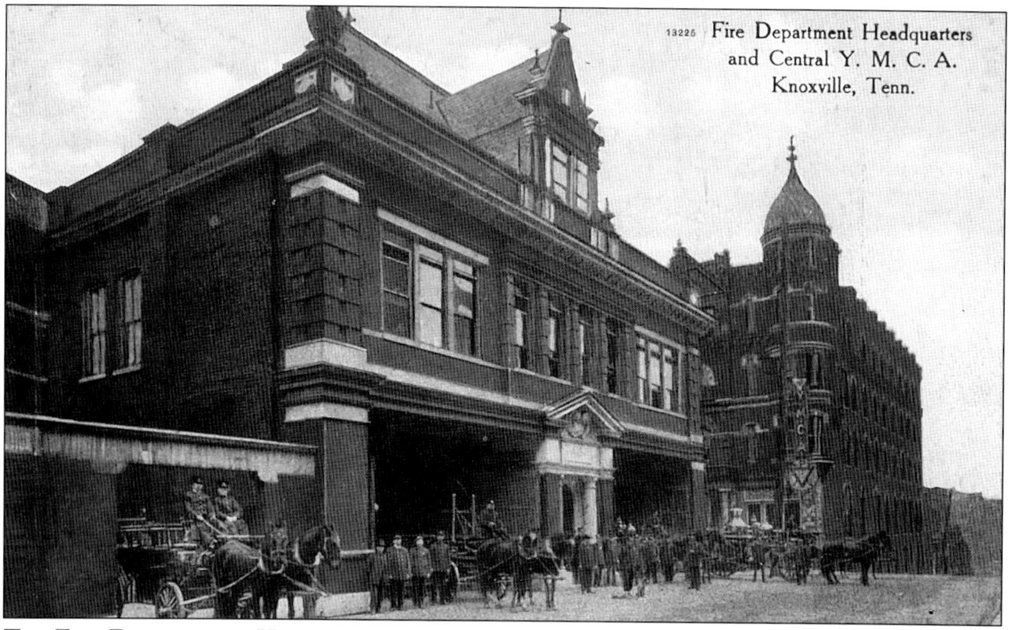

THE FIRE DEPARTMENT HEADQUARTERS AND THE CENTRAL **YMCA.** (Published by M. Howard, Knoxville.) The Knoxville Fire Company was established in 1822; however, the first hook and ladder truck was not purchased until 1868. Here we see a proud showing of firemen and their equipment sometime around 1905. This building, as well as the nearby YMCA, was razed in 1977 when Summit Hill Drive was created for better access to the Tennessee Valley Authority headquarters.

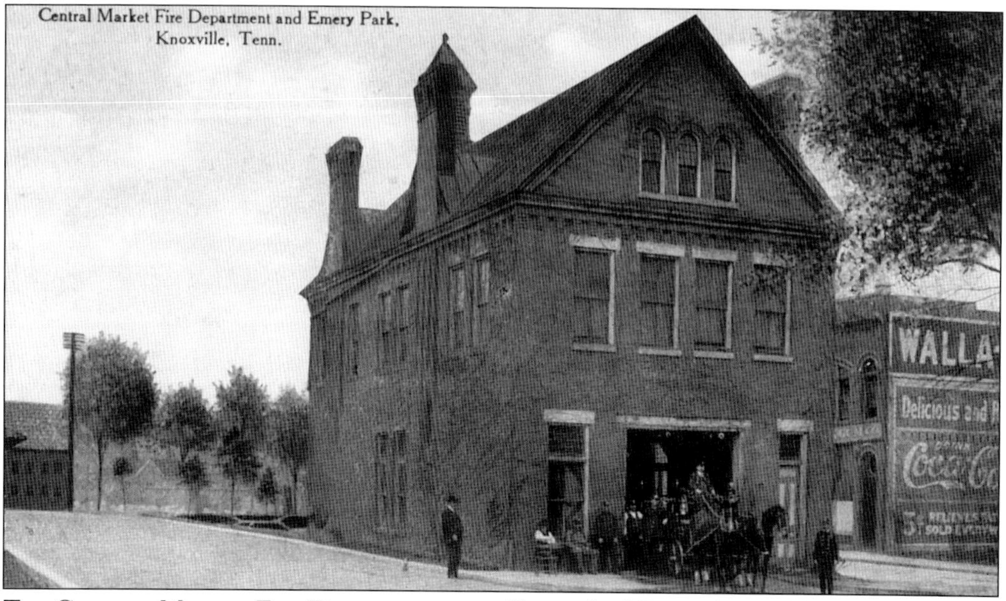

THE CENTRAL MARKET FIRE DEPARTMENT AND EMERY [*SIC*] PARK. (No publication data.) The Emory Park Fire Department building seems to date from about 1900. Located at the northern end of Gay Street just a block east of Broadway, it was part of a cluster of varied businesses. Next door to the fire station we see a chewing gum factory which sports a Coca-Cola sign. Emory Park, the first in the city, has since been paved over for parking space.

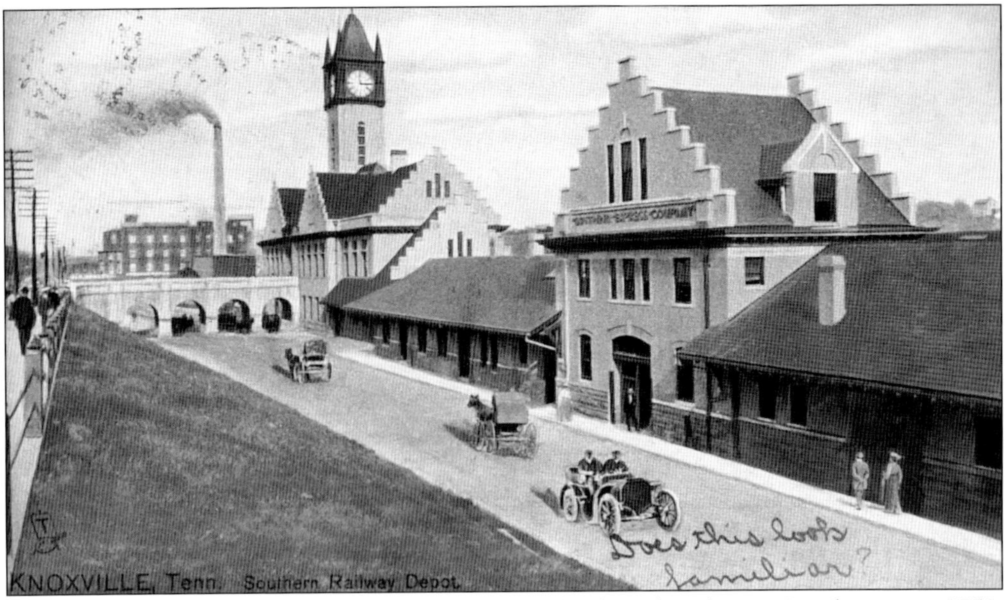

The Southern Railway Depot. (Published by Raphael Tuck and Sons, London; series 2750; card sent 1908.) The Southern Railway Station, with tower and weathervane, was built at the north end of Gay Street in 1904 according to the designs of Frank P. Milburn. For 75 years train travel was "the way to go"; however, competition with the automobile and airplane decimated passenger traffic, and on August 12, 1970, regularly scheduled passenger train service ended for Knoxville. The building, without its tower, is now occupied by an architectural firm.

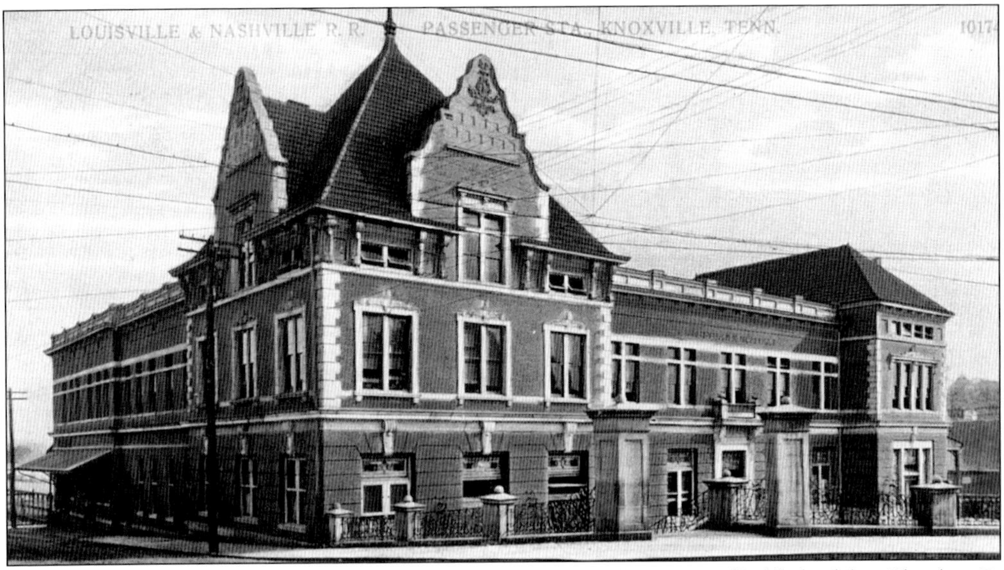

The Louisville and Nashville Railroad Passenger Station. (Published by Charles C. Cullen Company, Knoxville.) In 1905 the Louisville and Nashville (L & N) gained entrance to Knoxville, breaking Southern's monopoly. Completed in 1906, its ornate passenger depot became a landmark; it had stained-glass windows and tiled floors laid in Oriental carpet patterns. The Ladies' Waiting Room had a private entrance, rocking chairs, a fireplace, and desks furnished with L & N stationery. The station was renovated in 1982 for the World's Fair and has since housed two restaurants.

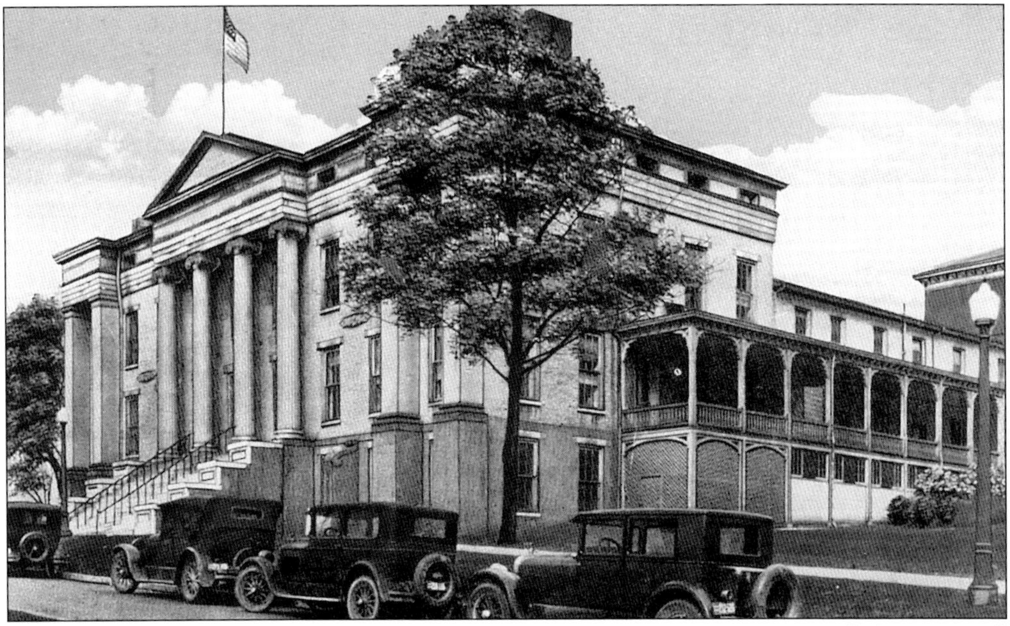

City Hall, Knoxville. (Published by Standard News Company, Knoxville.) City Hall was built as the Deaf and Dumb Asylum in 1848. It was used by Civil War soldiers as a hospital, first by the Confederates, then by the Federals. Then it served the Tennessee School for the Deaf until 1924, when the school was moved to Island Home and the building became city hall. Located at the corner of Henley Street and Western Avenue, it has undergone significant renovation.

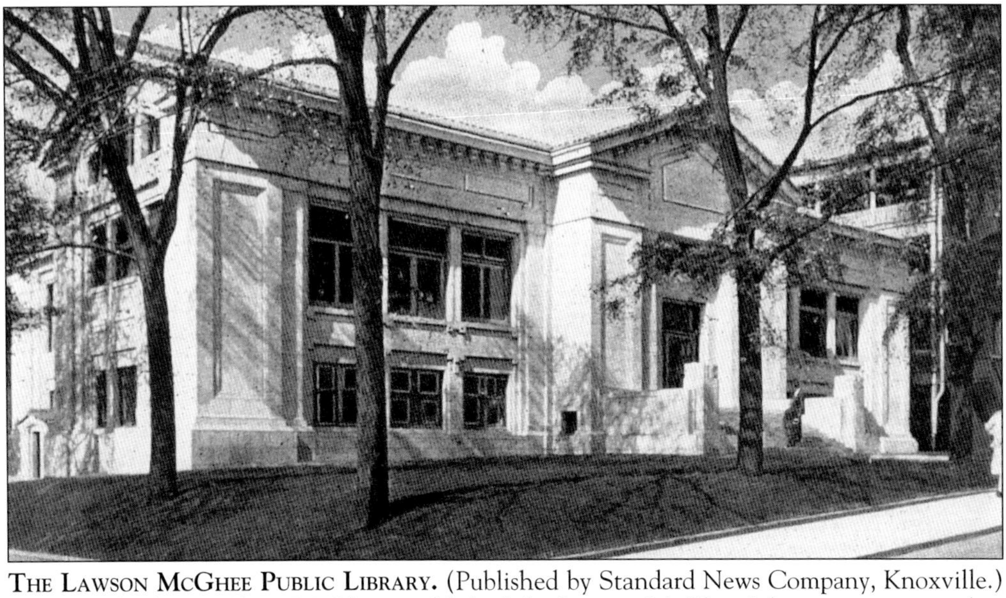

The Lawson McGhee Public Library. (Published by Standard News Company, Knoxville.) In 1885 Charles McClung McGhee established the Lawson McGhee Library as a memorial to his daughter with one of the largest philanthropic gifts in Knoxville history. The first building at Gay and Vine was sold and the money used to finance a new building at Market and Commerce (pictured here), which opened in 1917. This building was razed when the new library was built in 1971.

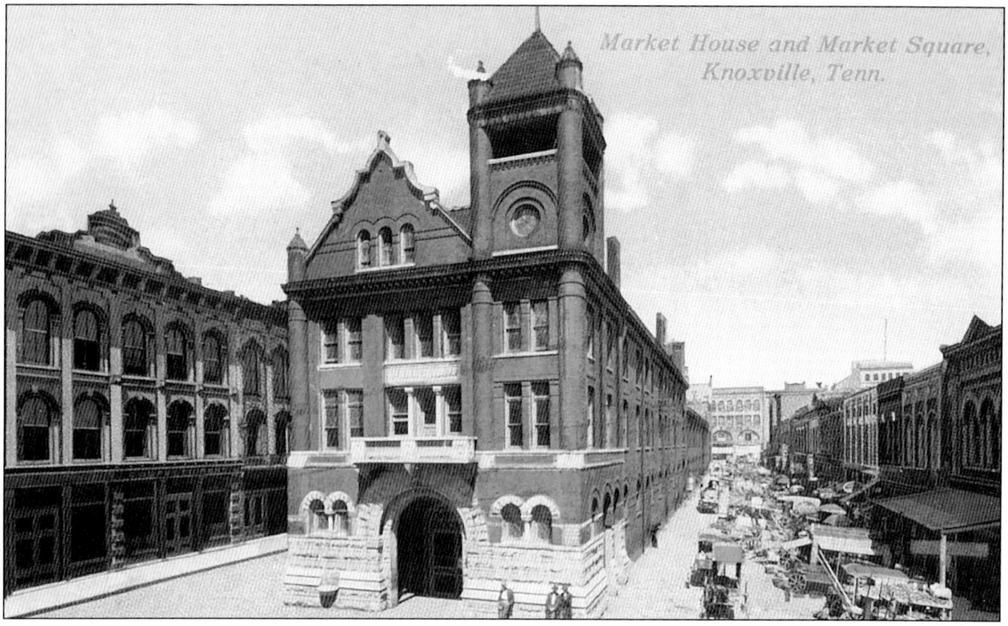

THE MARKET HOUSE AND MARKET SQUARE. (Published by Octochrome.) This building was erected in 1897. Permanent stalls inside the building offered bakery products, fresh meats, produce, and country butter. Along the outside of the building, wagons offered home-grown vegetables and fruits in season. The market never ceased to be a popular center for the sale of flowers and fresh foods. The building burned in 1960, and Market Square became a pedestrian mall.

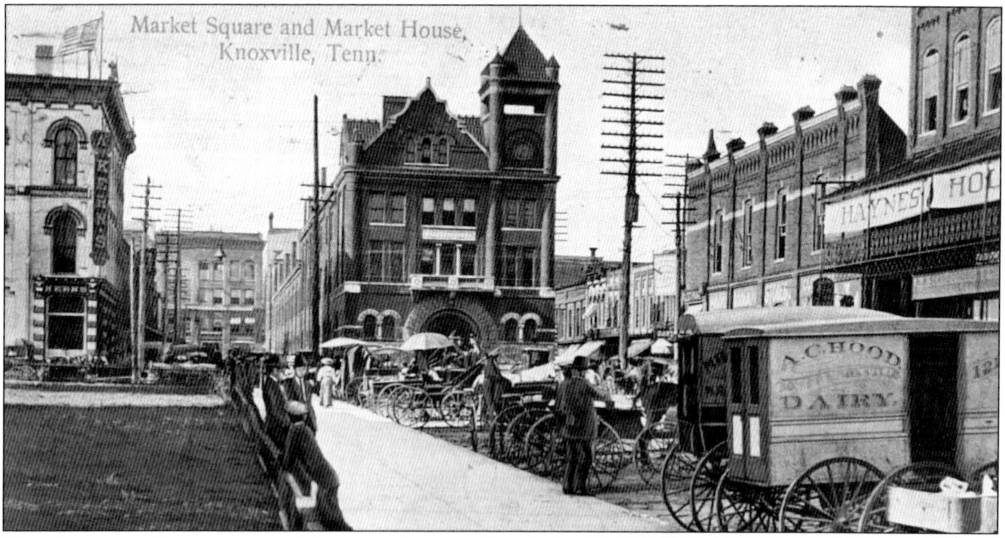

THE MARKET SQUARE AND MARKET HOUSE. (Published by International Post Card Co., New York; card sent 1910.) The viewer here is approaching the west side of the Market House, with typical wagons and vendors lined up along the street. The building at left is Kern's Confectionery, opened in 1872, an ice cream parlor owned by Peter Kern (1835–1907), whose bread and cakes became known all over the South. The building still stands on the corner of Union and Market. From 1910 to 1965 Cole Drug Store was here. Kern's Bakery was later expanded and moved to Chapman Highway.

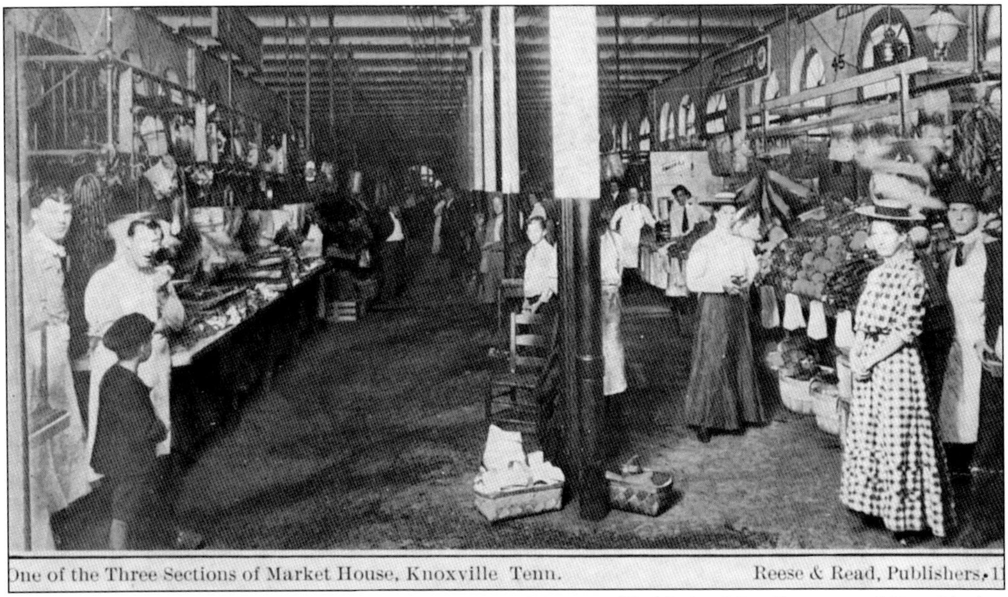

ONE OF THE THREE SECTIONS OF THE MARKET HOUSE. (Published by Reese and Reed.) An interior scene in the Market House shows meat and vegetable stalls patronized by customers who are dressed in the styles of 1907–10. Big sandwiches could be obtained here for 5¢, and many Knoxvillians made a day of shopping here, with a delicious lunch at mid-day. In spite of the pervasive fish smell in certain areas, people always enjoyed coming to the market.

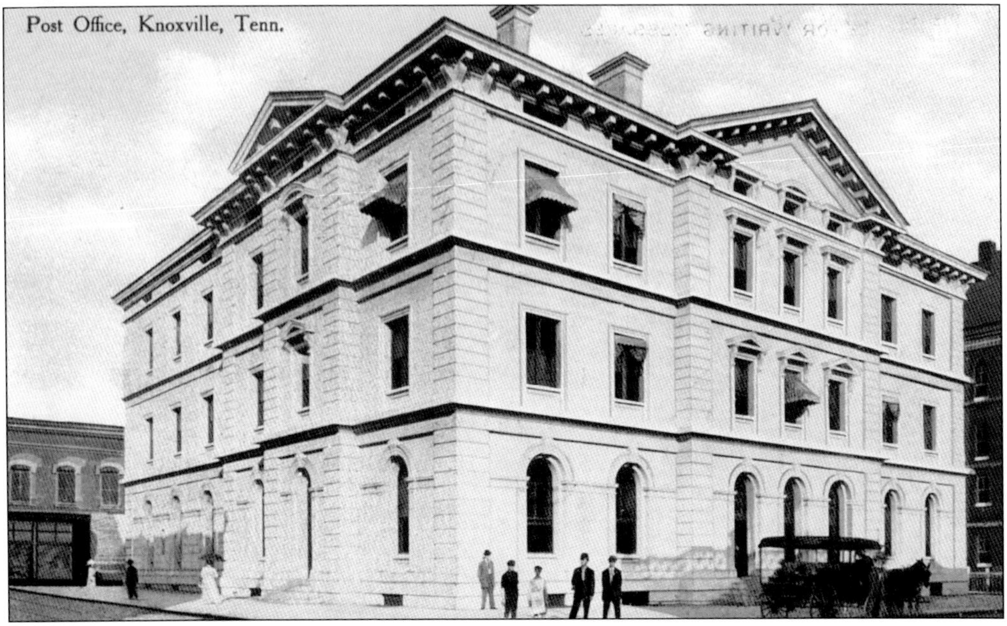

THE POST OFFICE. (Published by S.H. Kress; card sent 1910.) Probably the first building in Knoxville to be designed by a professional architect was the U.S. Post Office and Custom House, completed in 1874 from designs by Alfred B. Mullett. Located at the corner of Clinch and Market, it is solidly built with iron beams and exterior walls of local marble. In 1934 the Tennessee Valley Authority occupied the building; in 1976 it was restored to become the East Tennessee Historical Center.

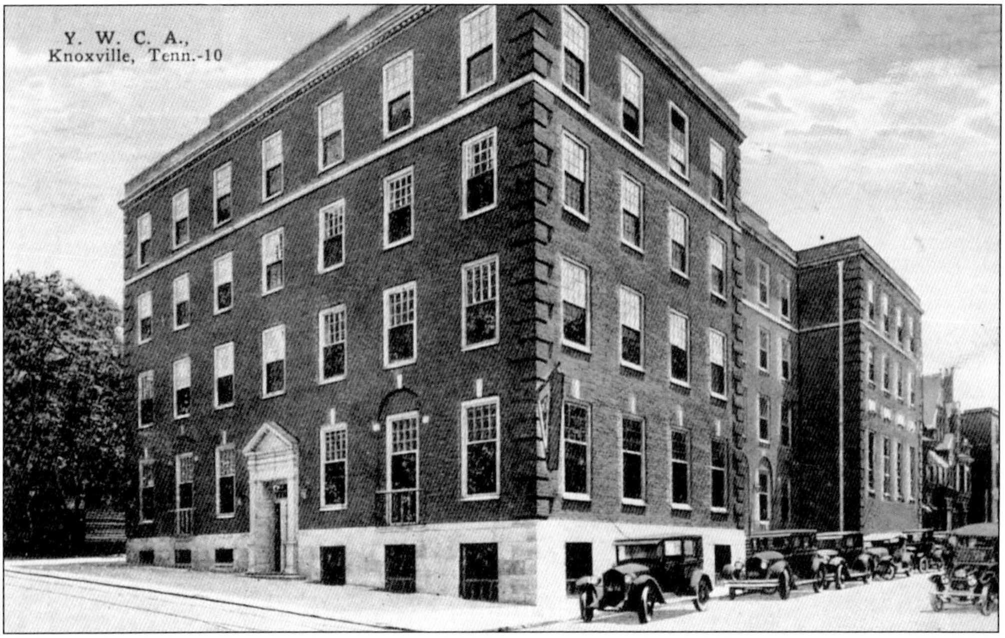

The YWCA, Knoxville. (No publication data; card sent 1928.) The Young Women's Christian Association was first organized in Knoxville in 1899. The pictured building, located at 420 Clinch Avenue, was built in 1926 from the Neo-Georgian design of Barber and McMurry, the prestigious Knoxville architectural firm.

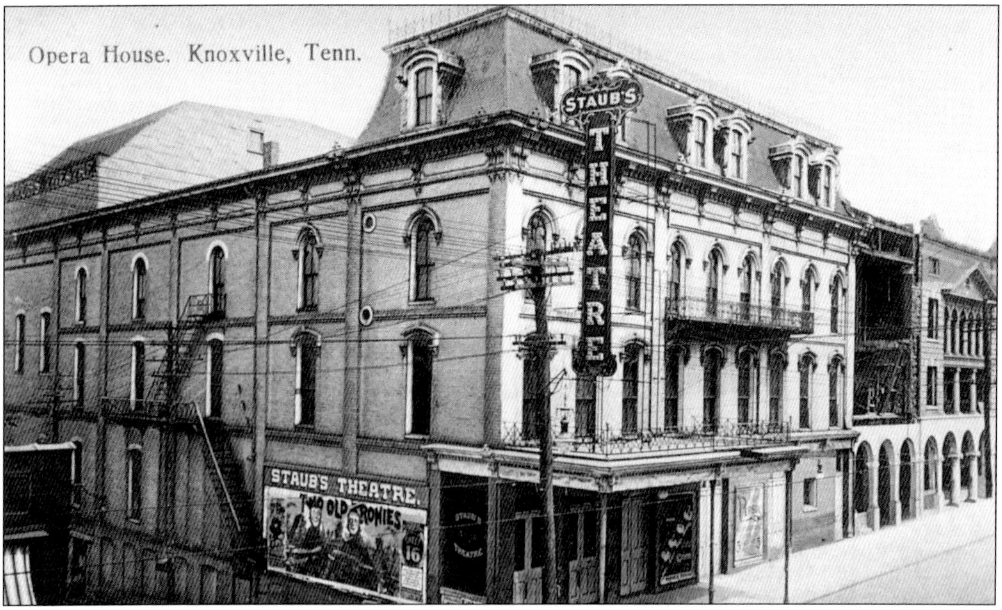

The Opera House, Knoxville. (Published by S.H. Kress.) This popular theatre was built in 1872 at the corner of Gay and Cumberland. Peter Staub (1827–1904), its builder, was an immigrant Swiss tailor who became one of Knoxville's most important businessmen. The three-story structure seated 1,400 people. For many years it was the principal showcase for traveling theatrical companies, but changing times forced it to close in 1919. In 1920 it reopened as Loew's; in 1922 it became the Lyric. After steady decline, it was torn down in 1956.

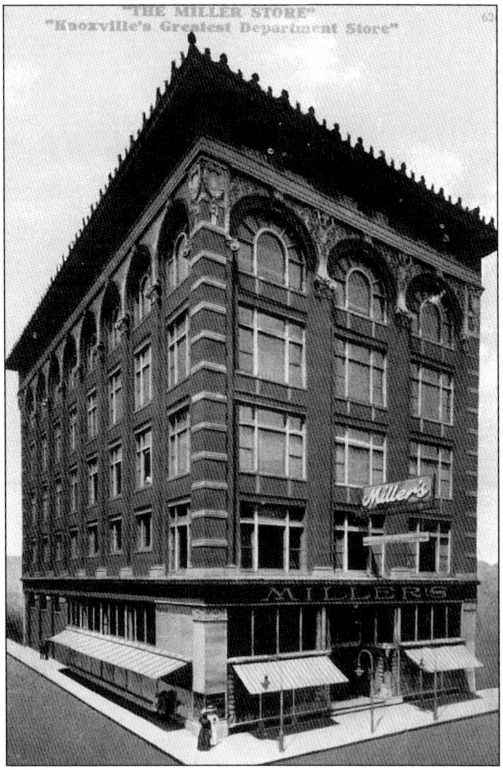

The Miller Store, "Knoxville's Greatest Department Store." (No publication data.) Located on the west side of Gay Street at Union, Miller's Store was designed and built in 1905 by R.F. Graf and Sons. For many years it was one of Knoxville's prestigious department stores; it closed in 1973 and was converted into an office building with an impressive glass-windowed facade.

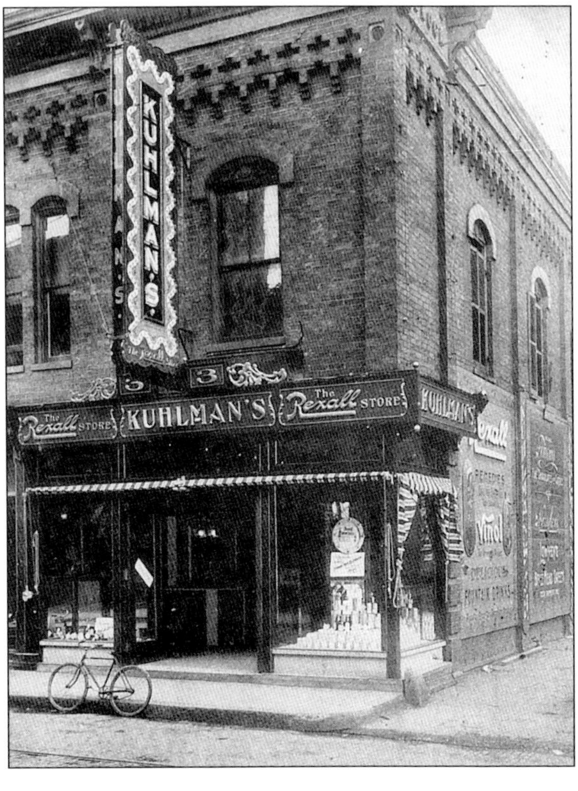

Kuhlman's Drug Store No. 3. (Published by W.D. Kuhlman; card sent 1912.) When this card was mailed, Nathan Kuhlman was operating three drugstores, two on Gay Street and one on Clinch Avenue. Here we see his No. 3 store, "the Rexall Store." Kuhlman also placed advertising banners festooned across Gay Street which attracted much attention.

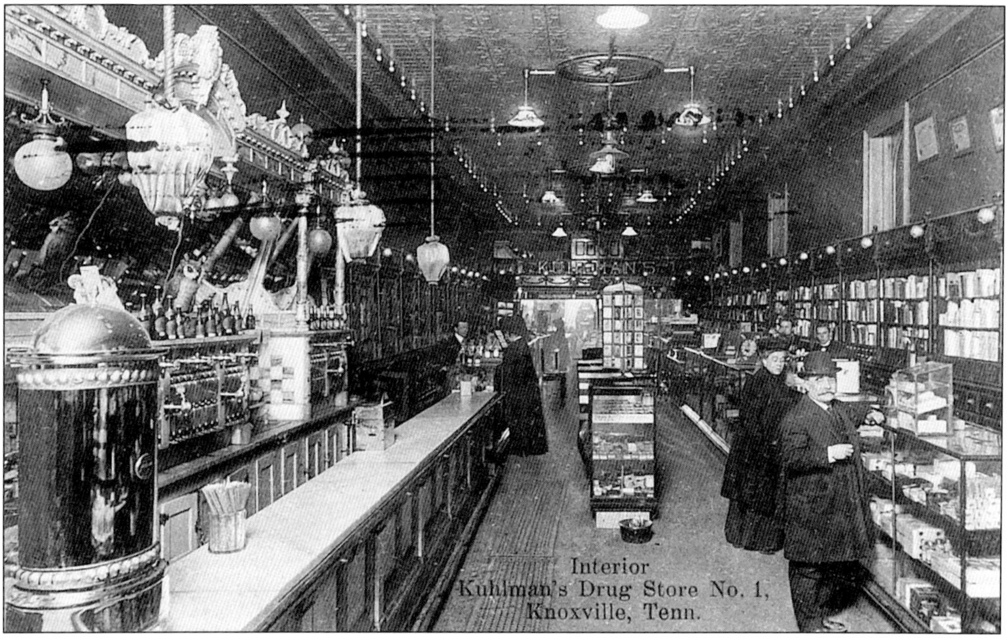

THE INTERIOR OF KUHLMAN'S STORE NO. 1. (Published by W.D. Kuhlman; card sent 1908.) Located at 301–303 Gay Street, Store No. 1 provided an exciting array of articles to buy and possibilities for refreshment at the soda fountain seen at left. In the center there is a postcard rack on the display case, and the ever-present spittoon sits on the floor.

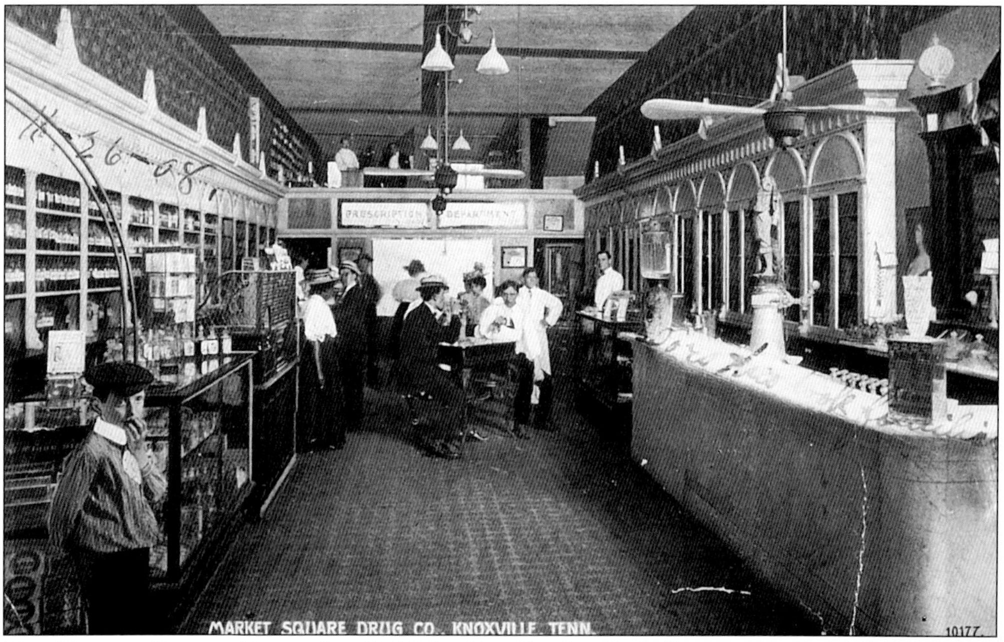

THE MARKET SQUARE DRUG CO. (Published by Charles C. Cullen; card sent 1908.) A typical drugstore of the time, the Market Square Drug Co. featured a soda fountain beneath a fan, seen at right. At left, beyond the glass display case, is the cash register behind a golden cage, and in the center distance customers enjoy their drinks at small tables. The prescription department is seen at rear. The postcard rack (at left center) was a prominent accessory to all drugstores.

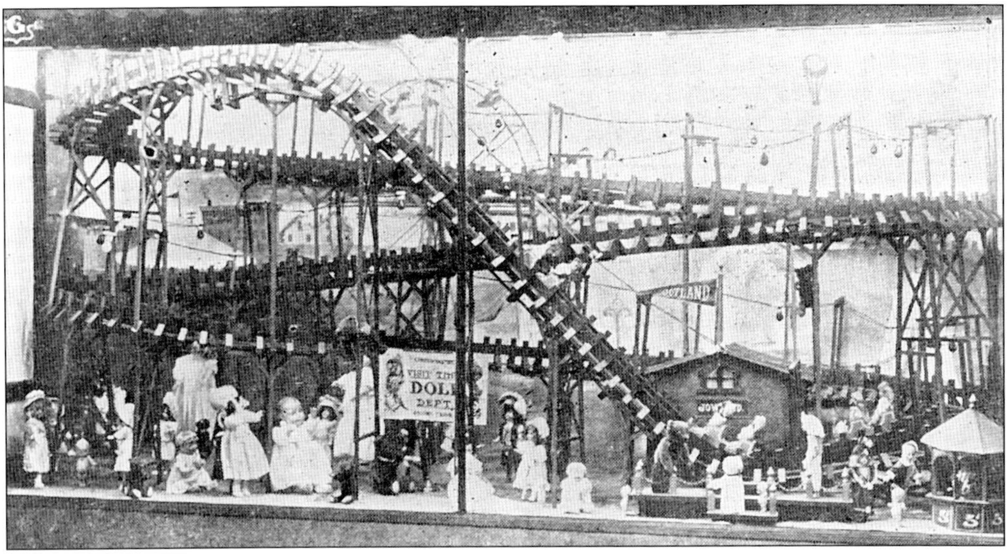

A DOLL'S ROLLER COASTER AS SHOWN IN S.H. GEORGE AND SONS GAY STREET WINDOW. (No publication data.) S.H. George and Sons, at Gay Street and Wall Avenue, was another popular department store of the early 1900s. This picture shows a Christmas-decorated window; on the back of the postcard the management expresses "The Season's Greetings—with sincerest wishes for a Christmas happily remembered." Rich's of Atlanta purchased S.H. George in 1952.

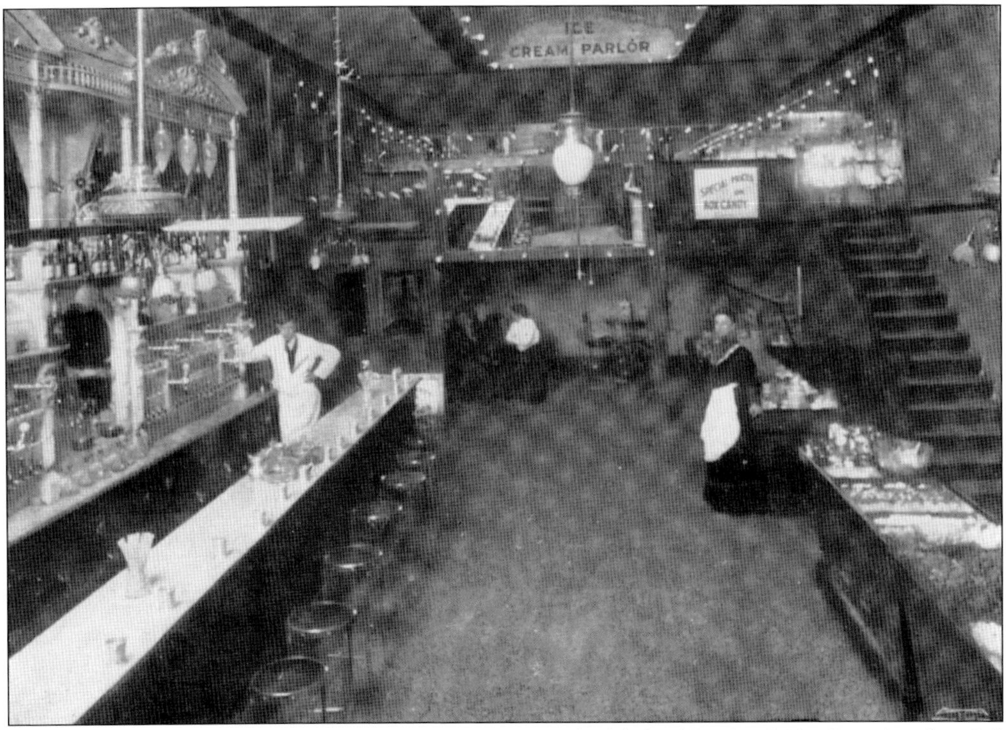

G.W. CARDEN'S CONFECTIONERY, 315 GAY STREET. (Published by Art Mfg. Co., Amelia, O.) A confectionery ("a place where sweet things are sold") was an appropriate place to take a girlfriend in 1907. It featured a soda fountain, seen on the left, as well as ice cream, candies, and cakes. This establishment has its "cream parlor" at the rear.

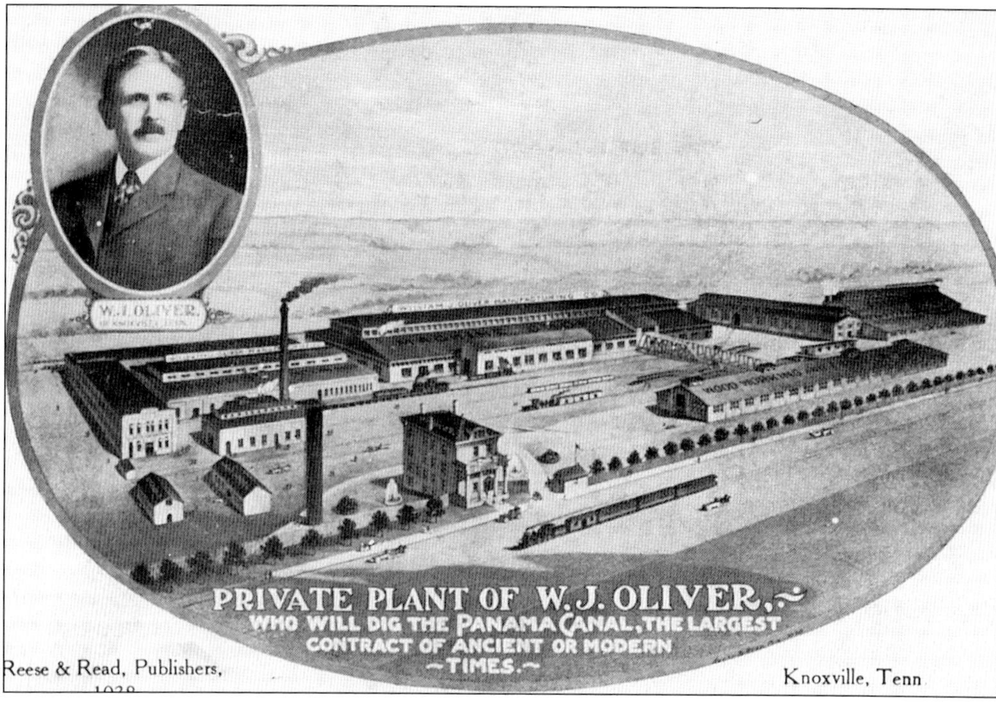

THE PRIVATE PLANT OF W.J. OLIVER. (Published by Reese and Reed, Knoxville.) William J. Oliver (1867–1925) founded in 1905 the Oliver Manufacturing Company, which made railroad and construction equipment. On Dale Avenue, the plant was the largest of its kind in the South; it made steel dump cars for the Panama Canal construction, and in World War I it manufactured artillery shells. Also a contractor, Oliver built the Clinch Avenue viaduct, the first concrete structure of its kind in Knoxville.

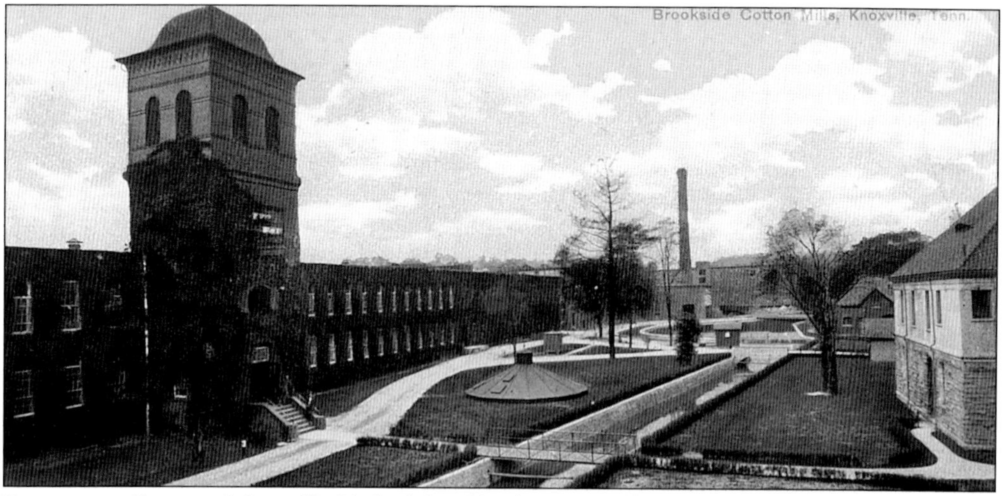

BROOKSIDE COTTON MILL. (Published by Charles C. Cullen; card sent 1911.) The textile mills in Knoxville experienced rapid growth between 1880 and 1910. Brookside Cotton Mill, founded in 1885, was by 1902 the largest employer of textile workers in the city. Nearby at Pickle School one classroom was set aside for the children who worked half-days at Brookside. No youth between 14 and 16 could be employed unless he attended school a portion of each day.

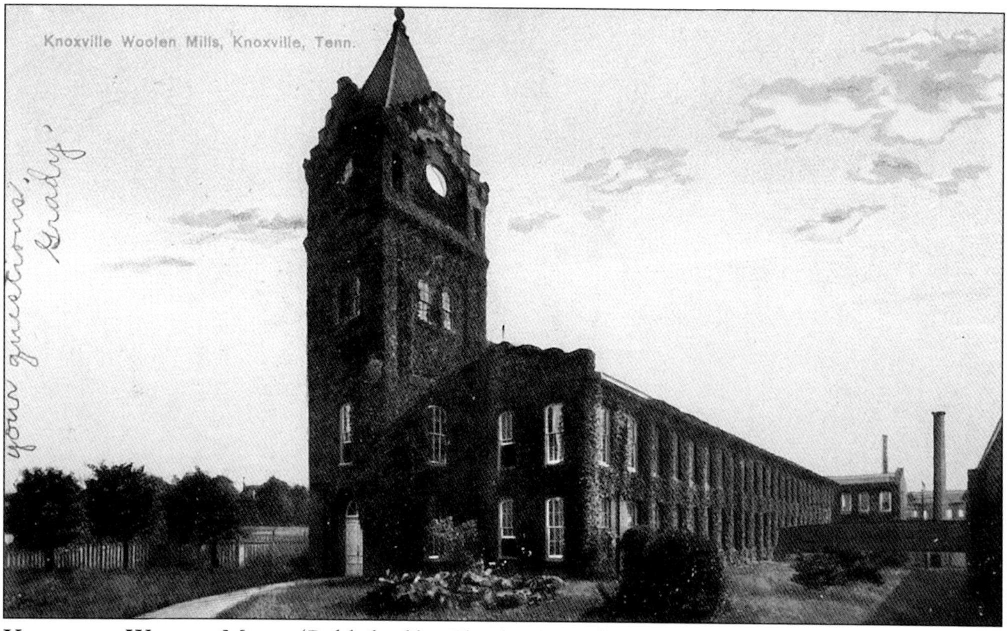

KNOXVILLE WOOLEN MILLS. (Published by Charles C. Cullen; card sent 1911.) Charles McClung McGhee and E.J. Sanford owned much of the stock in Knoxville Woolen Mills, which after 1884 was one of the city's largest industrial employers. William Cary Ross, vice-president and treasurer, notes in his memoirs that when he discovered its product had gone out of use, in 1911 he liquidated "while we could pay our debts." Subsequently the mill became Appalachian Mills, maker of men's knitted underwear.

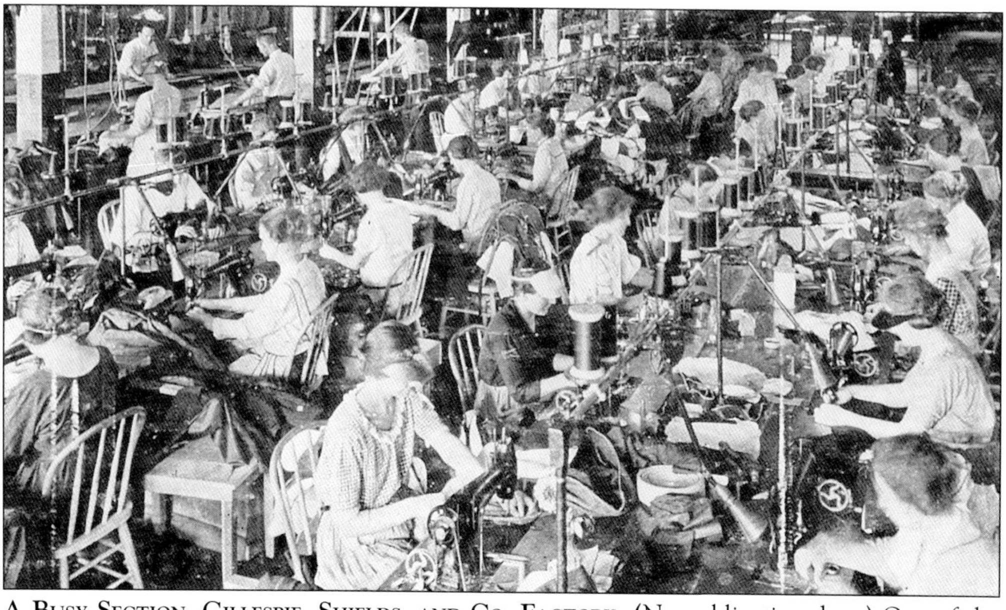

A BUSY SECTION, GILLESPIE, SHIELDS, AND CO. FACTORY. (No publication data.) One of the many enterprises of William S. Shields, who came to Knoxville in 1888 to organize the City National Bank, was the factory pictured here which made clothing known by its "Shield Brand." The back of this card says, "See Shield Brand clothing before you buy—and you will see the greatest values ever shown in a medium priced line."

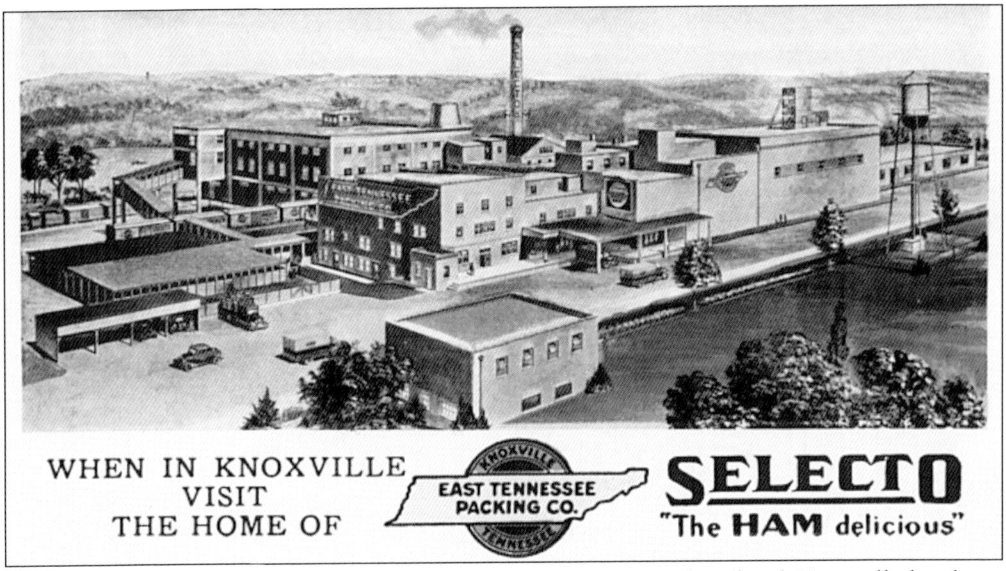

SELECTO "THE HAM DELICIOUS." (Published by E.C. Kropp, Milwaukee.) Knoxville has been called the livestock center of the South; it has been the home of several packing plants. This postcard shows the East Tennessee Packing Company, which dates from 1893. Other similar enterprises are T.L. Lay Packing Company (1920), the Union Livestock Yards (1932), and the Knoxville Abattoir Company, dating from 1899.

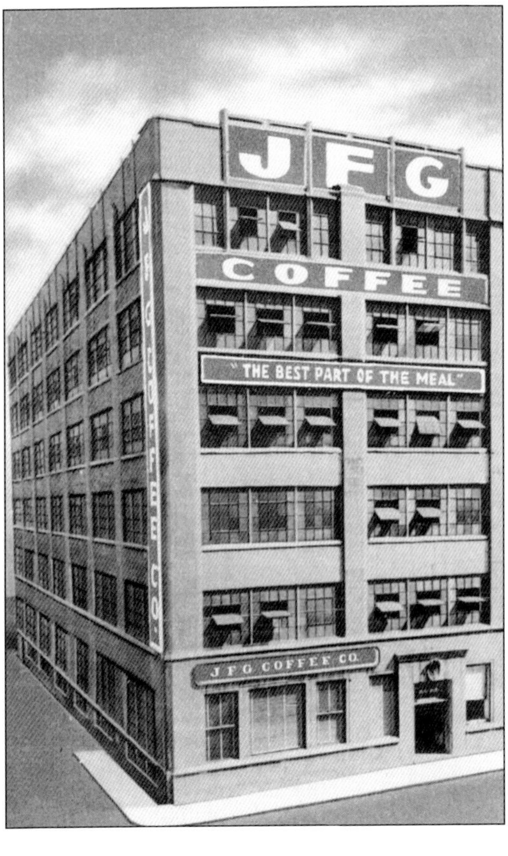

THE JFG COFFEE CO. (No publication data.) This advertising card for the local coffee firm, founded by James Franklin Goodson, shows the building much as it appears today at 200 Jackson Avenue. The back of the card presents a questionnaire about instant coffee. The firm currently manufactures, in addition to coffee, peanut butter, mayonnaise, and salad dressing, products distributed throughout the South.

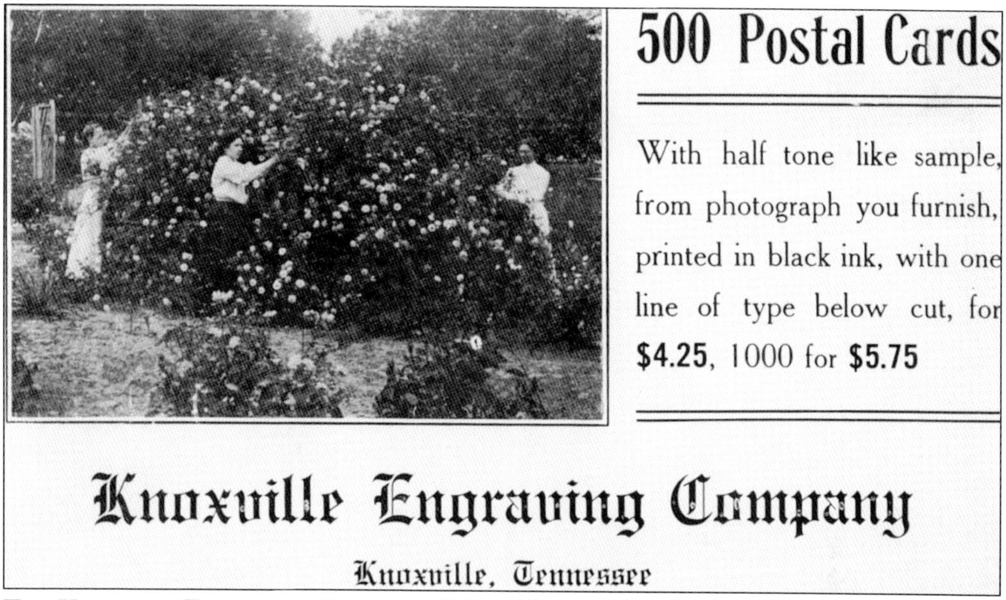

THE KNOXVILLE ENGRAVING COMPANY. (No publication data.) This advertising card for the Knoxville Engraving Company was printed before 1907, as indicated by the women's attire and the card's undivided back. Only the address of the recipient was permitted on the back of postcards before 1907. "Postal cards" were already a big business at this time.

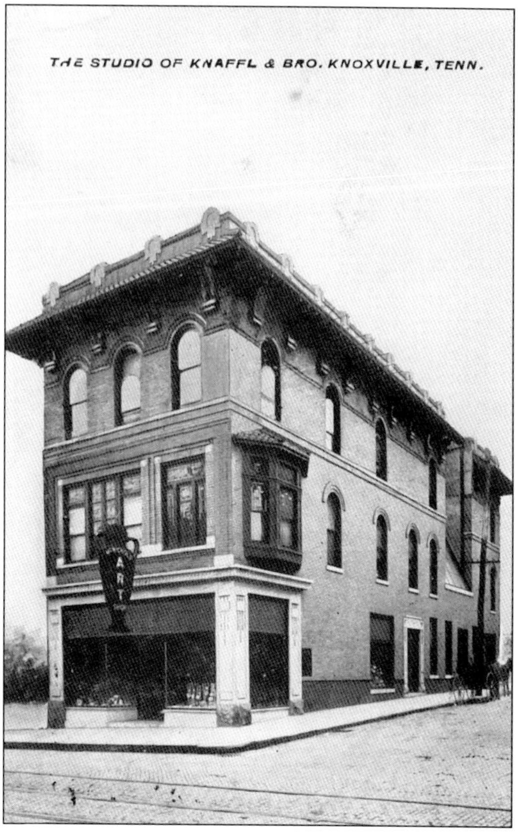

THE STUDIO OF KNAFFL AND BRO. (Published by Knaffl and Bro.; card sent 1910.) The first Knaffl photographic studio was opened in 1884 by Joseph Knaffl and his brother Charles, and was eventually located at Church and Gay Streets. The following is imprinted on the back of this card: "We created this model new home to supply your wants quickly." In 1909 James H. Brakebill joined Joseph Knaffl to open the studio of Knaffl and Brakebill, long esteemed for their portrait photography.

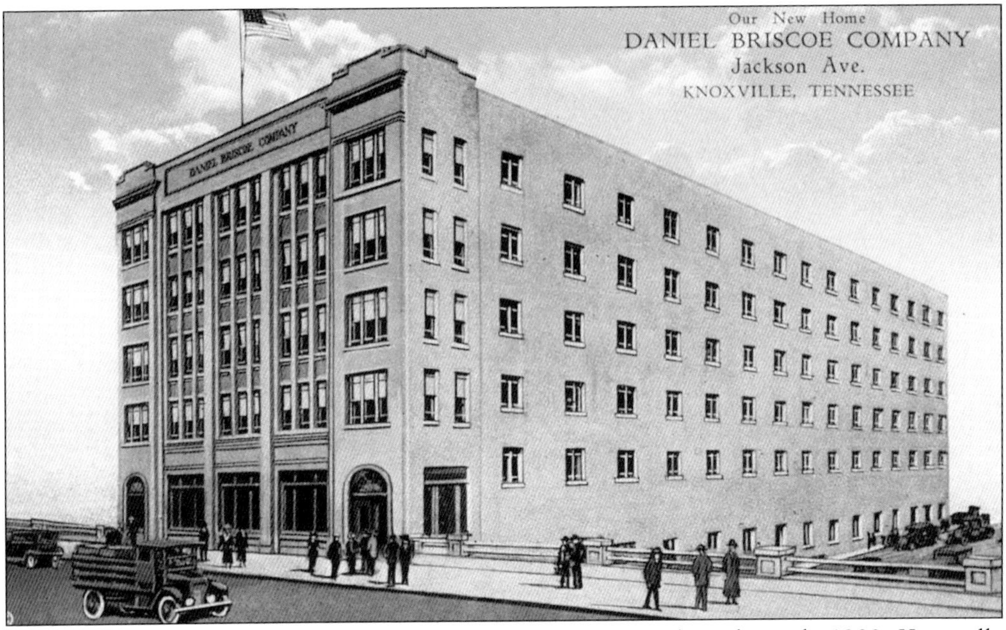

The Daniel Briscoe Company. (Published by Daniel Briscoe.) In the early 1900s Knoxville was the third largest jobbing center below the Ohio River, and Gay Street from Union to Jackson was crowded with warehouses. Many of the men who founded these businesses became rich and influential citizens. One was Daniel Briscoe, whose wholesale warehouse stood for many years at 326–328 Gay Street. He handled "dry goods, notions, furnishings, and ready-to-wear." This card announces his move to Jackson Avenue.

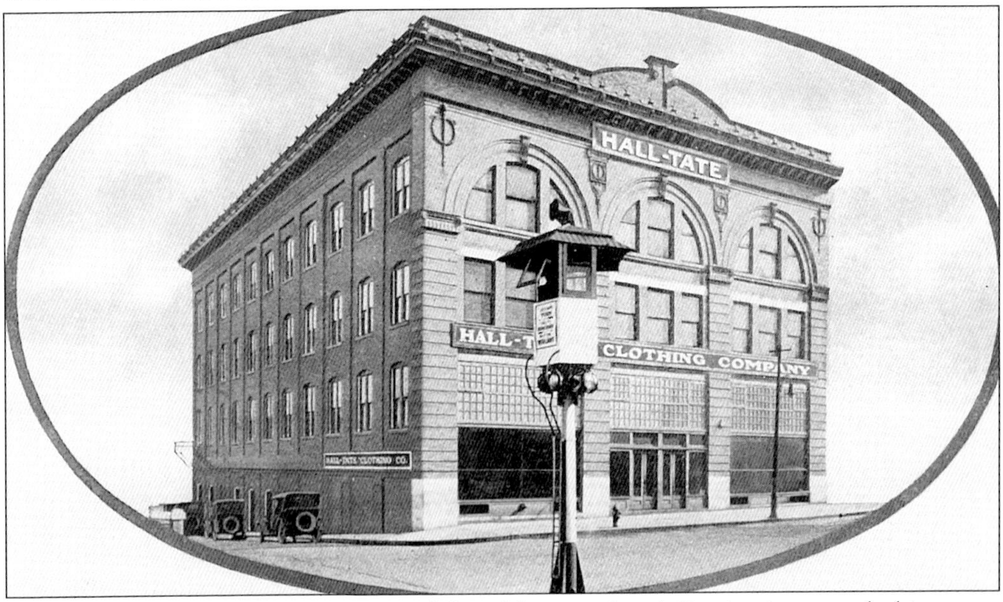

The Hall-Tate Clothing Company. (No publication data.) Originating as a clothing store founded by James S. Hall in 1865, Hall-Tate was first located at 16 Market Street. After 1897 the firm began to manufacture men's suits; in 1924 it moved to 318–320 Gay Street and added departments for women. The firm was sold in 1940 and became Tate-Wynn. This card dates from about 1925.

THE BICKLEY CLOTHING COMPANY. (Published by Harry G. Brown, Atlanta.) Bickley's was located at 314 Gay Street. This card advertises its "complete line of clothing for men and boys—men's suits, boy's suits, men's pants, boys' knee-pants, odd coats, overcoats, mackinaws, etc."

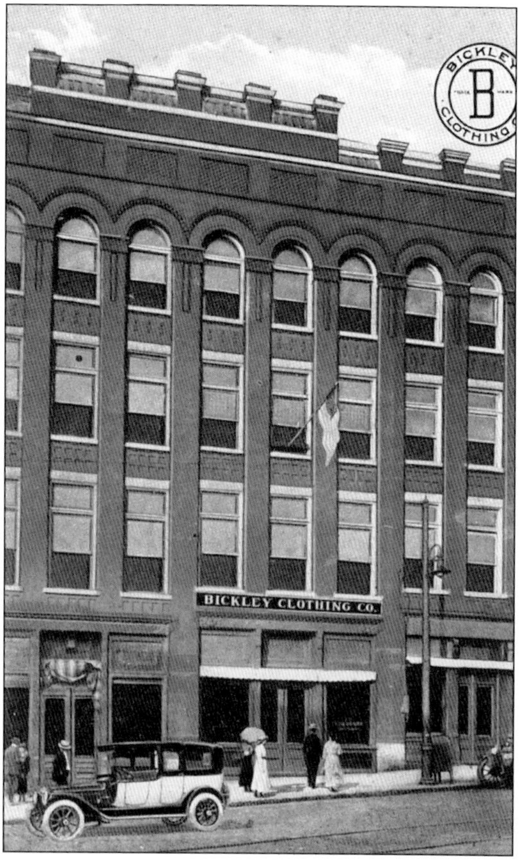

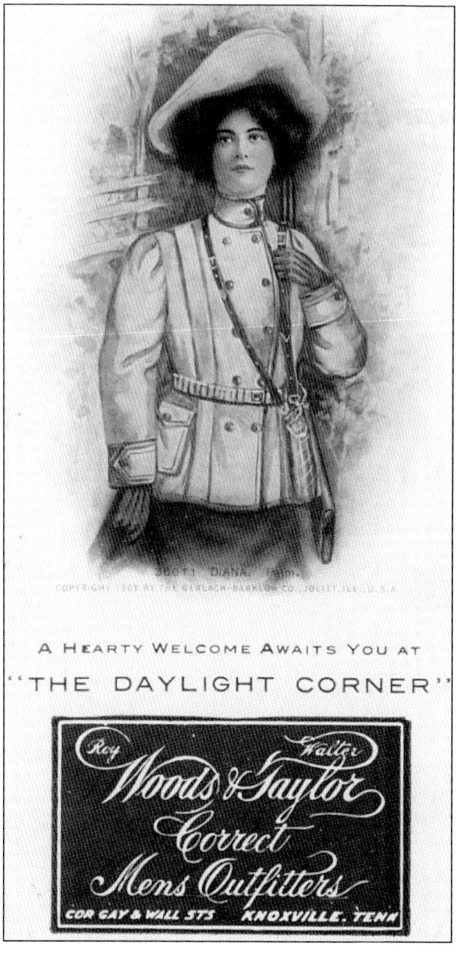

WOODS-TAYLOR, "MEN'S OUTFITTERS." (No publication data; card sent 1912.) Roy Woods and Walter Taylor were located at 323 South Gay Street in 1912 and were known as "Men's outfitters." By 1920 they advertised as "outfitters for the family." By 1951 the name had changed to Woods-Taylor-Cox and the store was at 514 Gay Street. The model in this 1908 picture is named "Diana" and carries a hunting rifle.

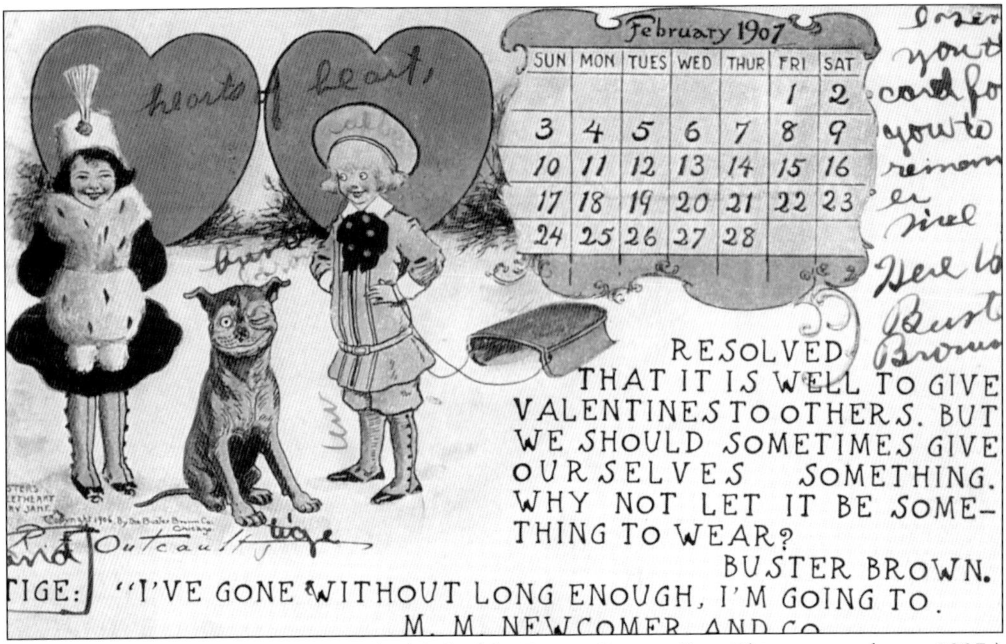

M.M. Newcomer and Company. (Published by Buster Brown Co., Chicago; card sent 1907.) The artist Richard Outcault drew many images for early postcards; he frequently featured Buster Brown and his dog Tige in appropriate holiday and amusing situations. This Valentine card is a clever advertisement for M.M. Newcomer Company, located in the 400 block of Gay Street. It occupied five floors of a former jobbing house.

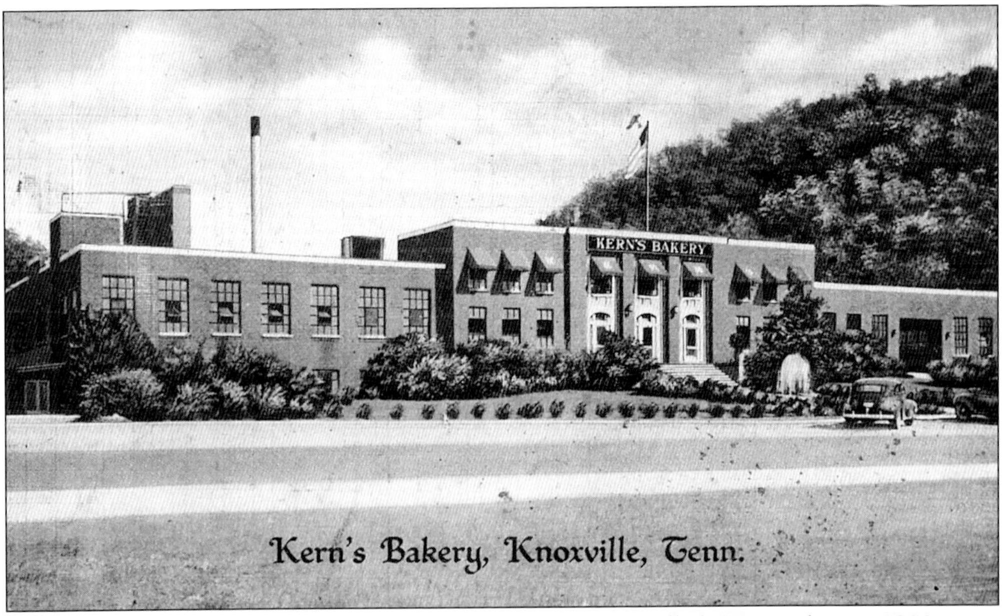

Kern's Bakery. (Published by Graphic Arts Agency, Knoxville.) We see here a 1930s view of the home of Kern's bread and cakes, the outgrowth of Peter Kern's early confectionery on Market Square. This large establishment on Chapman Highway is a landmark of Knoxville's commercial history.

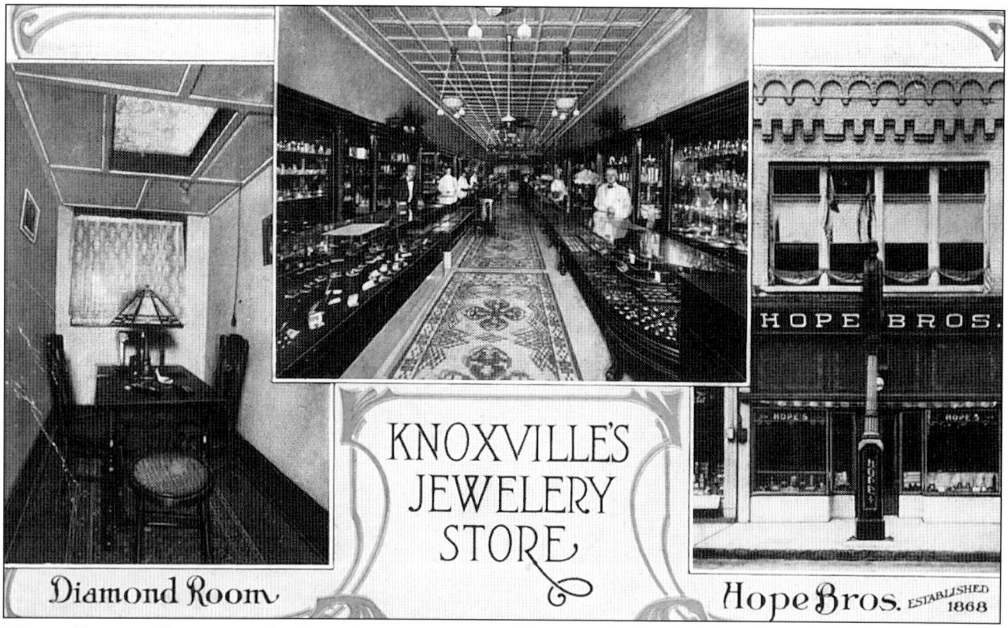

Hope Bros., Knoxville's Jewelery Store. (Published by Curt Teich, Chicago; card sent 1917.) Hope Bros. Jewelers, established in 1868, was located "at the clock" on Gay Street. Most Gay Street pictures show this landmark clearly; however, this card shows the clock sideways and it is almost invisible. The Diamond Room, pictured at left, reveals a Tiffany lamp, one of the beautiful products of a famous glass maker. In 1934 Kimball's Jewelers moved into the Hope address.

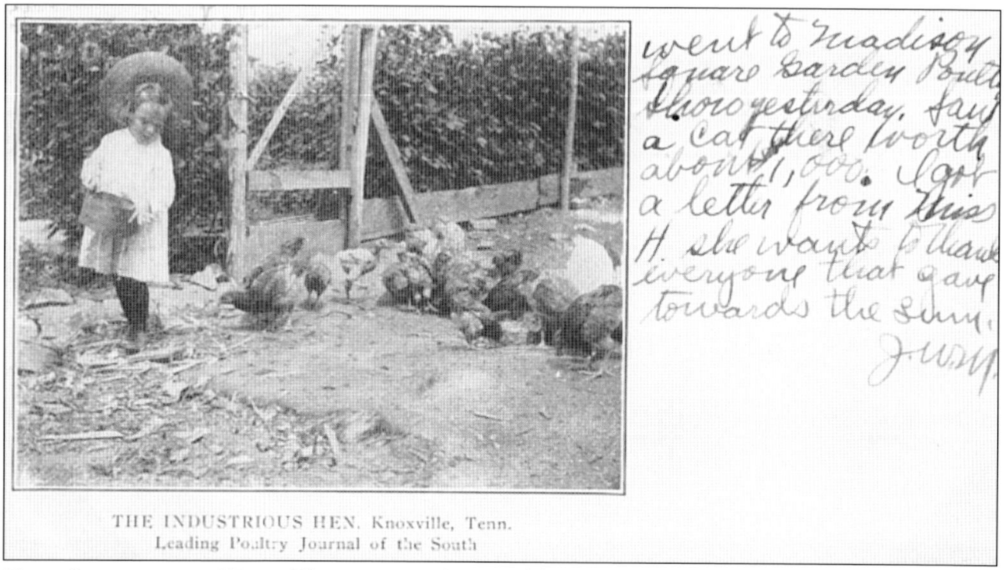

The *Industrious Hen*, Knoxville. (No publication data; card sent 1907.) Among Knoxville's many publications we find the *Industrious Hen*, "leading poultry journal of the South." This is an early advertising card published before 1907, when messages on postcards were required to be written on the front of the card, with only the addresses on the back. Typically the picture was small enough to permit a short message on the white space at the right.

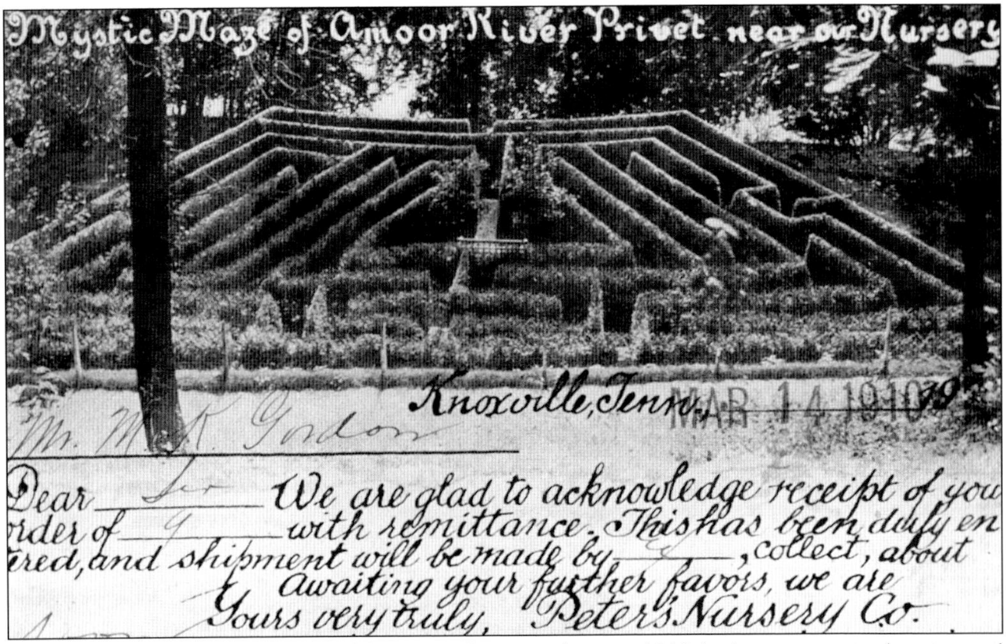

PETER'S NURSERY CO. (No publication data; card sent 1910.) An interestingly pictured advertisement, this Peter's Nursery postcard acknowledges an "order with remittance." Postcard advertisements have been used by businesses since the turn of the century as a quick and direct method of corresponding with customers.

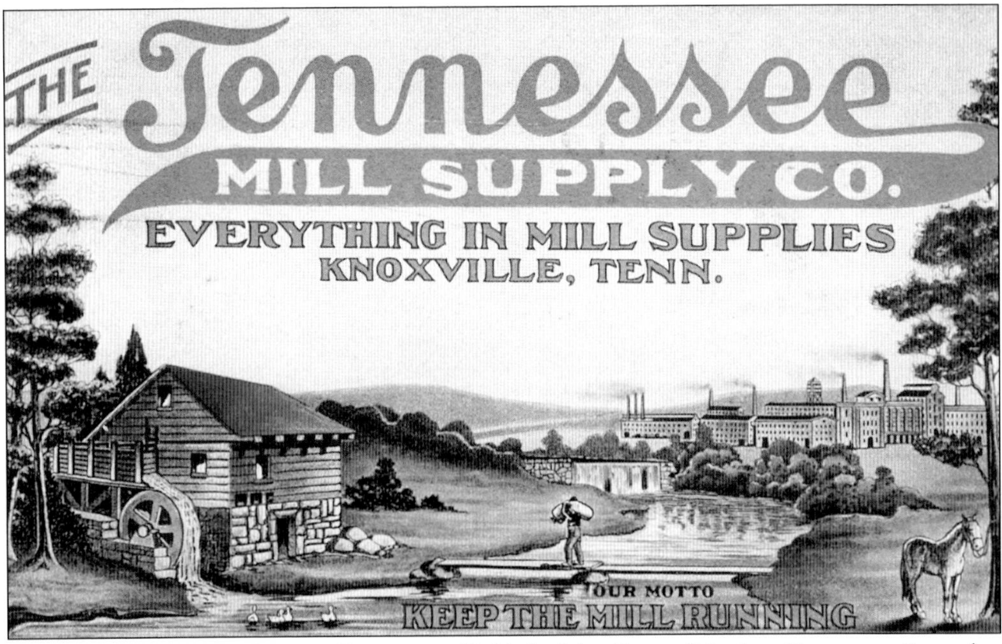

THE TENNESSEE MILL SUPPLY COMPANY. (Published by Stone Printing Company, Roanoke, Virginia; card sent 1909.) In 1900 Tennessee Mill Supply Company was one of Knoxville's principal wholesale companies and manufacturing plants. We see here an unusually neat and colorful advertising card mailed September 29, 1909, which says, "We thank you for remittance of $1.26 which we have credited."

Three

Homes, Churches, and Personal Life

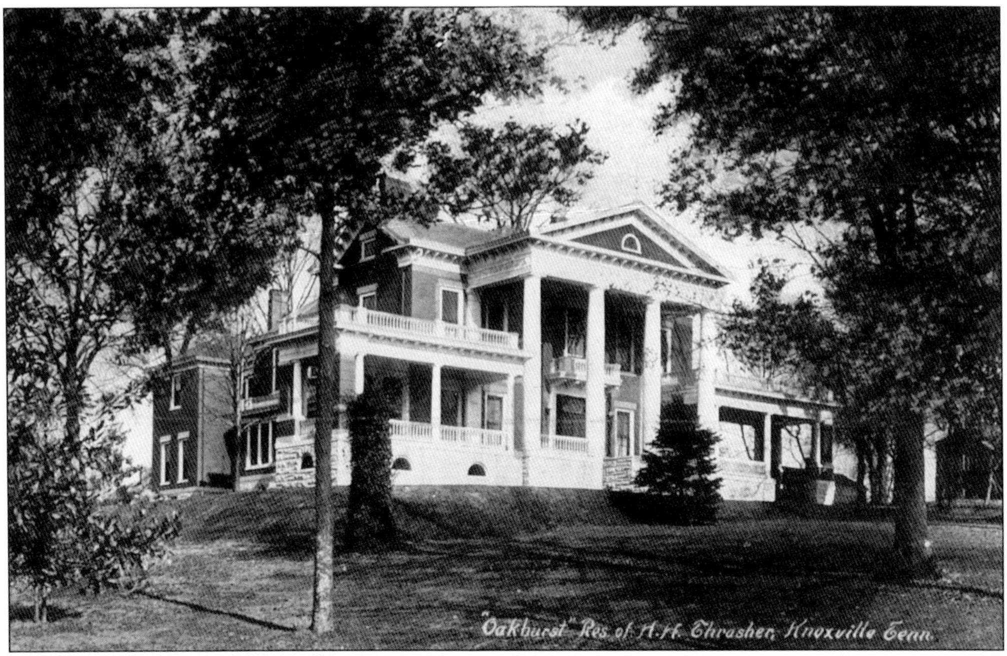

"Oakhurst," the Residence of H.H. Thrasher. (Published by CC&C Co.) In 1912 H.H. Thrasher was a partner in the firm of Thrasher and Gunter, contractors, located at 708 Gay Street; he was also vice-president of the Climax Coal Company. The Thrasher home at 2633 Kingston Pike has had a number of tenants. In 1920 it was remodeled and became the Thrasher Nursing Home, after which it became Howard-Henderson Hospital. Today it houses Big Brothers and Big Sisters of Knoxville.

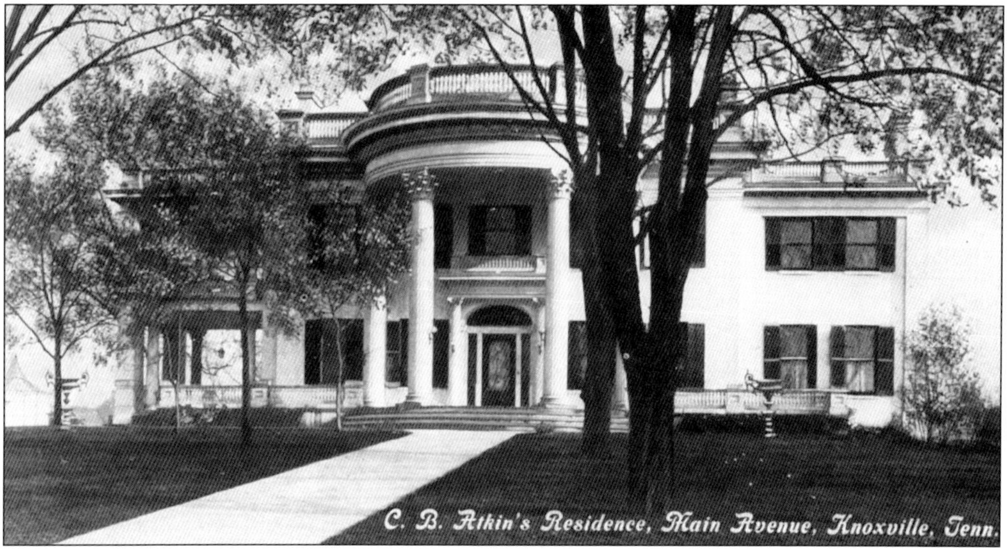

C.B. ATKIN'S RESIDENCE, MAIN AVENUE. (Published by S.H. Kress.) The Clay Brown Atkin house at 518 West Main was the old Perez Dickinson house built in 1830, bought by Atkin in 1905 and remodeled by George Barber, Knoxville architect. C.B. Atkin's fortune came from Oakwood Manufacturing Company, which made mantels; he became Knoxville's first millionaire. In 1949 the house was torn down, but the staircase and portico were saved and added to the Kingsport home of Harvey Brooks.

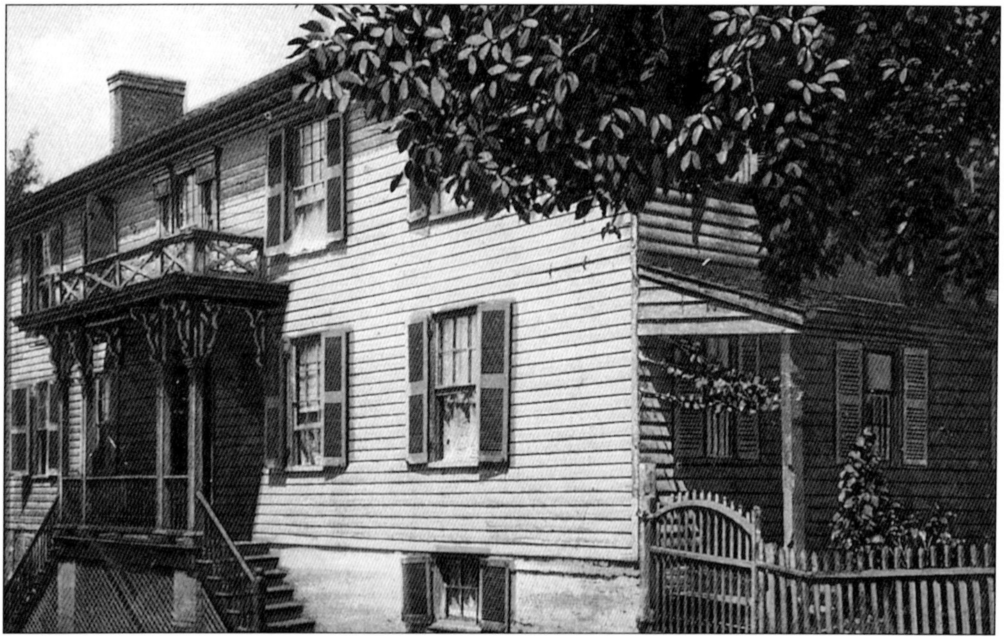

THE RESIDENCE OF GOVERNOR W.G. BROWNLOW. (Published by Souvenir Post Card Co.) William G. "Parson" Brownlow (1805–1877) lived at 211 Cumberland Avenue for 28 years. He was an outspoken man of many accomplishments—editor of the Knoxville *Whig* (1849–61), Unionist, the Reconstruction governor of Tennessee (1865–69), and U.S. senator (1869–75). Many famous guests visited here, including six presidents—Andrew Johnson, Grant, Hayes, McKinley, Teddy Roosevelt, and Taft.

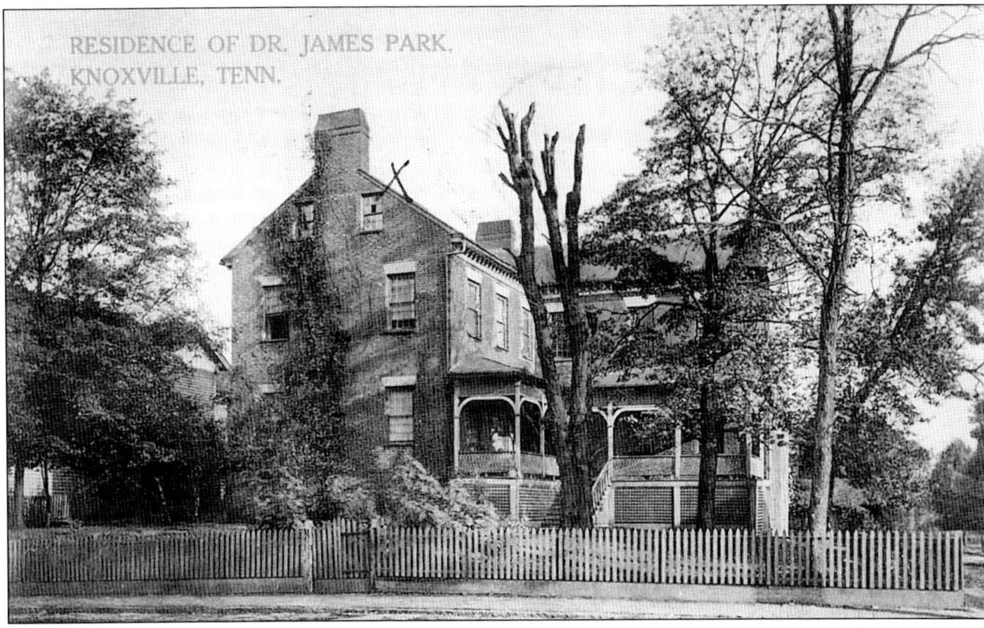

The Residence of Dr. James Park. (Published by M. Howard, Knoxville; card sent 1911.) James Park, a pioneer merchant, built this house in 1812; his family lived here for three generations. He was Knoxville's mayor from 1818 to 1821 and again from 1824 to 1826. The house, still standing at Cumberland and Walnut, has been the medical library and museum of the Knoxville Academy of Medicine since 1945.

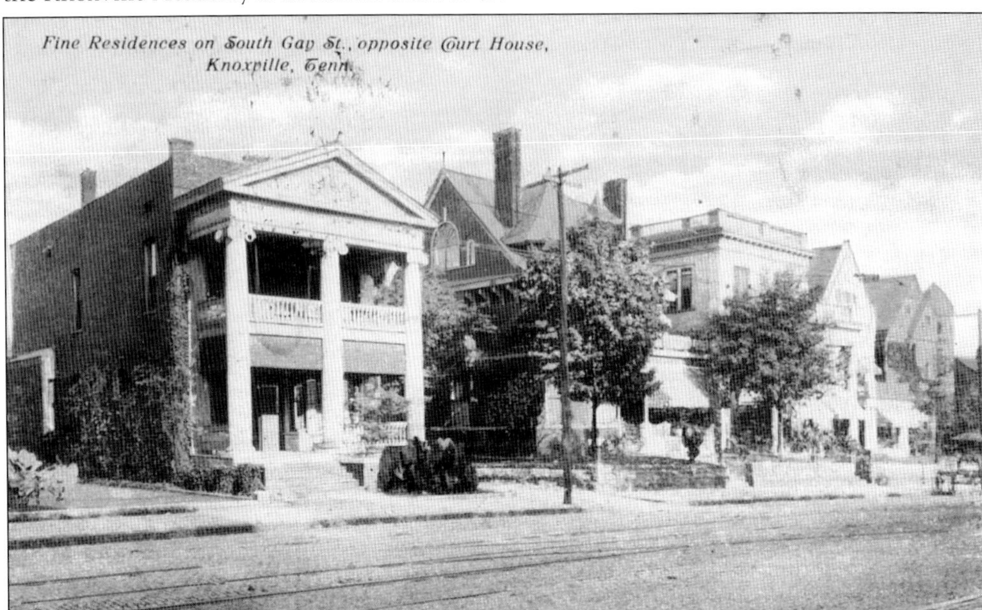

The Fine Residences on Gay Street opposite the Courthouse. (Published by Chapman Drug Co., Knoxville; card sent 1912.) These fine residences of the Ward, Beeler, Cunningham, Knaffl, and Hurst families faced the Courthouse across Gay Street until 1925, when they were demolished for the construction of the Tennessee Terrace Hotel. Refinanced and renamed, the Andrew Johnson Hotel emerged here in 1929.

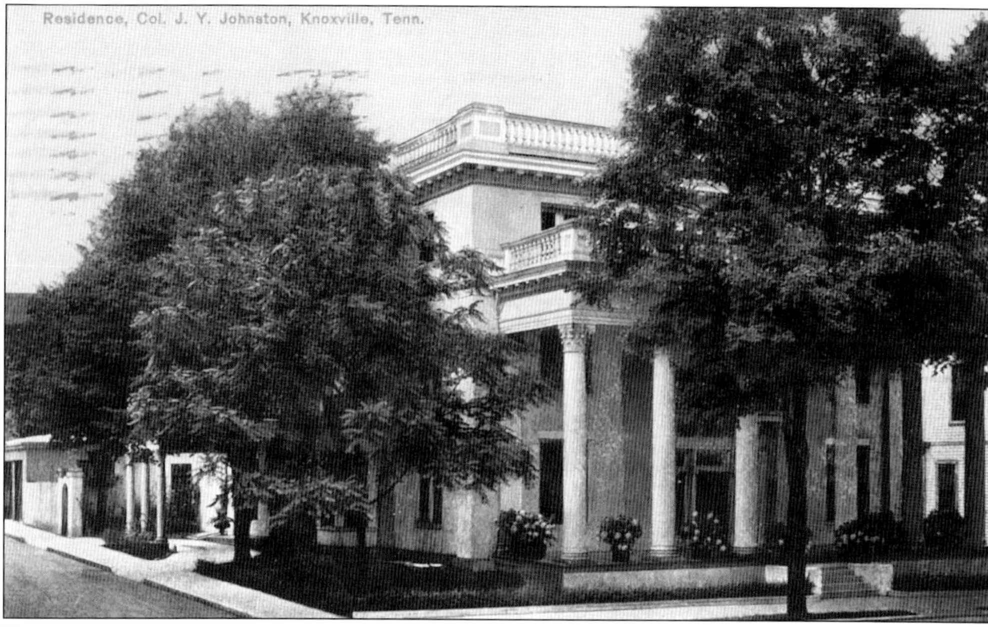

The Col. J.Y. Johnston Residence. (Published by Charles Cullen; card sent 1910.) Col. J.Y. Johnston, a former Confederate officer, occupied this home located at 421 West Main Avenue at Walnut after 1909. Earlier it had been the home of the Benevolent and Protectorate Order of Elks. Colonel Johnston moved here when his former mansion, bounded by East Fifth, North Central, North Fourth, and Lamar Streets, was sold to the City and demolished to build Knoxville High School.

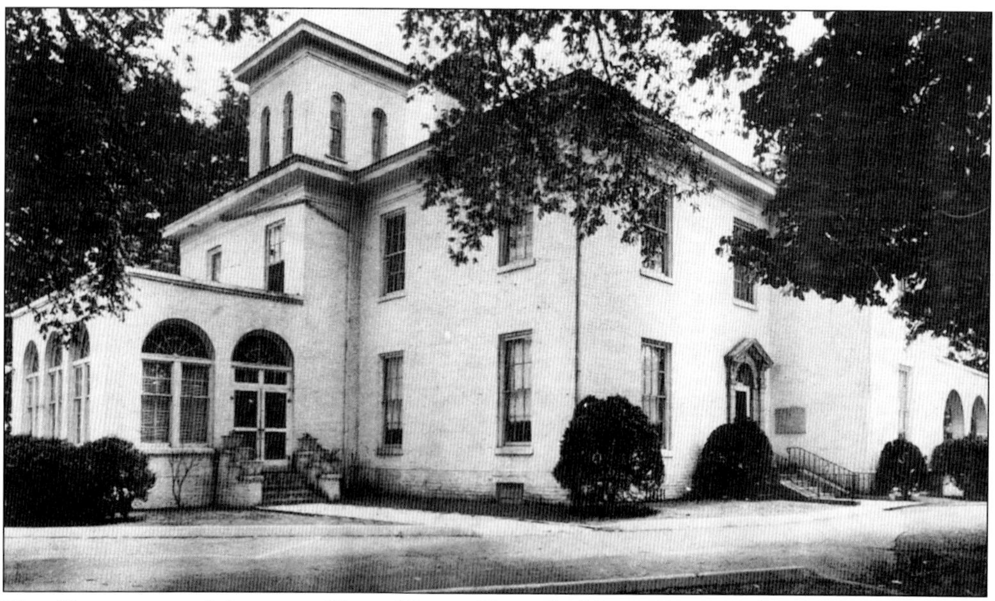

The Confederate Memorial Hall (Bleak House). (No publication data.) Bleak House, at 3148 Kingston Pike, is a 15-room antebellum mansion of handmade brick, built in 1856 by Robert H. Armstrong. In 1863 it was used as the headquarters of Gen. James Longstreet during the Siege of Knoxville; bullet holes are still visible in its brick facade. It was purchased in 1959 by the United Daughters of the Confederacy for a chapter house and a memorial.

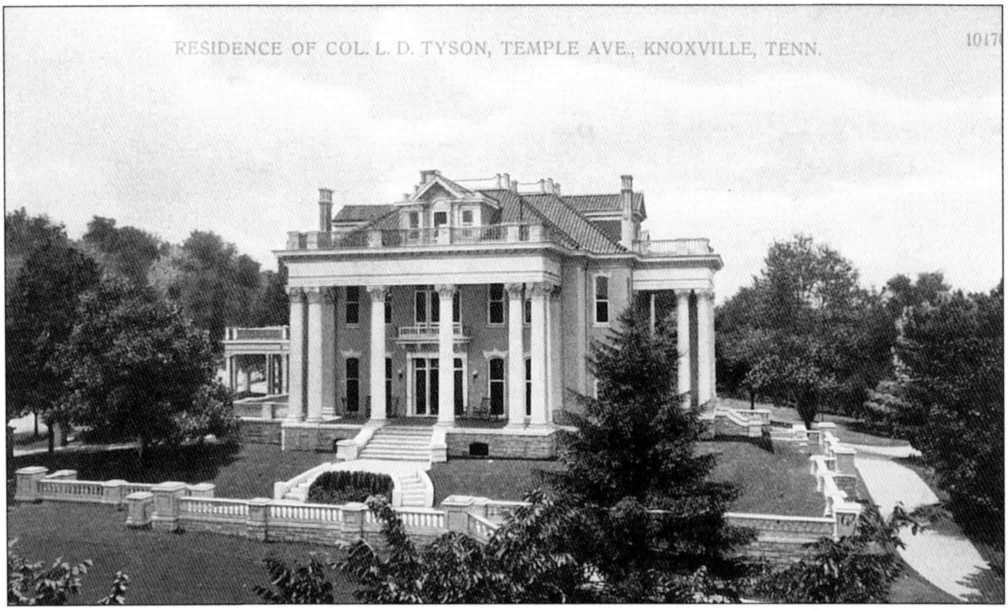

THE RESIDENCE OF COL. L.D. TYSON. (Published by Charles C. Cullen, Knoxville.) Brig. Gen. Lawrence D. Tyson came to Knoxville in 1891 as the university's commandant of cadets. He achieved prominence in the Spanish-American War, in World War I, and as a U.S. senator. He bought the *Sentinel* in 1923, and was in many ways an illustrious citizen. The University of Tennessee has owned the house since 1954.

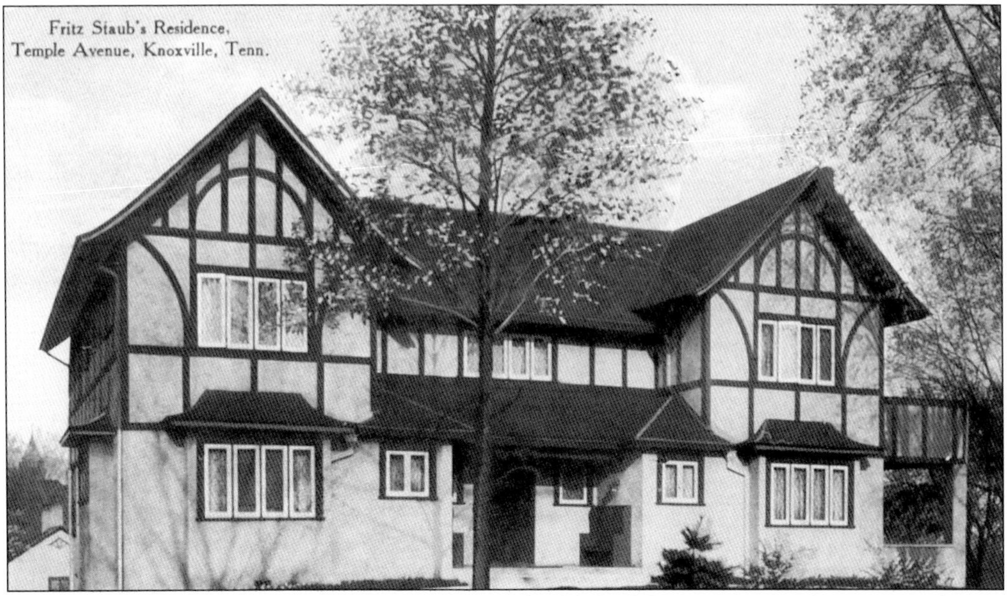

FRITZ STAUB'S RESIDENCE, TEMPLE AVENUE. (Published by S.H. Kress.) Fritz Staub was the son of Peter Staub, the prosperous tailor and mayor of Knoxville who opened Staub's Theatre. In 1885 Fritz became manager; under his direction the theatre was remodeled, greatly increasing the seating capacity and the beauty of the interior. His residence on Temple Avenue (now Volunteer Boulevard) was a gracious home which exhibited the wealth and style of its owner.

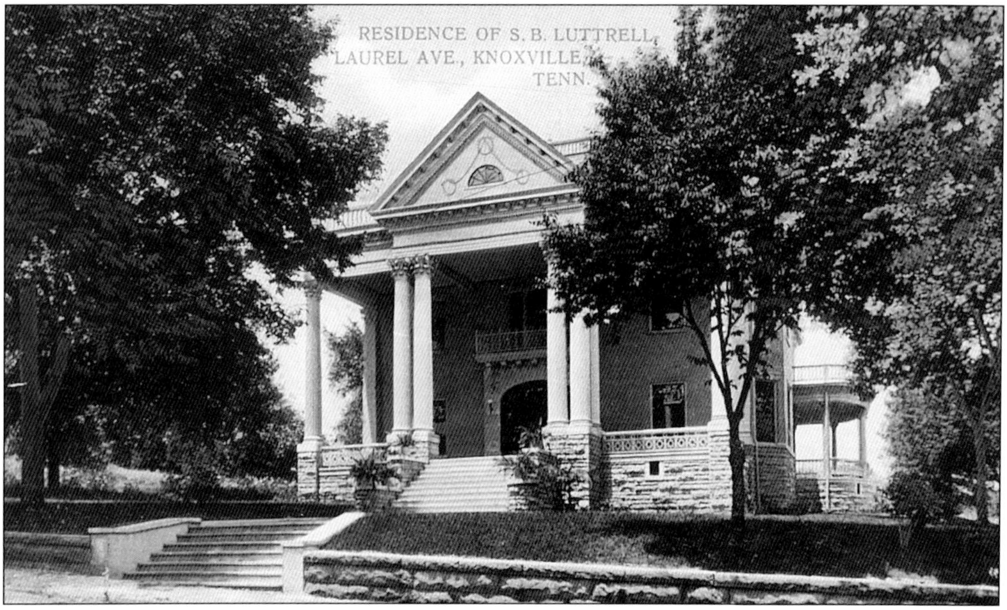

The Residence of S.B. Luttrell, Laurel Avenue. (Published by Charles C. Cullen.) Samuel B. Luttrell (1844–1933) was one of Knoxville's "merchant princes"—a hardware merchant with various business and political interests. He was a stockholder in many corporations, and served for a short time as mayor (1879–80). His Classical style mansion at Laurel Avenue and Fifteenth Street reflected his wealth as well as the architectural preference of the time. The site is now a parking lot.

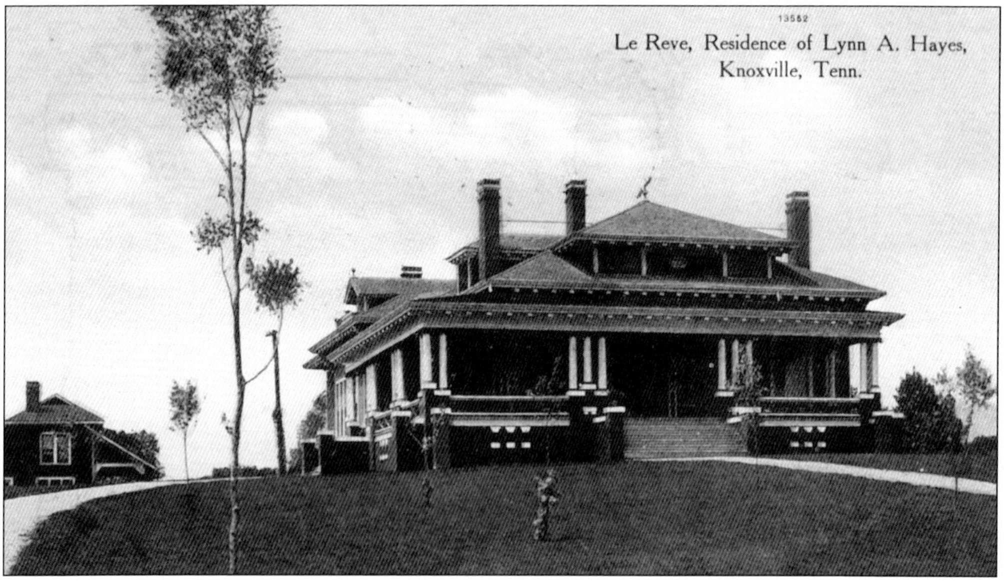

Le Reve, the Residence of Lynn A. Hayes. (Published by W.D. Kuhlman, Knoxville; card sent 1912.) In the early 1920s Lynn Hayes was associated with George Brown, whose store sold hardware, seeds, and agricultural implements at 306–310 South Gay Street; later he became partner in the Cruze-Lyon-Hayes Company, which sold hardware and was one of the sponsors of the Appalachian Exposition in 1911. The Hayes home at 994 Broadway, where it still stands, was designed by Charles Hayes for his brother.

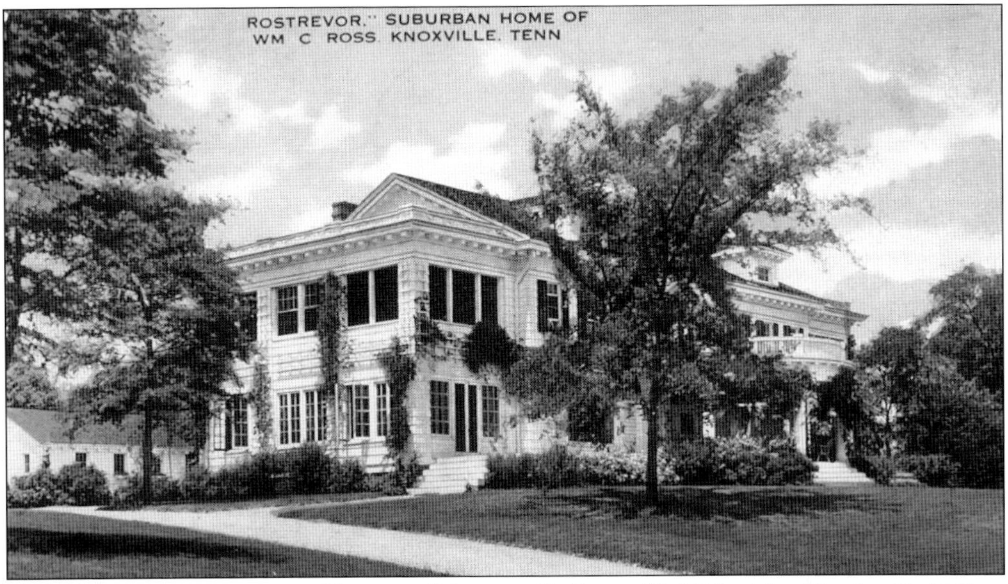

ROSTREVOR, THE SUBURBAN HOME OF WILLIAM C. ROSS. (Published by Charles C. Cullen; card sent 1915.) William C. Ross (1879–1956) built his home on Lyons View Pike in 1910. An outstanding Knoxville industrialist, he contributed much to the planning and landscaping of his house. It was notable for its commanding presence on a hilltop, from which the Tennessee River and a full sweep of the Smoky Mountains could be seen.

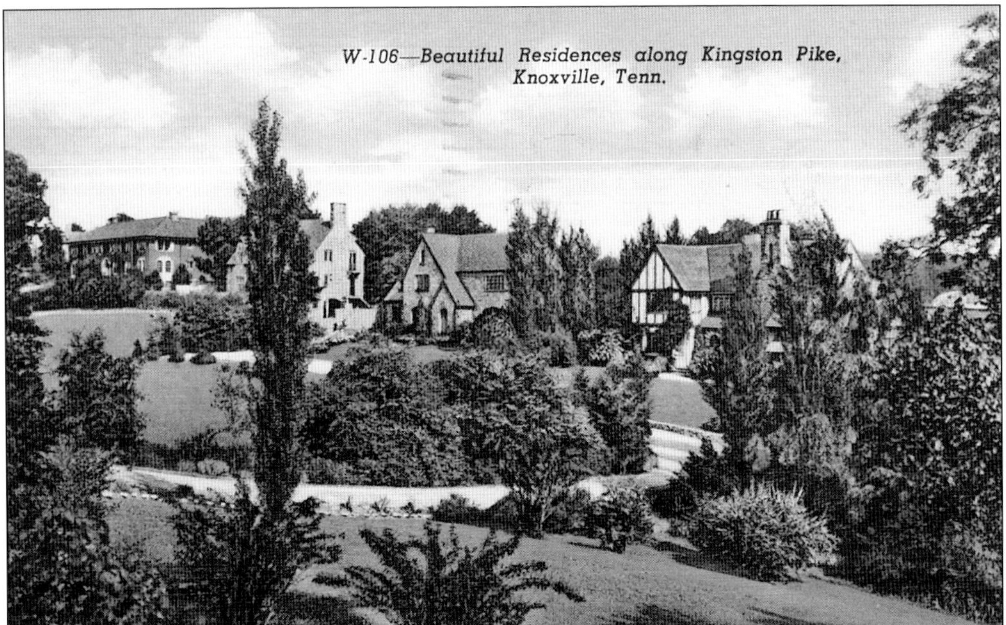

BEAUTIFUL RESIDENCES ALONG KINGSTON PIKE, KNOXVILLE. (Published by Werner News Agency, Knoxville.) Kingston Pike was an important roadway as early as 1795. Originally 30 feet wide, it was later widened to 50 feet and extended to the town of Kingston. It has always been the choice for beautiful and elegant homes, some of them now memorials to its historic past. They include "Statesview," "Crescent Bend," "Westwood," and "Bleak House."

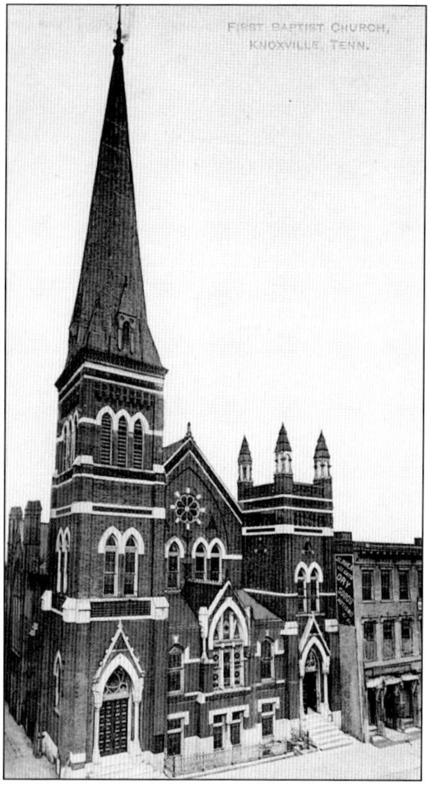

The First Baptist Church. (Published by Monroe Howard.) The old First Baptist Church, designed by Joseph F. and Albert B. Baumann, was erected on Gay Street in 1887, where it stood until 1924, when its congregation moved to their new edifice on Main Street. Its steeple provides a landmark in many early pictures of Gay Street.

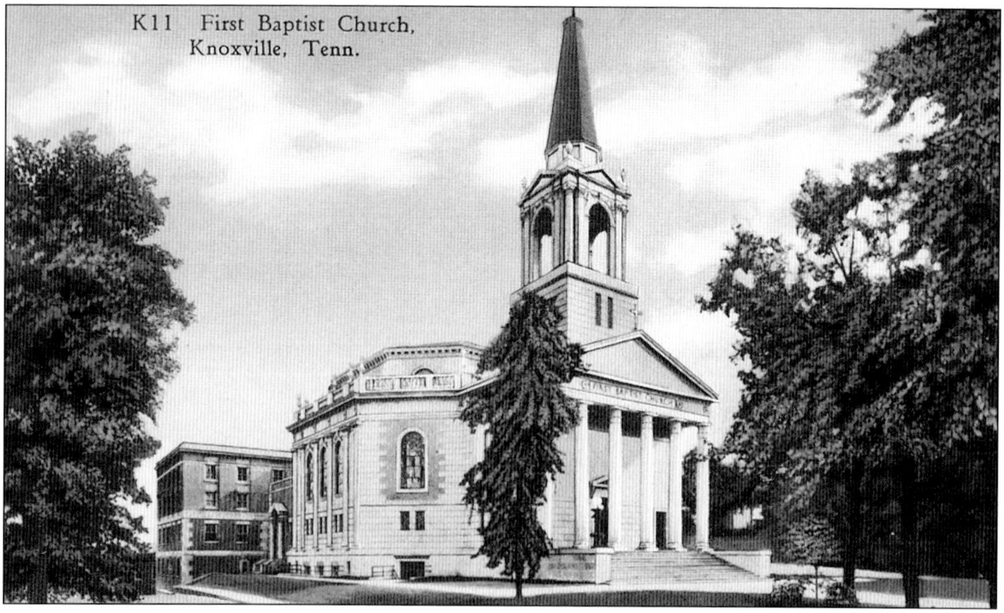

The First Baptist Church. (Published by Curt Teich; card sent 1944.) The First Baptist Church at 510 Main Avenue succeeded the previous one on Gay Street. Designed by Dougherty and Gardner of Nashville, it was built in 1923–24 on the site of the old McClung house. Constructed of gray brick and Indiana limestone, it cost $500,000. It has one of the largest congregations in the county.

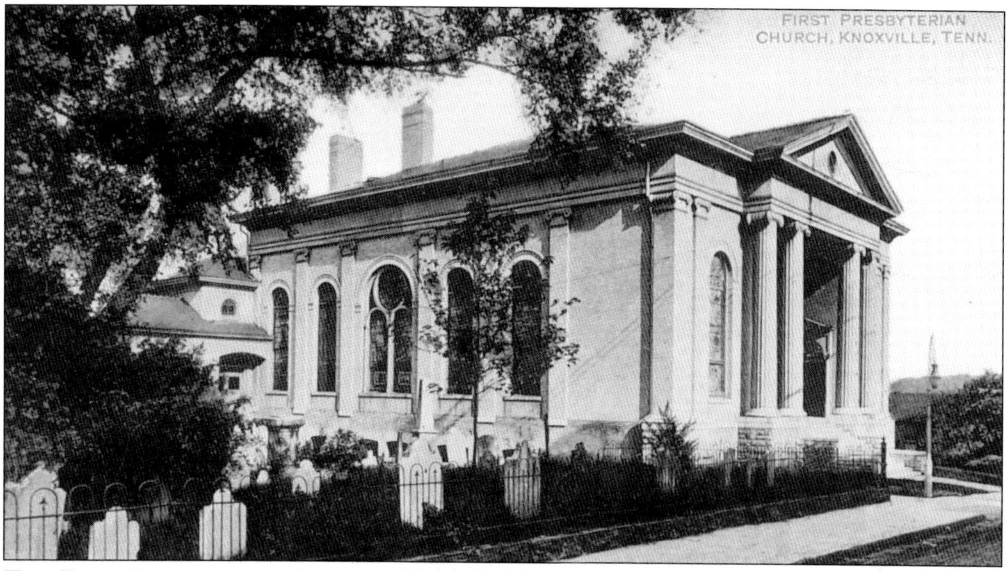

THE FIRST PRESBYTERIAN CHURCH. (Published by Monroe Howard, Knoxville.) Knoxville's oldest urban church, the First Presbyterian was organized about 1793 with James White, John Adair, and George McNutt as founding elders. The pictured building, erected in 1852, sits on the land reserved by James White. It was remodeled in 1869 after use as a hospital in the Civil War. In the adjacent graveyard are buried a number of early Knoxvillians, including James White, Samuel Carrick (the first pastor), and William Blount.

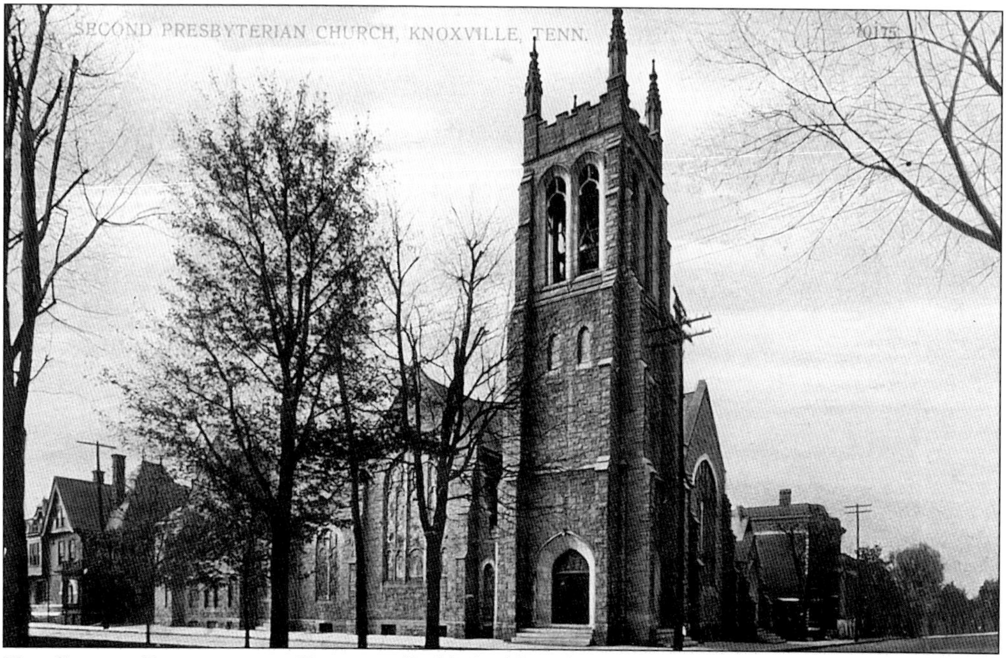

THE SECOND PRESBYTERIAN CHURCH. (Published by Charles C. Cullen, Knoxville.) The Second Presbyterian Church was organized in 1818 because of a split in the First Church congregation. An earlier church structure was built on Clinch Avenue at Market Street in 1860; however, the church in this picture was built at Church and Walnut Streets in 1906 and served the congregation here until it moved to Kingston Pike in 1957.

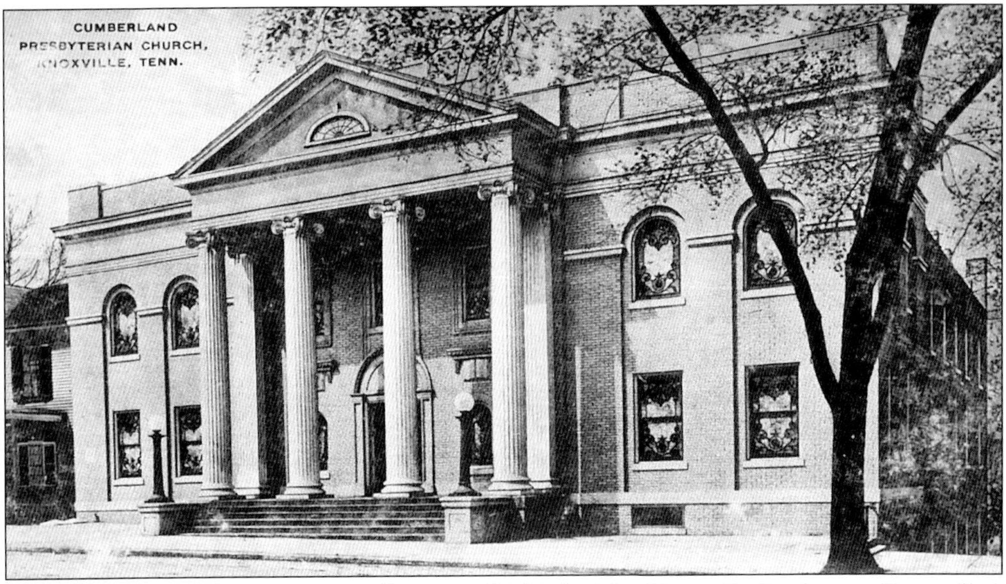

THE CUMBERLAND PRESBYTERIAN CHURCH. (Published by Howard's Bookstore, Knoxville.) Organized March 22, 1885, Knoxville's Cumberland Presbyterians built their church on Broad Street (now Broadway) next to the Old Gray Cemetery. It was remodeled in 1912 as shown in the picture. Here it remained until 1975, when the congregation moved to a new home at 6900 Nubbin Ridge Drive. The old Broadway church was torn down, and a new building on the site now houses the Knox Area Rescue Ministries.

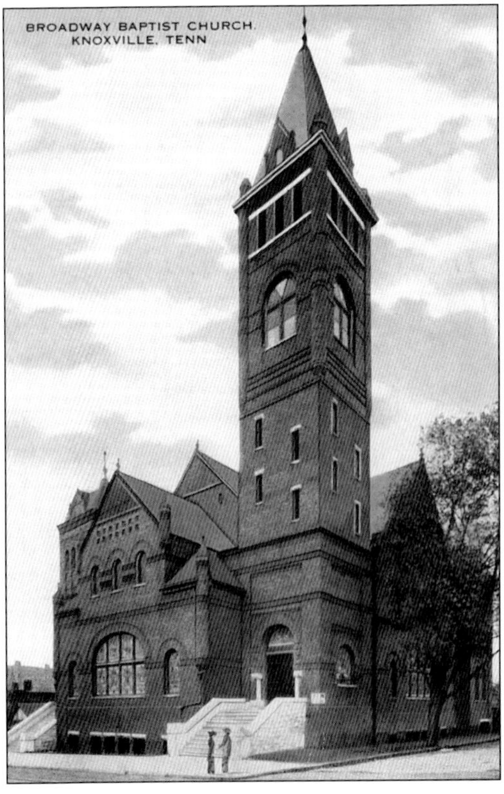

THE BROADWAY BAPTIST CHURCH. (Published by Commercial Chrome; card sent 1916.) Broadway Baptist was first organized in 1886 as Calvary Baptist; it then became Second Baptist, and subsequently Broadway Baptist. This building was completed in 1898 and burned in 1965. The new church edifice is at 815 North Broadway.

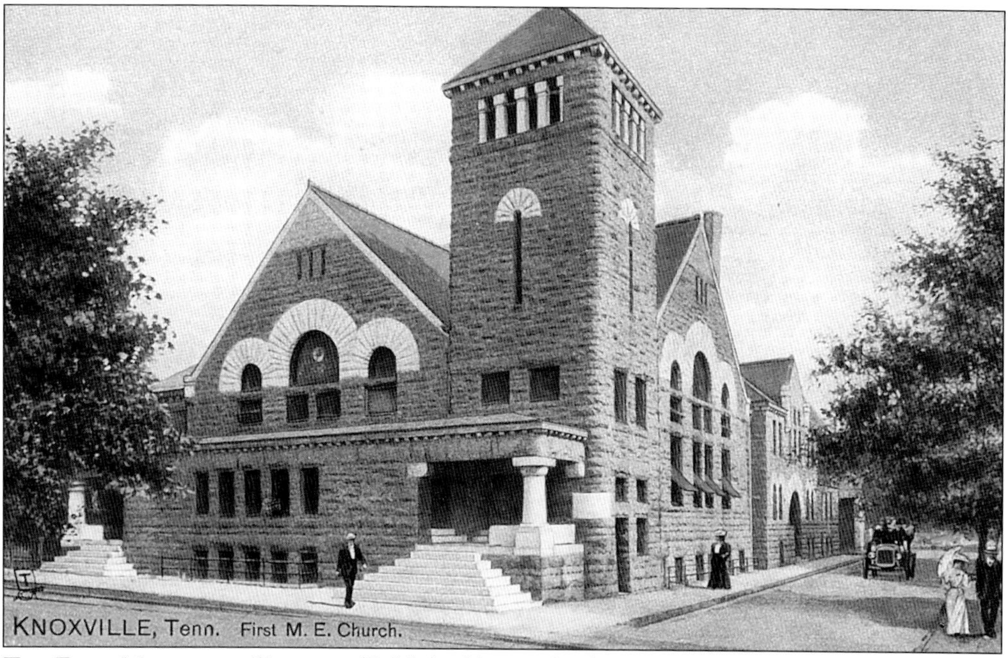

THE FIRST METHODIST CHURCH. (Published by Raphael Tuck and Sons, London; series 2721.) Built in 1893 on the southeast corner of Clinch Avenue and Locust Street, the First Methodist Church was Knoxville's best example of the style of the great American architect H.H. Richardson. The church was massively designed in the Romanesque manner, with heavy stone work and a bold tower. It has since been destroyed.

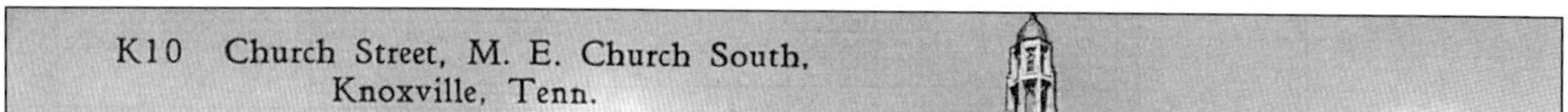

THE CHURCH STREET M.E. CHURCH. (Published by Asheville Post Card Company.) The name of the Church Street M.E. Church was transferred to this new edifice when the congregation moved from its original Church Street location in 1930 to 900 Henley Street between Main and Hill Avenue. Its modern Gothic style, designed by Barber and McMurry, exhibits throughout high standards of detailing and craftmanship.

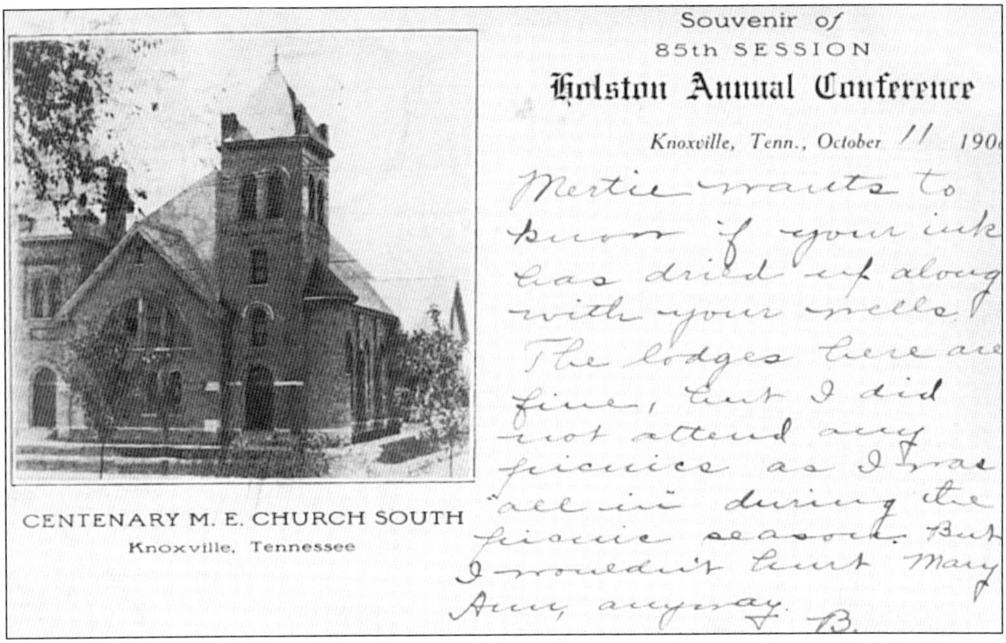

The Centenary M.E. Church South. (No publication data; card sent 1908.) One of the area's small Southern Methodist churches, the Centenary M.E. Church South was located at 120 Gill Avenue in 1908 when this card was sent. There are messages on both front and back of the card; on the back the sender advises, "Come to the Carnival, Gertrude. It's going to be great."

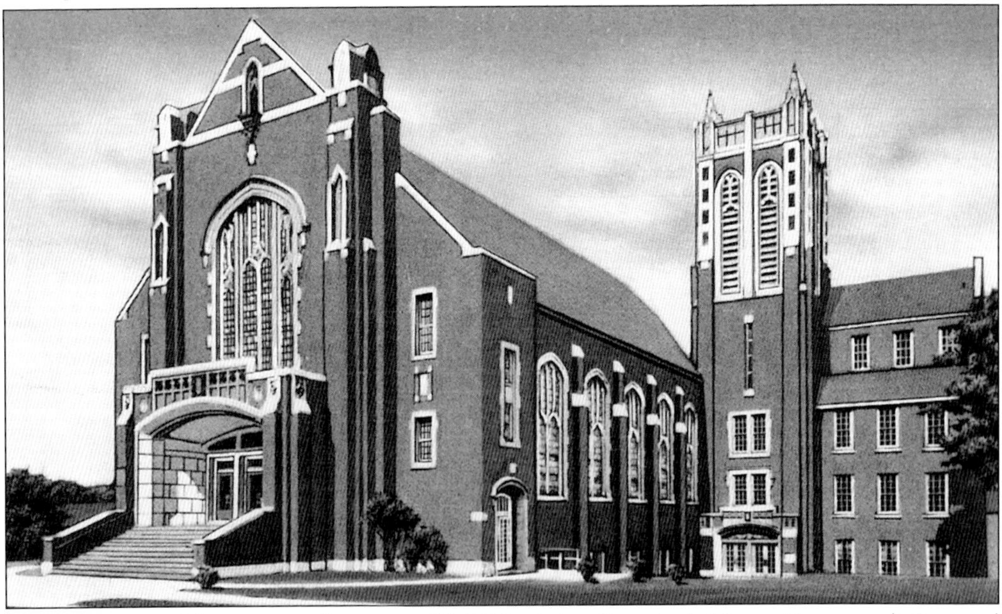

The Central Methodist Church. (Published by Standard News Company.) Located at 201 East Third Avenue, Central Methodist was formed by the union of the Broadway and Centenary congregations in 1924. This postcard, printed in the 1930s, informs us that "Central Methodist is Knoxville's largest church." Its massive Gothic structure overwhelms its small neighborhood.

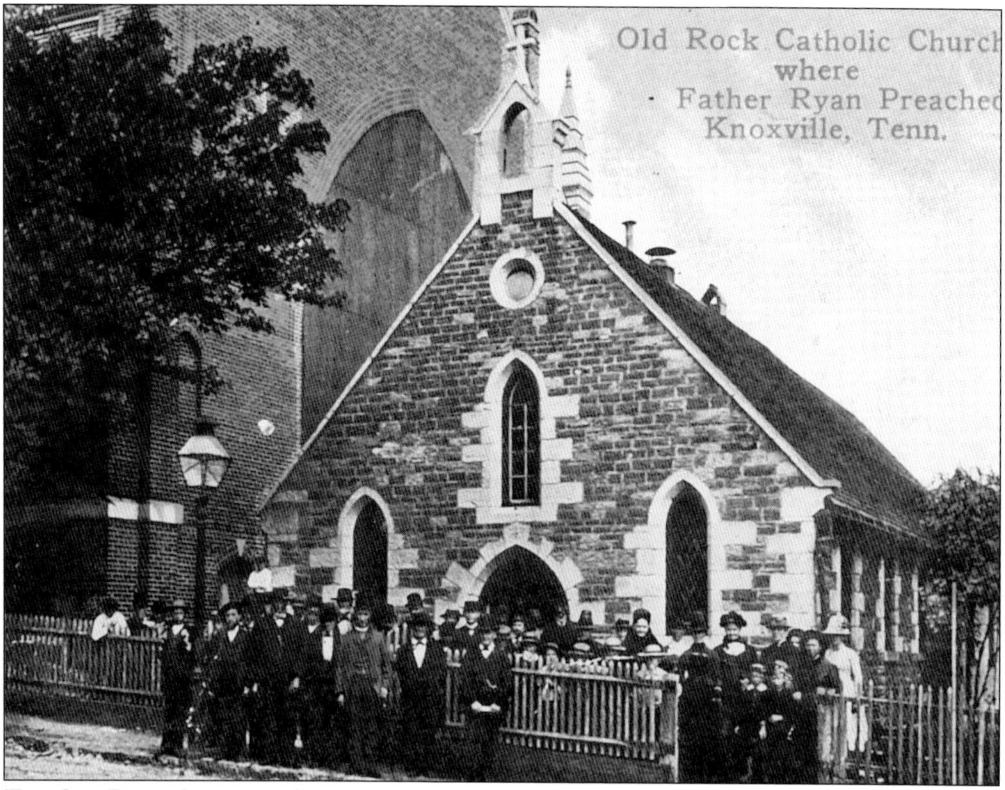

THE OLD ROCK CATHOLIC CHURCH WHERE FATHER RYAN PREACHED. (No publication data; card sent 1913.) Knoxville's first Catholic church, erected in 1852, was of Gothic design. Father Abram Joseph Ryan, known as "Poet-laureate of the Confederacy," was in charge of this church between May 1865 and July 1866. He wrote the famous poem "The Conquered Banner." The building was razed in 1886 to make room for the subsequent structure on Summit Hill.

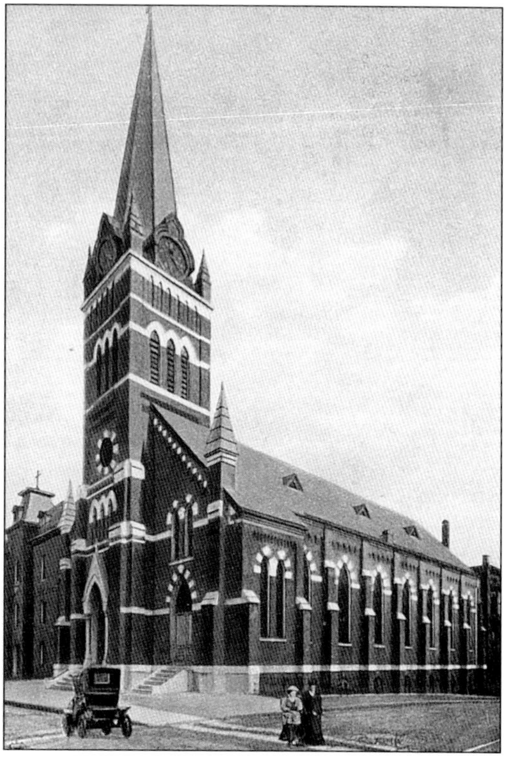

THE CHURCH OF THE IMMACULATE CONCEPTION. (Published by Raphael Tuck and Sons, London; series 2750; card sent 1921.) One of downtown Knoxville's oldest buildings, the Immaculate Conception Church was built at 414 West Vine Avenue in 1886 on the site of the old Rock Church. Designed in Gothic style by Joseph F. and Albert B. Baumann, it dominates its site on Summit Hill.

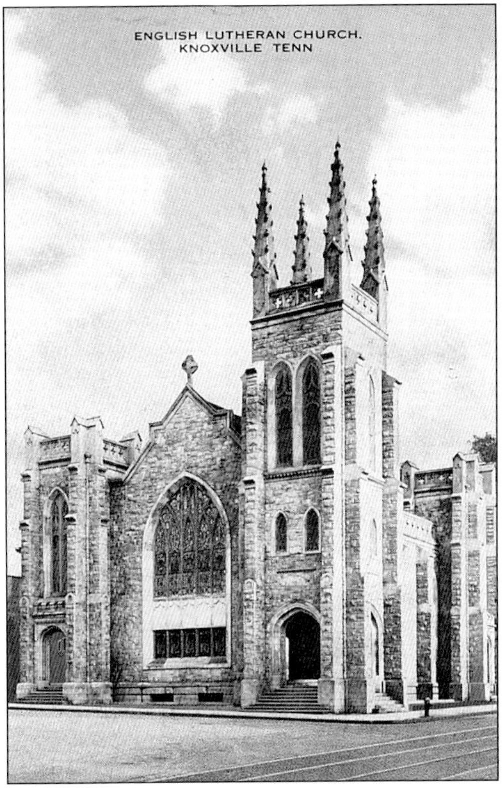

THE ENGLISH LUTHERAN CHURCH. (No publication data.) St. John's English Lutheran Church is located at 544 North Broadway at Emory Park. Built in 1912, the church was given by Mrs. Martha Henson as a memorial to her husband, James A. Henson, and was dedicated May 25, 1913. Designed by R.F. Graf, it contains many noteworthy stained-glass windows. In 1985 St. John's was placed on the National Register of Historic Places.

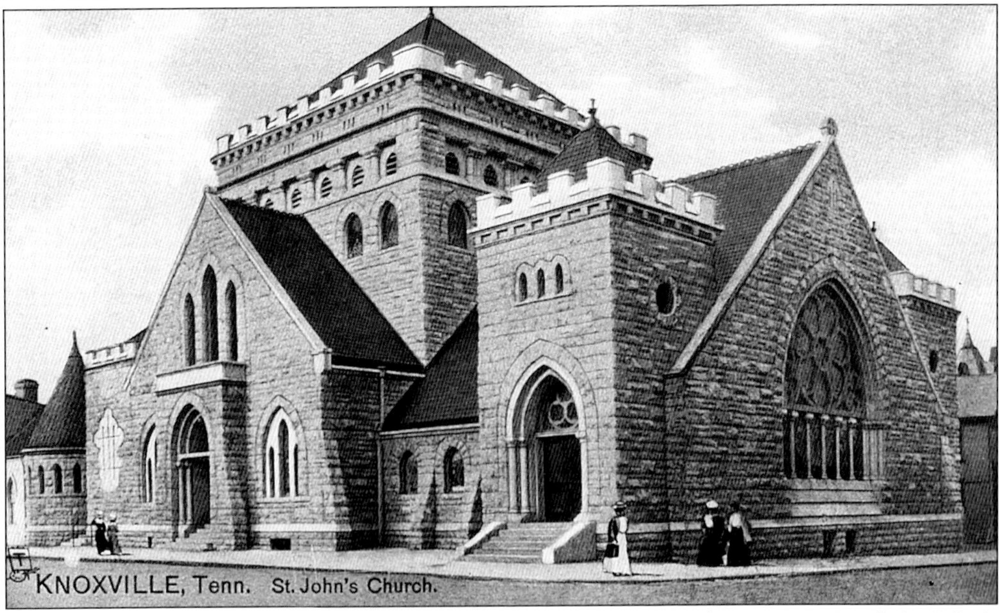

ST. JOHN'S CHURCH. (Published by Raphael Tuck and Sons, London; series 2721.) St. John's Episcopal Church has been on this site since 1845. The present sanctuary was built in 1892, from the designs of J.W. Yost of Columbus, Ohio, whose style was influenced by H.H. Richardson. Located at the corner of Cumberland and Walnut, the sanctuary became St. John's Cathedral in 1986.

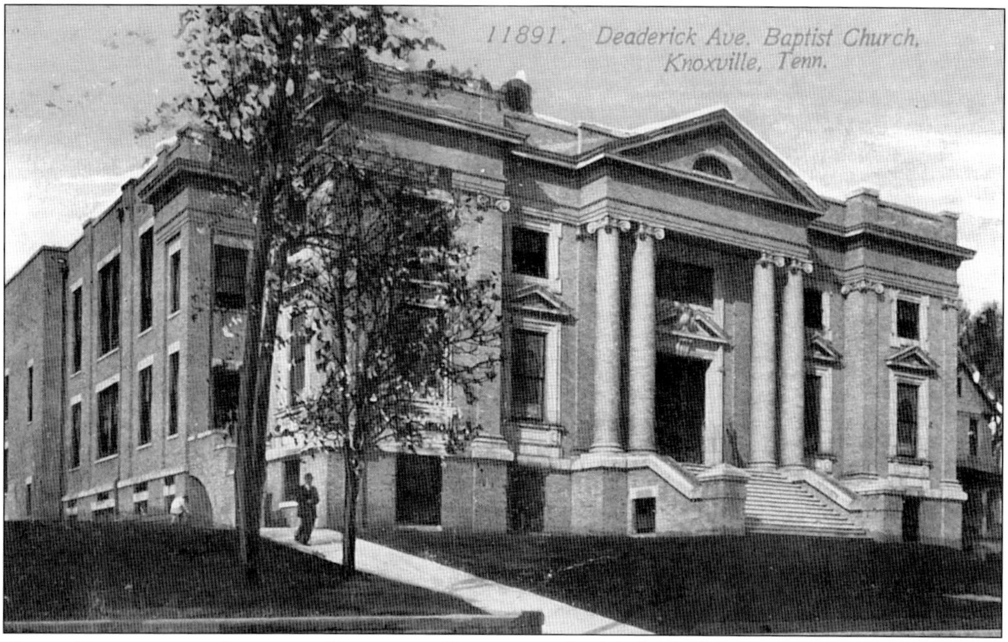

THE DEADERICK AVENUE BAPTIST CHURCH. (Published by Acmegraph, Chicago.) First known as Centennial Baptist Church, the Deaderick Avenue Church was organized September 13, 1892, the fourth Baptist congregation to emerge in Knoxville. Rev. J.K. Pace served as its first pastor; there were 87 charter members. This building at 307–309 Deaderick Avenue was designed in 1910 by R.F. Graf.

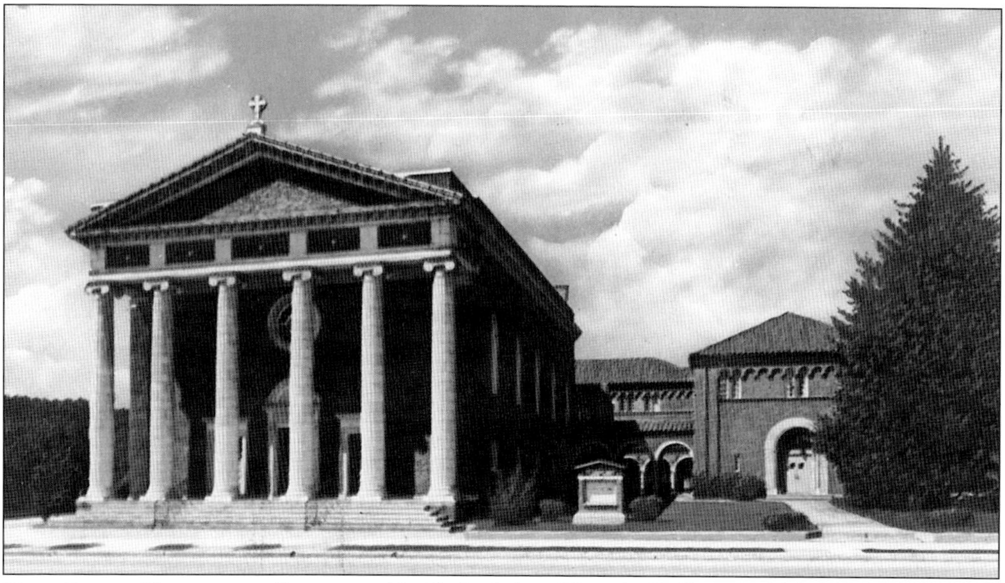

THE FIRST CHRISTIAN CHURCH. (Published by Church Bulletin Publication Company, Bowling Green, Kentucky.) The First Christian congregation, organized in 1874, moved twice from smaller locations before it built the present structure at 211 West Fifth Avenue at the corner of Williams Street. It was dedicated on February 7, 1915. It has monumental Ionic columns and a portico of terra cotta and brick; a new wing built in 1929 is primarily Romanesque in style.

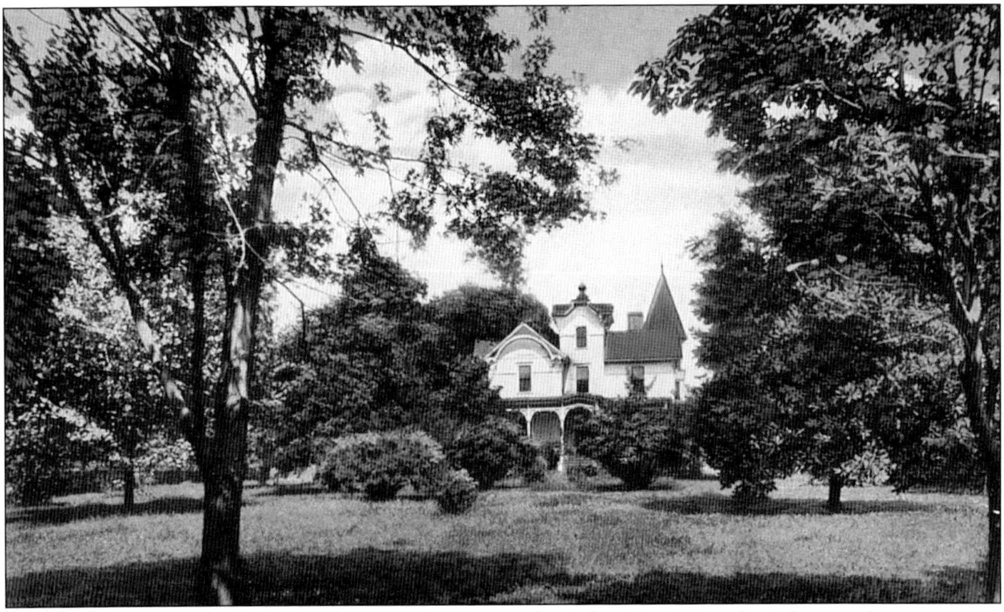

DR. GOETZ'S SANITARIUM. (Published by Knoxville Litho Co.) This building and its spacious grounds were originally utilized by the Fountain Head Hotel, which opened in 1886 in Fountain City. In 1900 Dr. Goetz bought the property for his sanitarium, where he treated nervous diseases and drug and alcohol addiction. It burned in 1920. Later the Manor Apartments were built on the site.

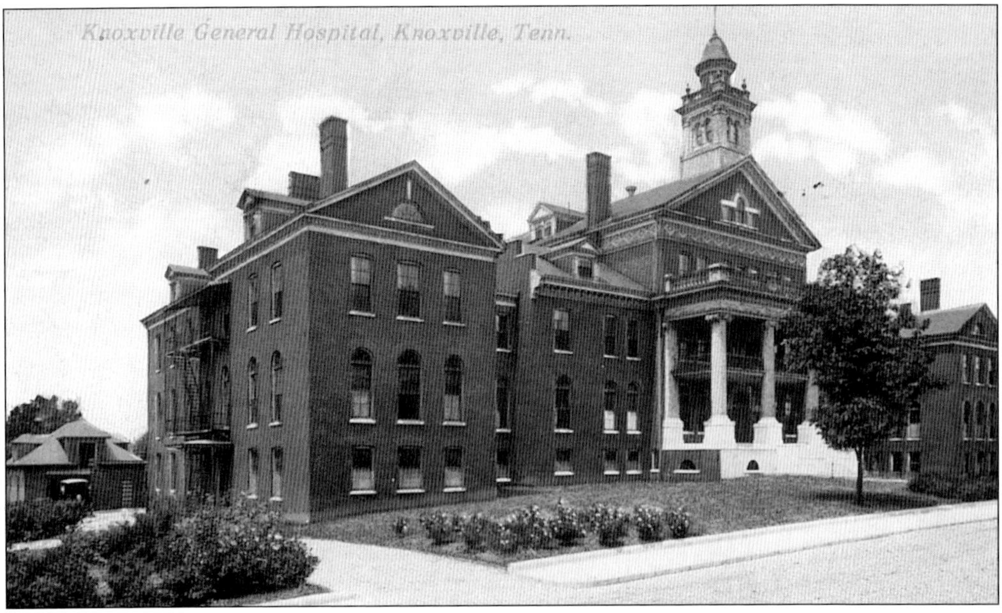

KNOXVILLE GENERAL HOSPITAL. (Published by Octochrome; card sent 1906.) Publicly owned Knoxville General Hospital faced privately owned Lincoln Memorial Hospital across Cleveland Place from about 1904. Knoxville General has been replaced by the Knox County Health Department Center. A novel, *By Dim and Flaring Lamps*, published by Mrs. Calvin Buehler in 1964, features a Knoxville nurse who begins her career at old Knoxville General in 1911.

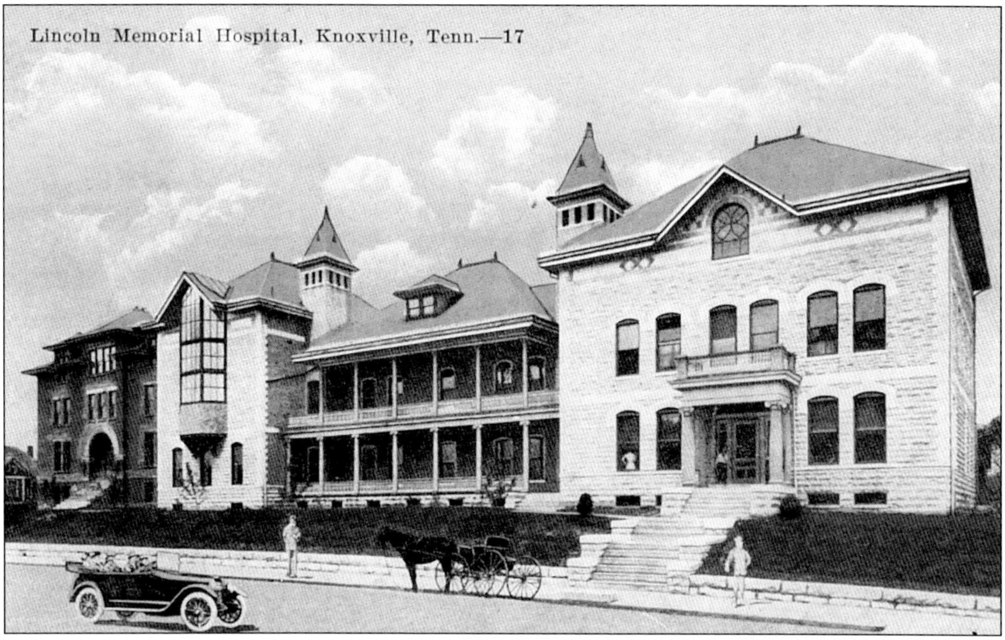

LINCOLN MEMORIAL HOSPITAL. (Published by E.C. Kropp, Milwaukee.) Many physicians were trained at Lincoln Memorial Hospital. Closely associated with the Tennessee Medical College (the red brick building at left), the buildings were sold to Lincoln Memorial University in 1909. The medical school closed in 1914; the hospital closed in 1918. These buildings were just across the street from Knoxville General Hospital.

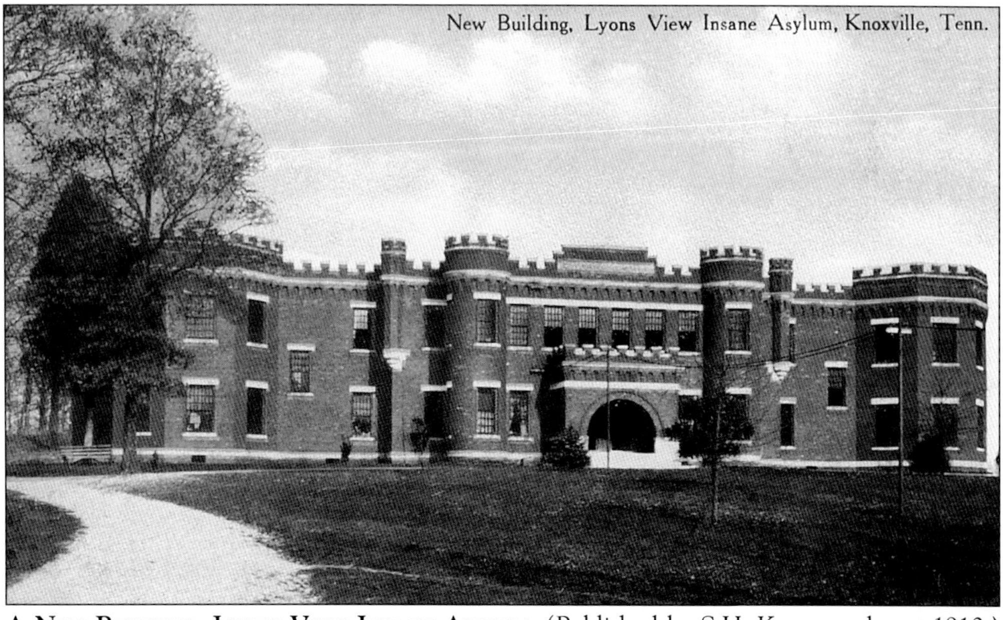

A NEW BUILDING, LYONS VIEW INSANE ASYLUM. (Published by S.H. Kress; card sent 1910.) Lyons View Insane Asylum was established in 1873; however, it was 1886 before the first patients arrived in Knoxville. The name and location of the facility has been known as "Lyons View" ever since William Lyon purchased the land in 1809. The official title has been changed several times; it is now the Lakeshore Mental Health Center.

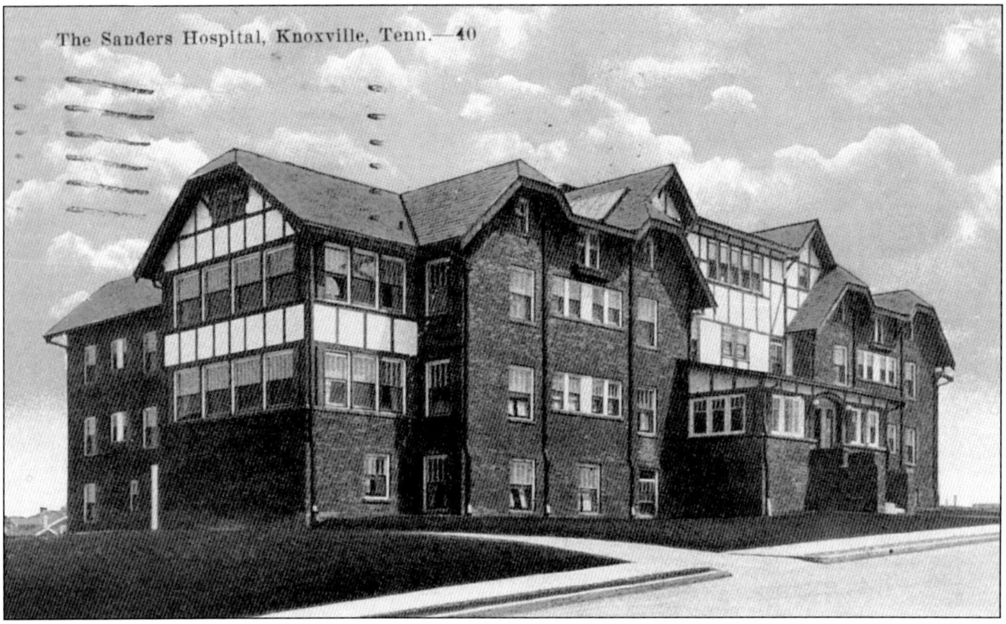

FORT SANDERS HOSPITAL. (Published by S.H. Kress; card mailed 1922.) The modest size of Fort Sanders Hospital in the 1920s, as seen on this postcard, does not forecast its prestigious development in later decades. Its center is now located at 1901 Clinch Avenue, with several associated facilities in other Knoxville locations.

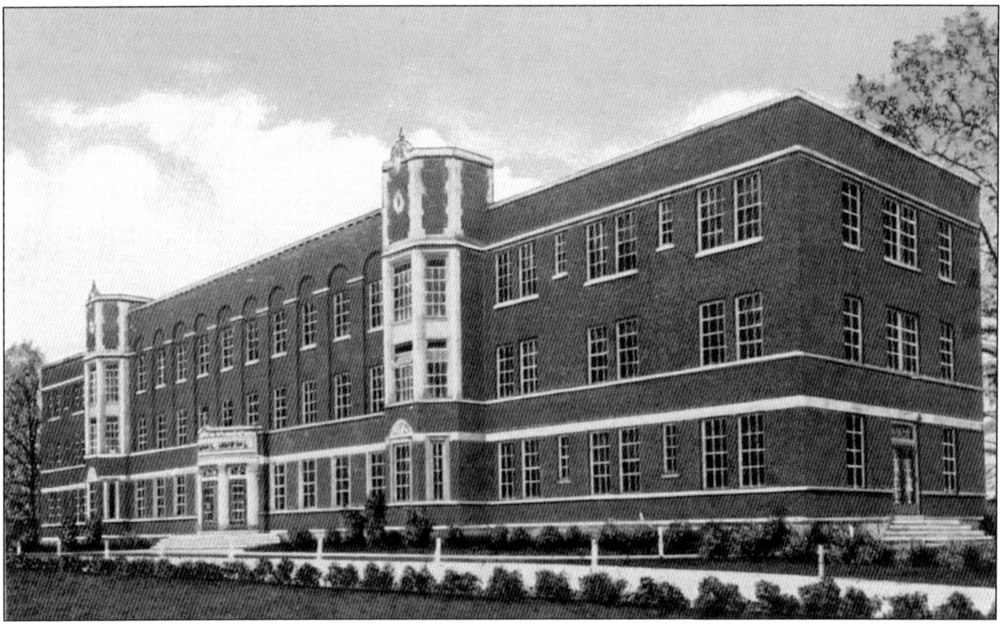

ST. MARY'S MEMORIAL HOSPITAL. (Published by Standard News Co., Knoxville.) St. Mary's Hospital was established on Oak Hill Avenue in 1928 by the Sisters of Mercy, who first came to Knoxville in 1898 to staff the parochial school. It was impossible then to forecast the enormous expansion of the hospital which has occurred since.

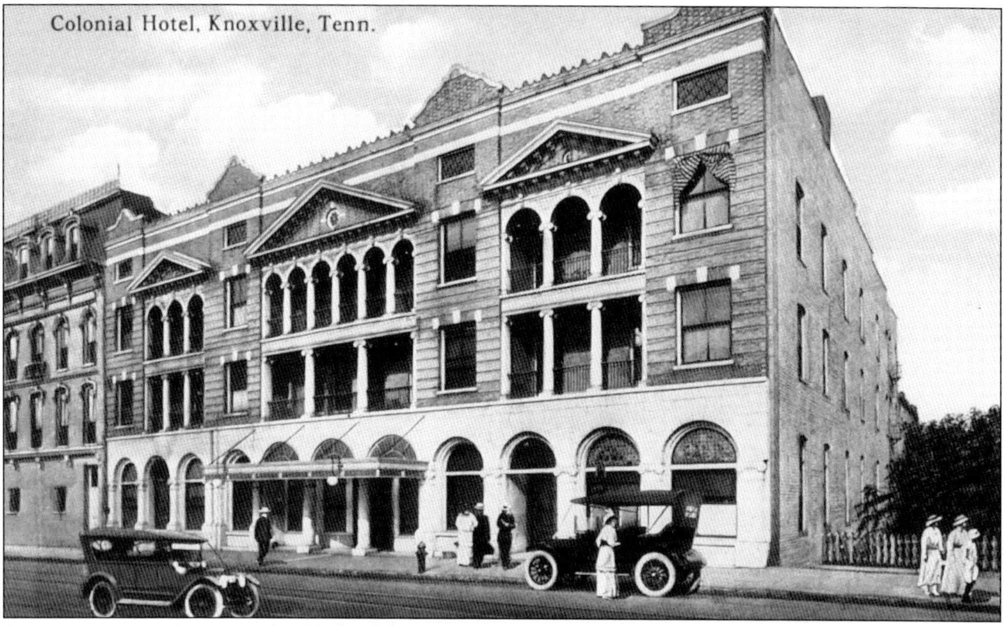

The Colonial Hotel. (Published by Knoxville Lithographing Co.) In the early 1900s the Colonial Hotel was located at Gay Street and Cumberland Avenue. Its advertising promised that it was "thoroughly equipped throughout with automatic sprinklers." Rooms without baths could be had for $1; rooms with private baths cost from $1.50 to $3. There was also "an excellent café with popular prices."

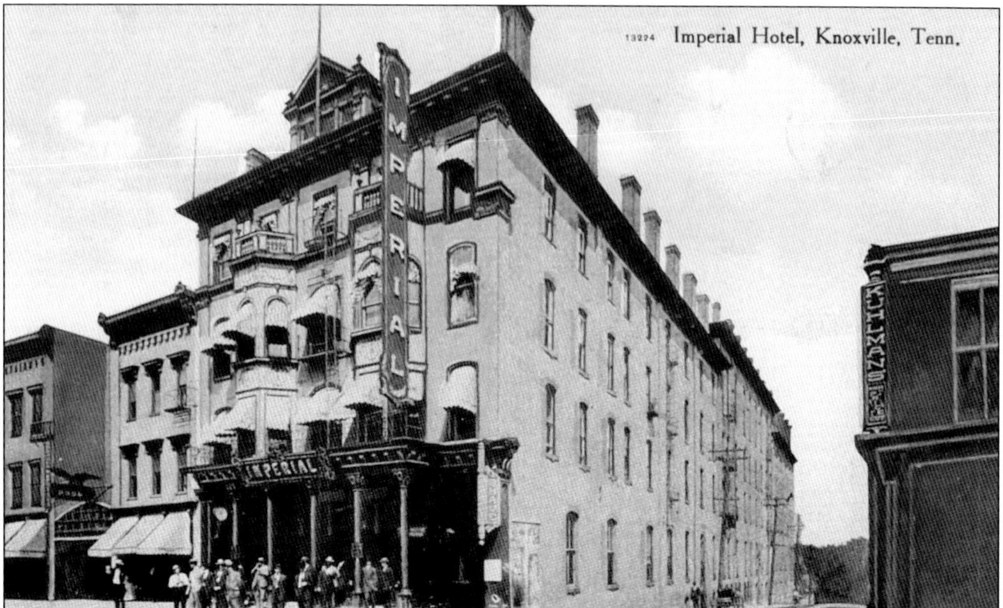

The Imperial Hotel. (No publication data.) The Imperial Hotel stood at the corner of Gay and Clinch and continued to be a popular "home away from home" until 1916, when it was destroyed by fire. It was replaced in 1919 by the Farragut, whose advertising made much of the fact that it was "completely fireproof."

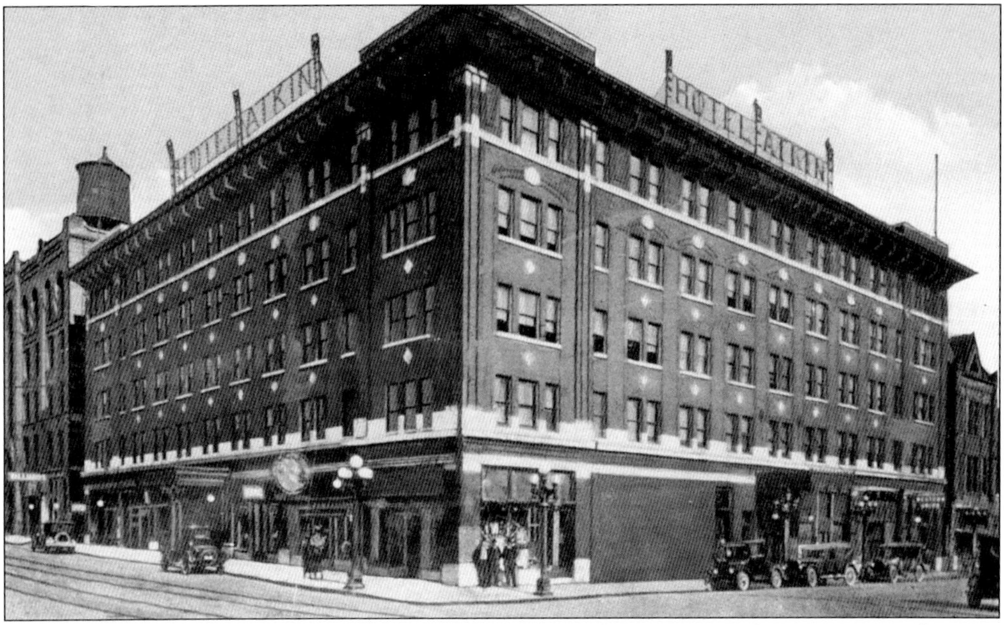

The Hotel Atkin. (No publication data.) On the northeast corner of Gay Street and Depot Avenue, the Atkin Hotel had "200 rooms, 150 with bath." It was immediately accessible to train passengers coming in at the Southern Depot across the street. It was said that one could get from the station to a room in five minutes. In later years, the Atkin disappeared; the area is now a parking lot adjacent to Regas Restaurant.

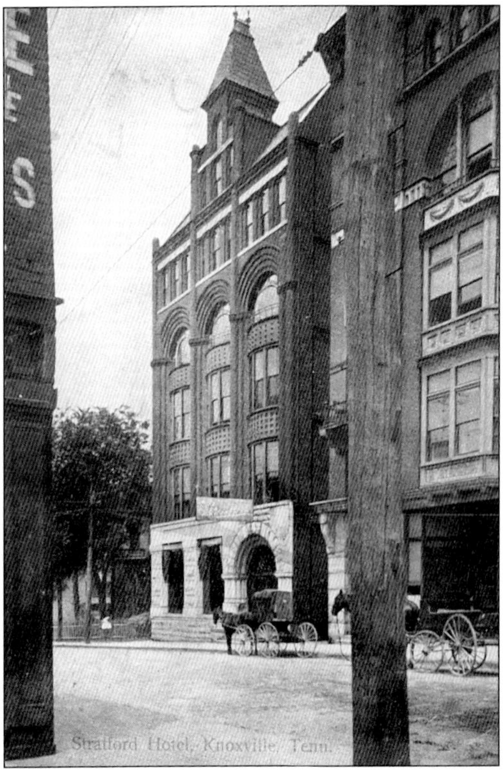

The Stratford Hotel. (Published by International Post Card Co., New York.) In the early 1900s the Stratford Hotel, located at 405 Wall Avenue, was owned by James G. Sterchi (1867–1932). The founder of the well-known chain of furniture stores whose main store was at 114 South Gay Street in Knoxville, Mr. Sterchi was also a farmer who supplied his hotel with fresh produce, milk, and eggs. This quiet street of downtown Knoxville is much changed today.

THE HOTEL FARRAGUT. (Published by CC&C Co; card sent 1920.) Named for Adm. David G. Farragut, this hotel was opened February 1, 1919. It was fireproof and had a ceiling fan in every room. The sender of this card says, "This is one of the many beautiful hotels in this city. Business is good here, and everyone seems to have plenty of money. Come south, young man!"

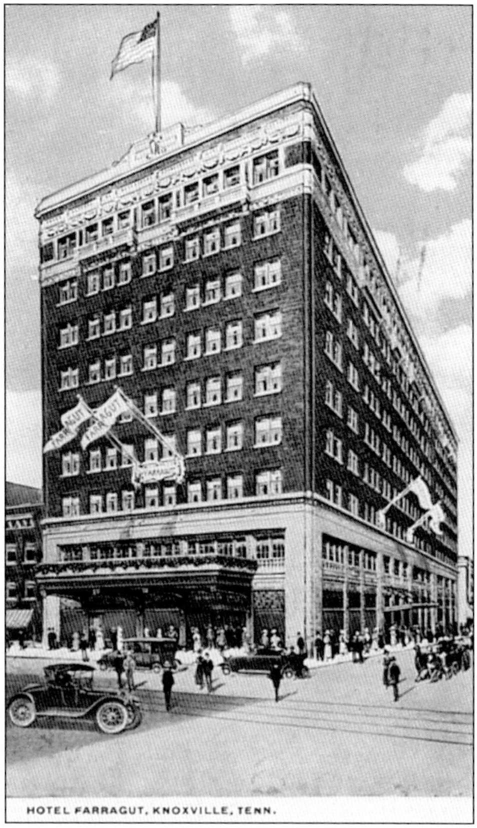

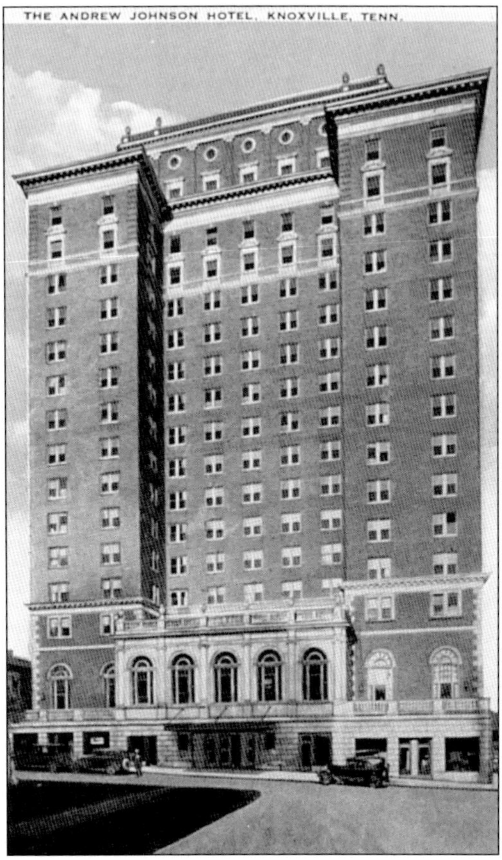

THE ANDREW JOHNSON HOTEL. (Published by Standard News Co., Knoxville.) Located on South Gay Street across from the Courthouse, the Andrew Johnson opened in December 1929, replacing several fine homes which had been demolished. Originally called the Tennessee Terrace, it was renamed the Andrew Johnson and operated successfully during the Depression. Its refined interiors and excellent service satisfied over 100 permanent residents. More recently it has been renovated for office use.

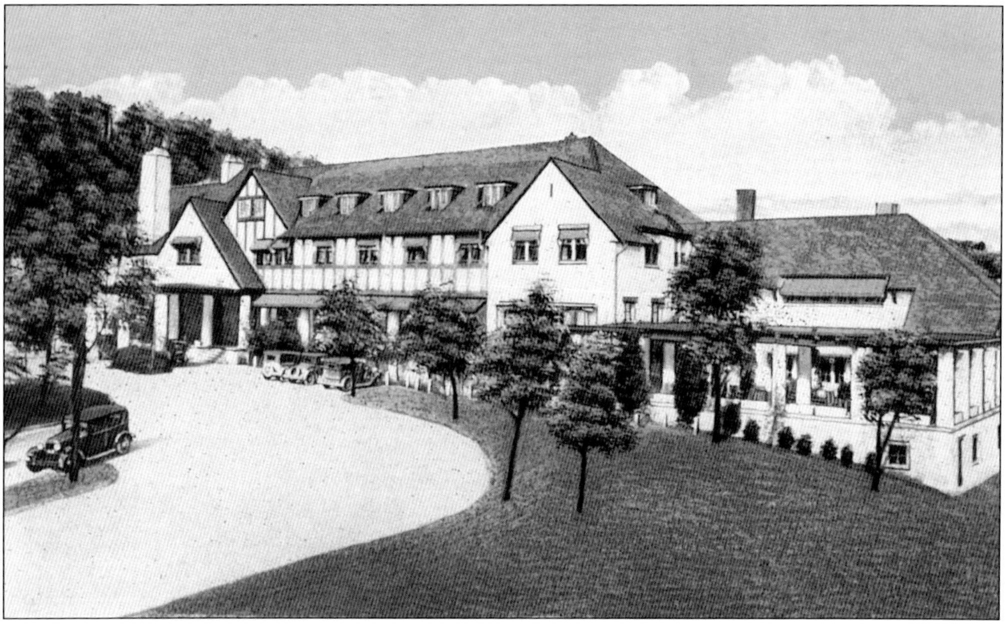

THE WHITTLE SPRINGS HOTEL. (Published by Standard News Co., Knoxville.) The old Whittle Springs Hotel offered in 1910 the good life for people with money and leisure. After the fire of 1919, the new hotel became Knox County's most important year-round resort. It offered "dances, dinners, and social events. Evening dinner $1.25." It still furnished the famous Whittle water "noted for its remarkable medicinal properties." It was razed in 1964.

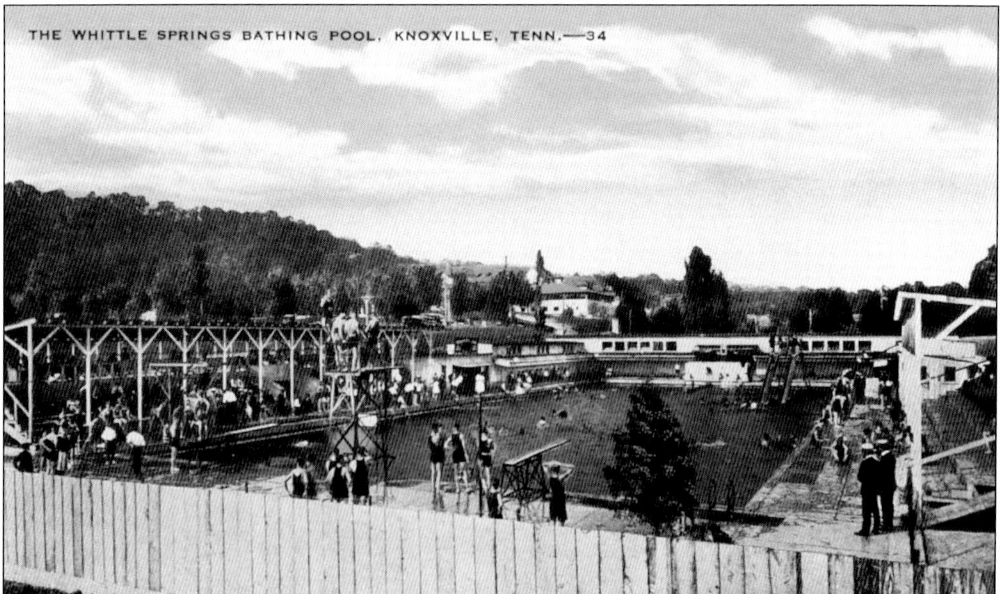

THE WHITTLE SPRINGS BATHING POOL. (Published by E.C. Kropp, Milwaukee.) Advertised as "the million-gallon swimming pool 80 x 180 feet," this recreational facility was a most popular spot for young and old alike. "Going to Whittles" to swim furnished fun and recreation for many a family. Nearby was a pavilion for dancing; there were tennis and croquet courts as well.

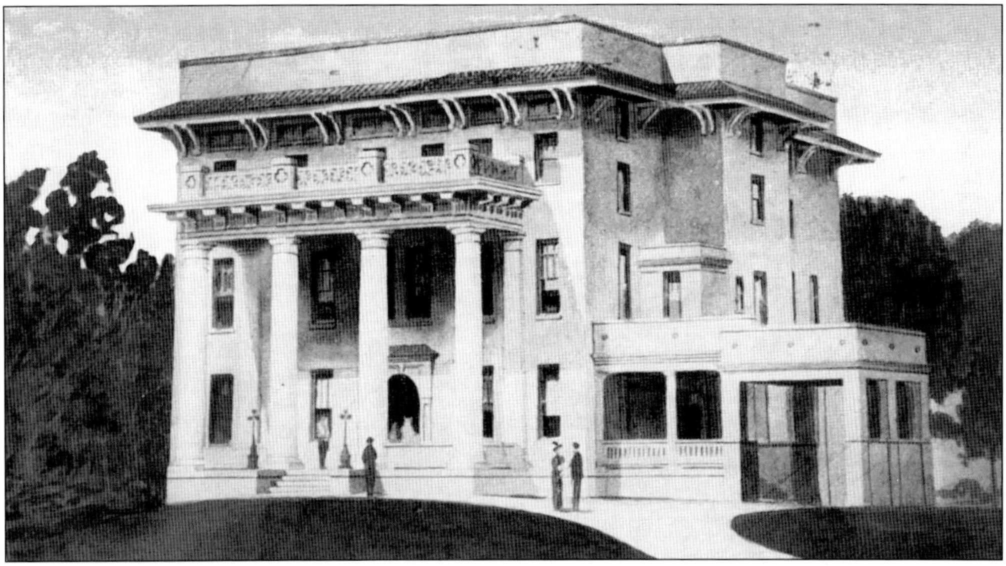

THE MASONIC TEMPLE. (Published by S.H. Kress; card sent 1916.) This building was designed as the home of Charles McClung McGhee (the Lawson McGhee Library donor) in 1872 by Joseph F. Baumann. Altered after Mr. McGhee's death in 1907 to serve as a Masonic Temple, it stands on Locust Street at Union Avenue.

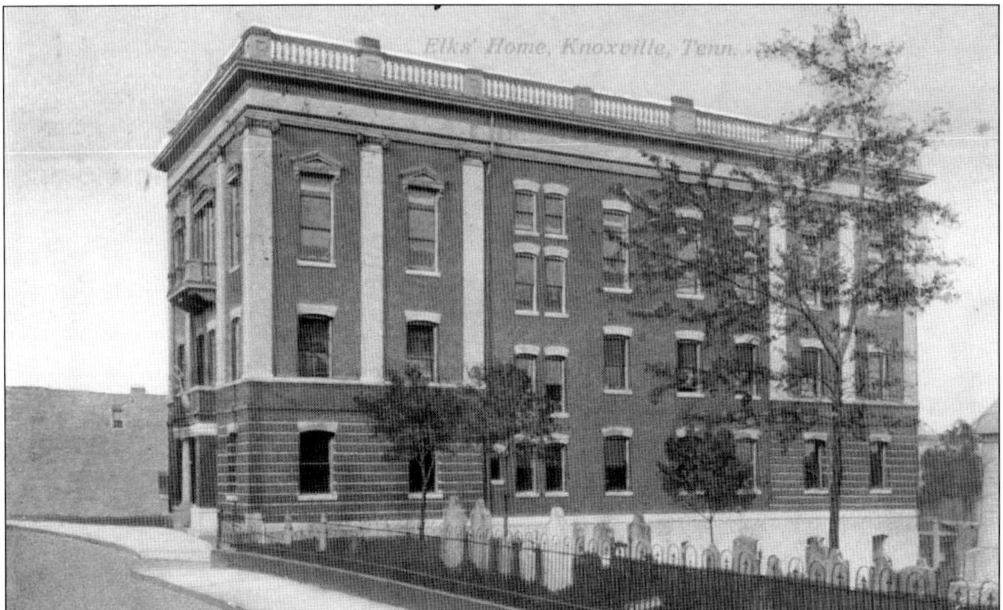

THE ELKS' HOME. (Published by Octochrome; card sent 1913.) Located on State Street near First Presbyterian Church, this Elks' Home, seen here in 1913, has disappeared as a result of downtown building projects. In 1909 it had replaced the BPOE Home at 421 Main Avenue when that building was bought by Col. J.Y. Johnston for his home. The north end of the First Presbyterian graveyard can be seen here at near right.

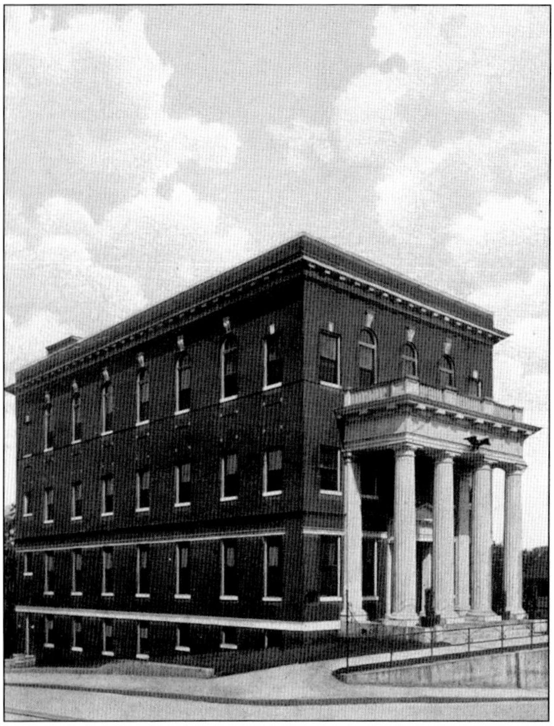

The Eagles Home No. 1009. (Published by Knoxville Eagles; card sent 1948.) Down the street from the Elks' Home, the Eagles Home No. 1009 stood in classic grandeur at 700 State Street. The home now having disappeared, a parking lot occupies the space. Currently, the Fraternal Order of Eagles No. 2698 dwells at 203 Walnut Street.

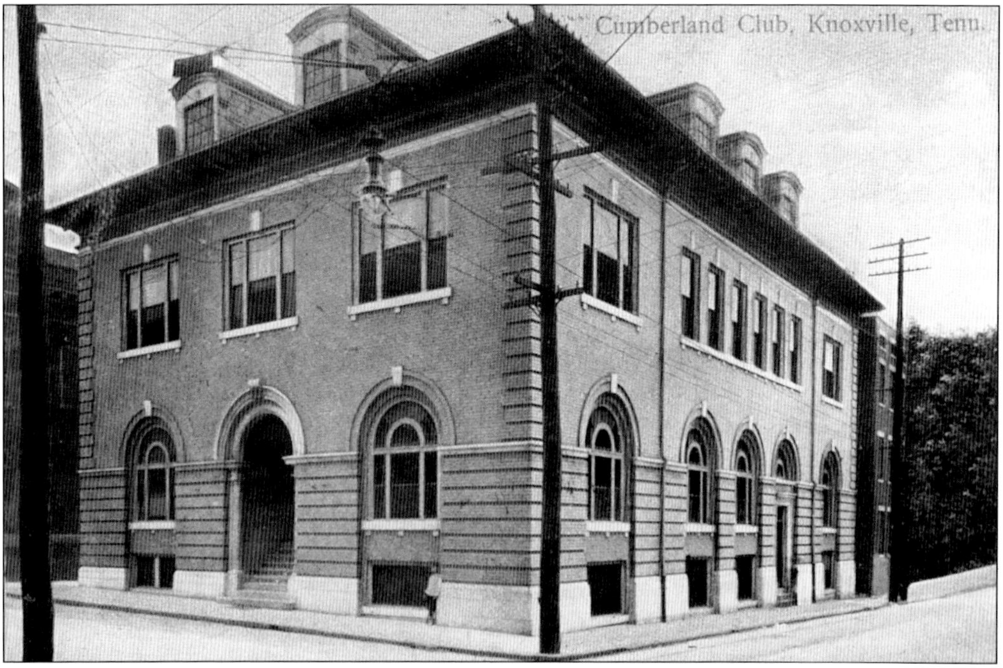

The Cumberland Club. (Published by International Post Card Co., New York.) The Cumberland Club owned this fine building at 601 Walnut Street in the early years of the century. The club was "a special group that met for the exclusive purpose of social enjoyment . . . among its members." In June 1915 it was accused of keeping liquor on the premises, a misdemeanor at the time.

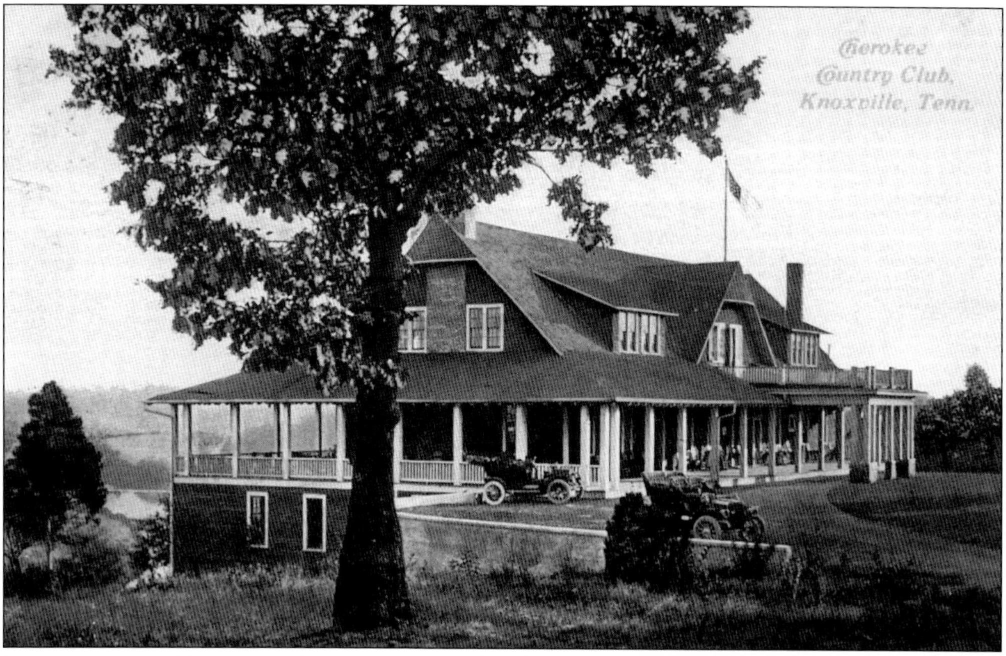

The Cherokee Country Club. (Published by Charles C. Cullen; card sent 1912). The first Cherokee Country Club was built in 1907 in Bearden, on Lyons View Pike, with a view from the back terrace of the horseshoe bend of the river. It also sported the first 18-hole golf course in Knox County, across the road from the front porch. This building lasted until 1928.

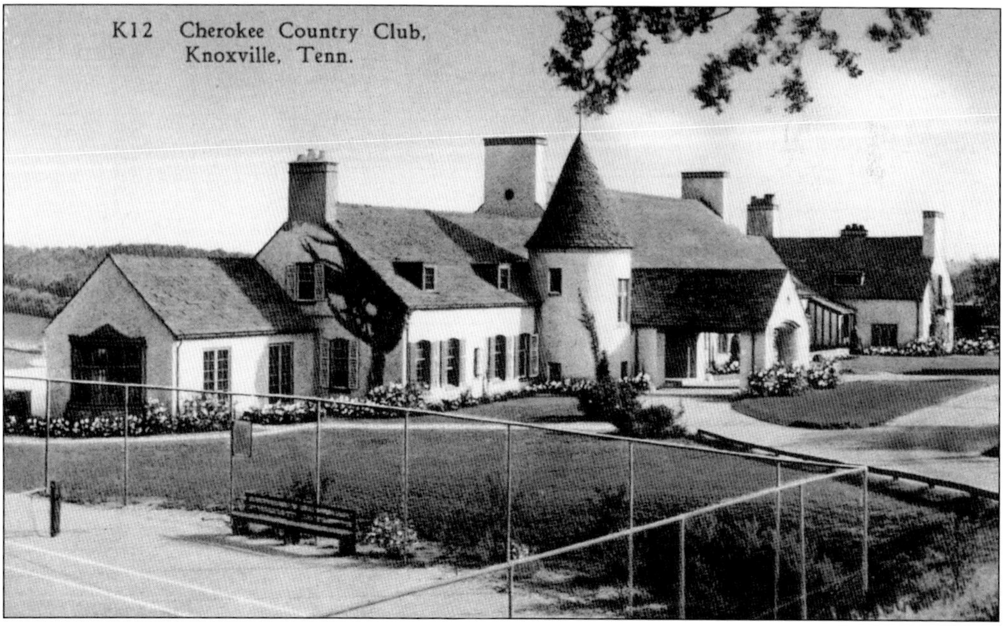

The Cherokee Country Club. (Published by Asheville Post Card Co.) The second Cherokee Country Club was designed in 1928 by Baumann and Baumann, Knoxville architects who planned many of Knoxville's more prestigious buildings. It replaced the older structure on Lyons View Pike and provided a new elegance. Soon it was called "the South's finest country club." It is located 4 miles west of downtown.

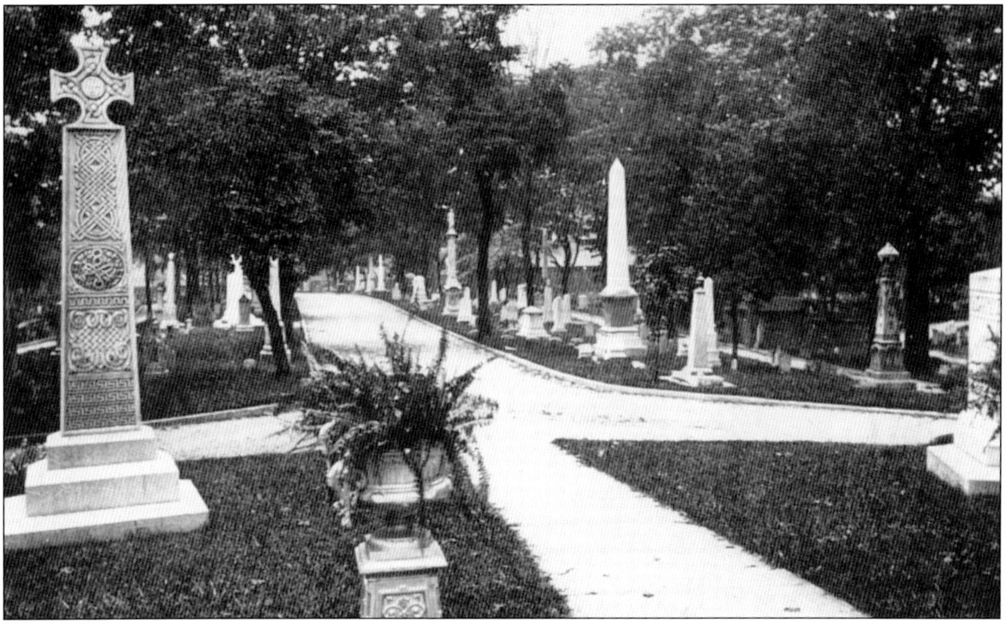

Old Gray Cemetery. (Published by Reese and Reed; card sent 1907.) Old Gray Cemetery, located on Broadway just north of downtown, was established in 1850, the name having been inspired by Thomas Gray's "Elegy in a Country Churchyard." Among the many unique memorials found in the quiet plots are those of William G. Brownlow and Lawrence C. Tyson.

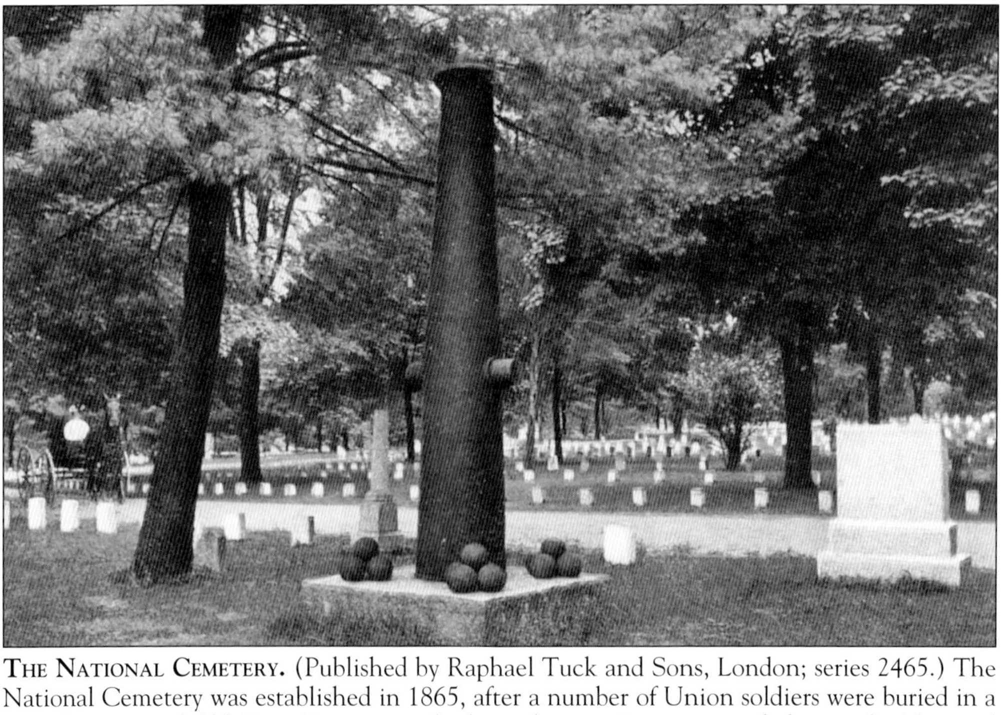

The National Cemetery. (Published by Raphael Tuck and Sons, London; series 2465.) The National Cemetery was established in 1865, after a number of Union soldiers were buried in a special section of Old Gray Cemetery, which is adjacent. It was expanded in to the National Cemetery and was given a separate entrance on Tyson Street. Another cemetery, established for Confederate soldiers, is located on Bethel Avenue.

THE CONFEDERATE MONUMENT. (No publication data; card sent 1908.) This marble monument, in the Confederate Cemetery at 1715 Bethel Avenue, was placed there in 1892 by the Ladies' Memorial Association of Knoxville. It honors the more than 1,600 Confederate soldiers who are buried there.

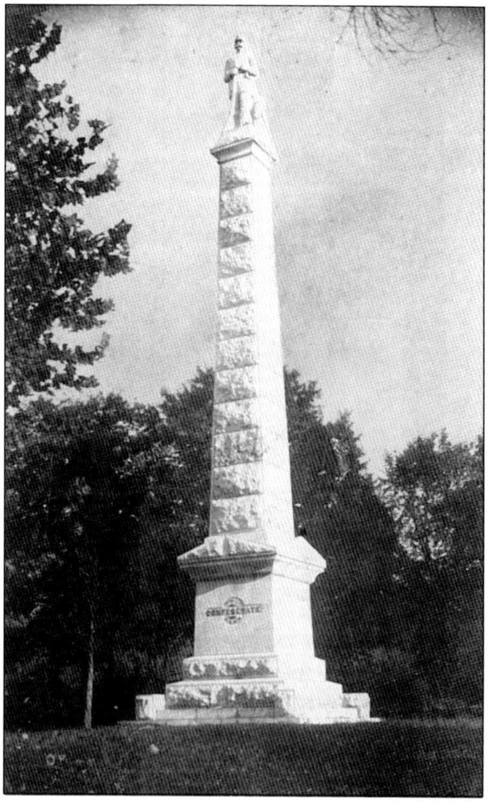

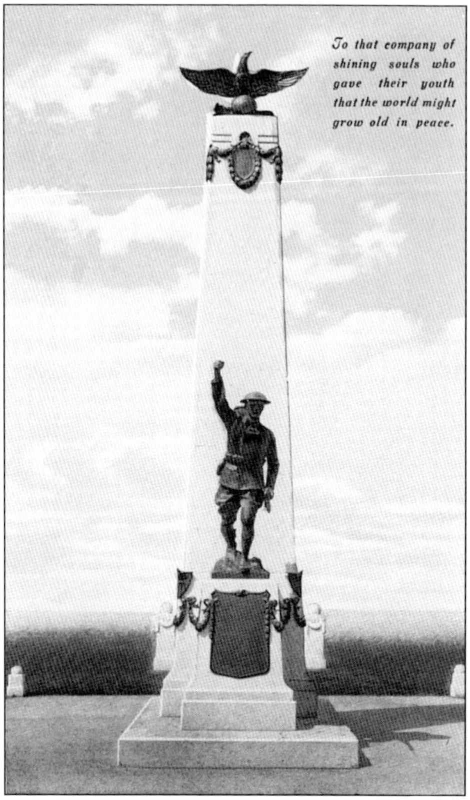

THE DOUGHBOY STATUE. (Published by CC&C Co.) The Doughboy Statue was erected in 1921 on the front lawn of Knoxville High School. It was given by the 117th Infantry, 59th BGE, 30th Division, 3rd Tennessee Infantry in memory of the Knox County soldiers (including 192 former Knoxville High School students and 9 teachers) who died during World War I. Gen. Lawrence D. Tyson conducted the dedication ceremonies.

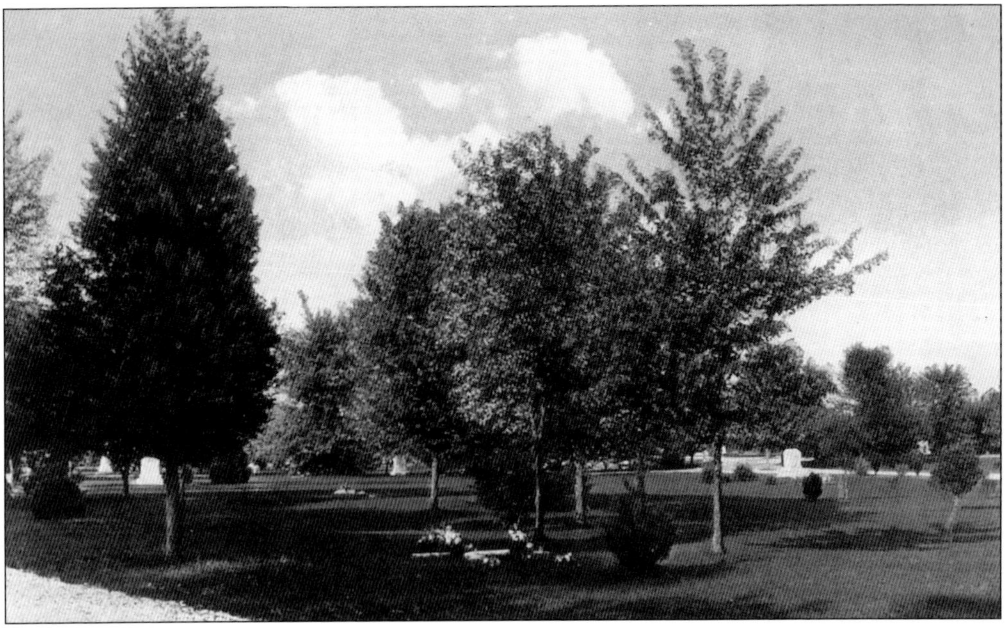

Greenwood Cemetery. (Published by Curt Teich, Chicago.) Located at 3500 Tazewell Pike, Greenwood Cemetery was opened in 1900, the first burial there taking place on July 2 of that year. Several celebrities are buried there, including Red Rector, entertainer, and James Agee, noted Knoxville author.

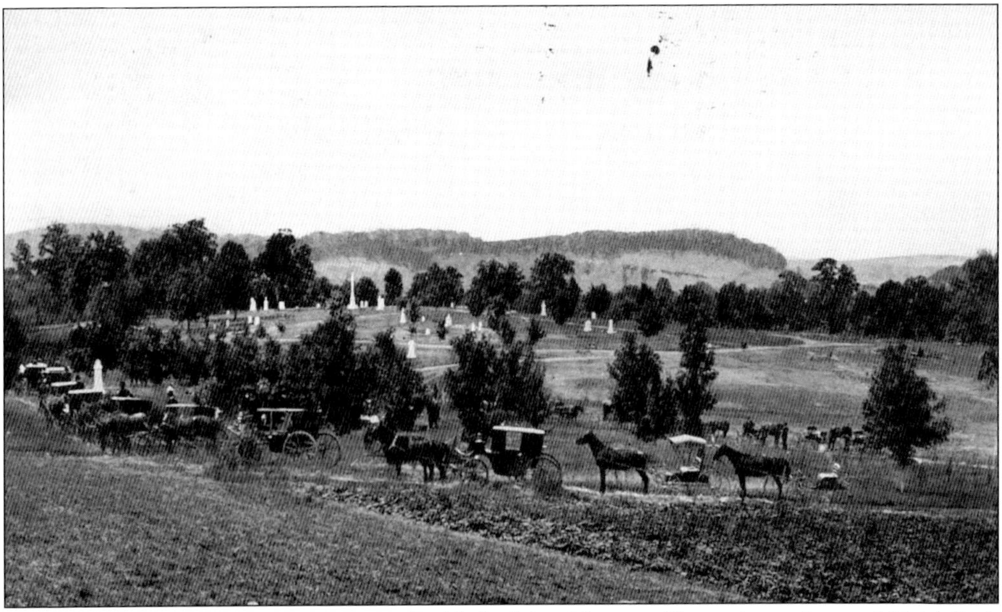

A Scene in Woodland Cemetery. (Published by Monroe Howard; card sent 1914.) It is possible that this card was misprinted; "Woodland" might have referred to "Woodlawn." In any case, a procession of horses and carriages seems to be lined up for a funeral service. In 1914 the grounds were not yet crowded with tombstones.

Four

Education

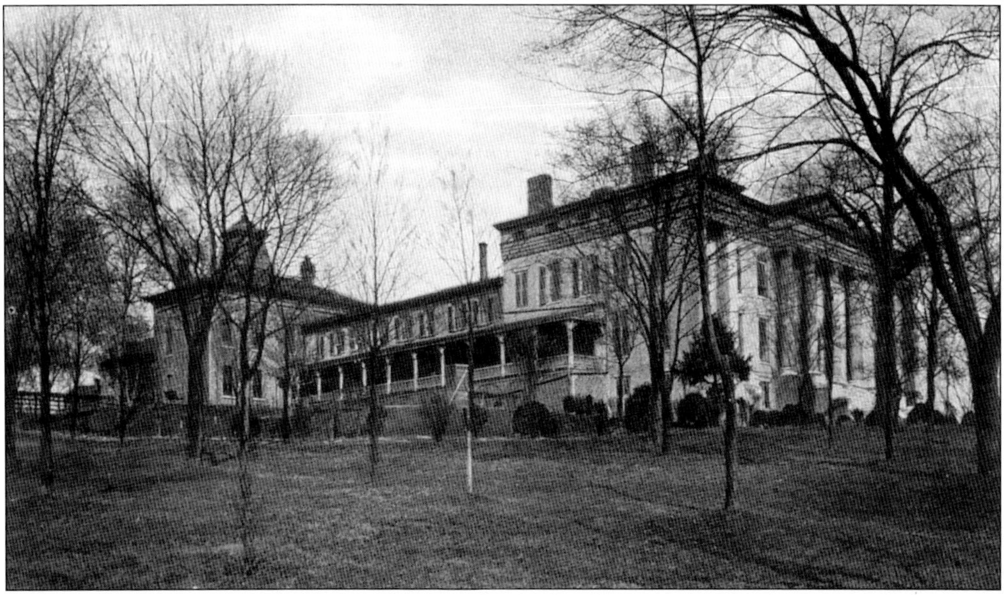

The Tennessee Deaf and Dumb School. (Published by International Post Card Co., New York.) The Tennessee Deaf and Dumb School occupied these buildings from 1851 to 1924, when the school was moved to Island Home. The City converted the buildings for use of the city hall and the Boyd Jr. High School. Boyd closed in 1938. The word "dumb" has long been omitted from the title; the school is now known as Tennessee School for the Deaf.

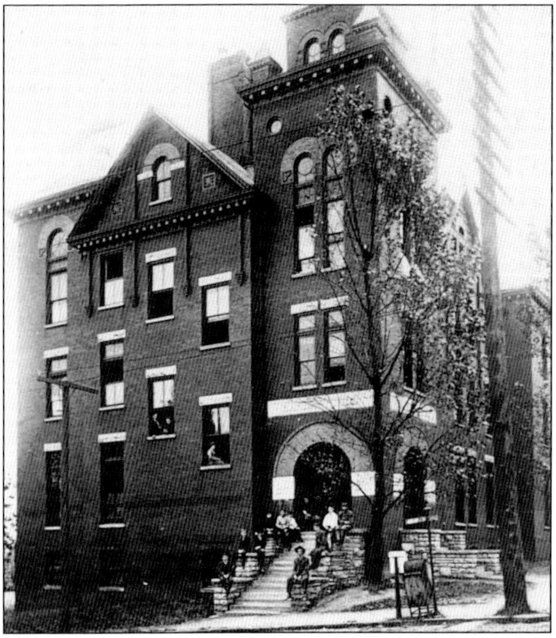

Baker-Himel School. (Published by Rotograph Co., New York; card sent 1907.) In 1889 Lewis M.G. Baker and Charles M. Himel opened their private school to prepare boys for college. Situated on Highland Avenue at Twelfth Street, it endured until its closing in 1913. For several years Baker-Himel graduates were admitted to the University of Tennessee and other colleges without further examination.

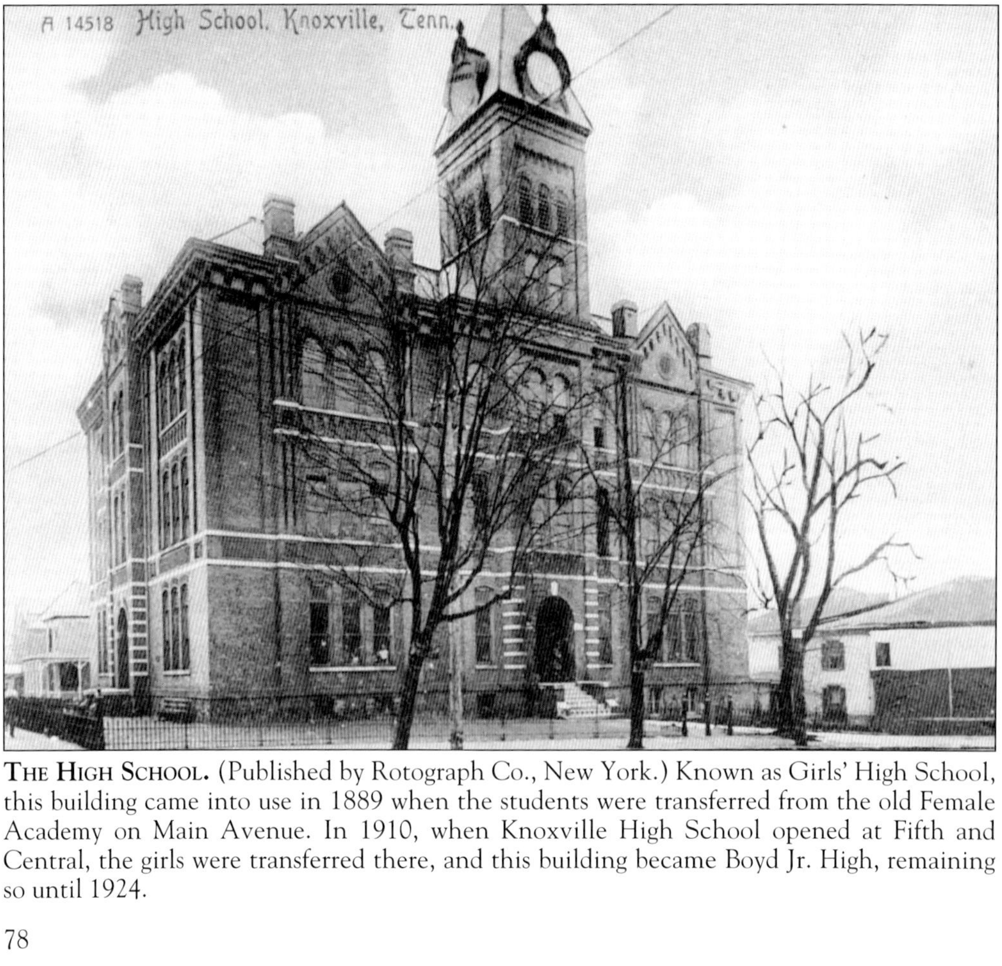

The High School. (Published by Rotograph Co., New York.) Known as Girls' High School, this building came into use in 1889 when the students were transferred from the old Female Academy on Main Avenue. In 1910, when Knoxville High School opened at Fifth and Central, the girls were transferred there, and this building became Boyd Jr. High, remaining so until 1924.

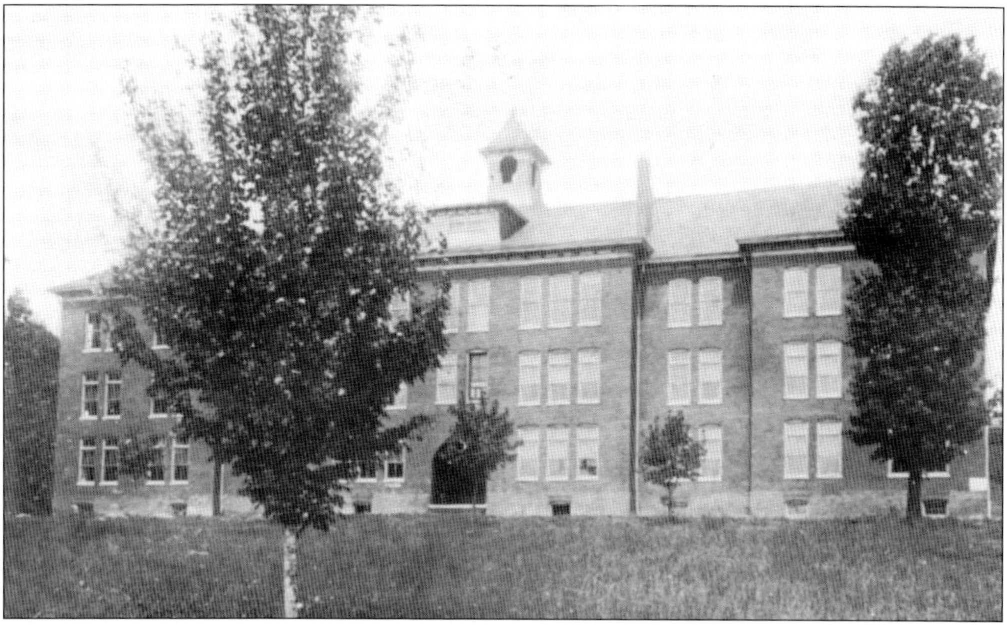

THE KNOX COUNTY HIGH SCHOOL. (Published by Reese and Reed.) Knox County's first courses in business were offered by Holbrook College, a short-lived institution in Fountain City, which opened in 1893 and closed in 1900. In 1906 the college property was purchased by Knox County and became Central High School. The outmoded building seen here was replaced by a modern one in 1931, which eventually became Gresham Middle School.

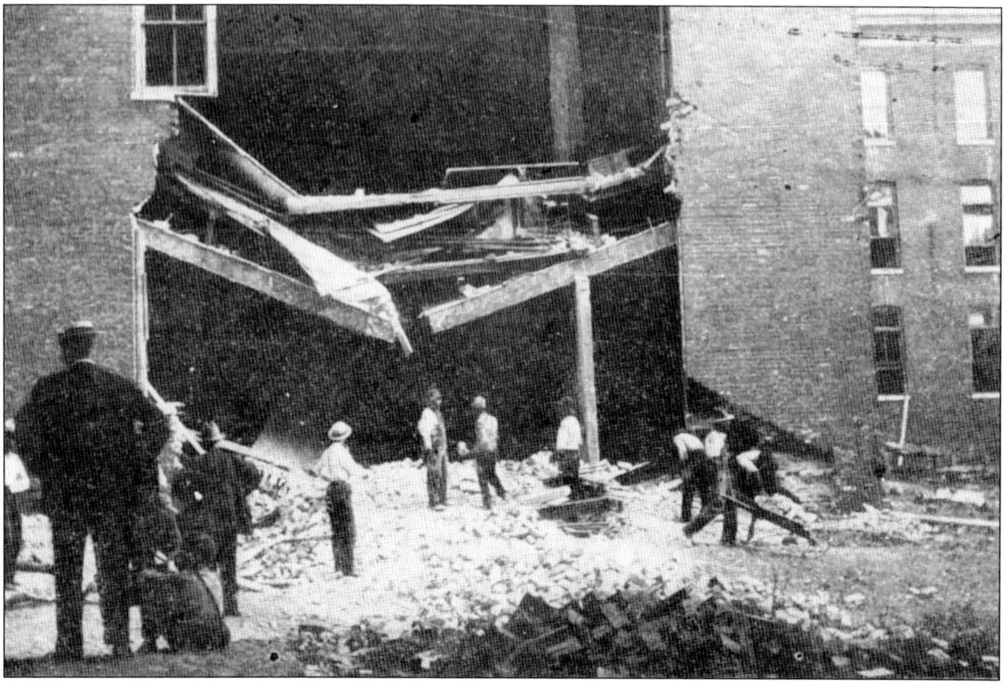

A "CAVE IN" AT CENTRAL HIGH SCHOOL, FOUNTAIN CITY. (Published by F.G. Asquith; card sent 1911.) An interesting local catastrophe is pictured here, which happened probably in early 1911. The sender says, "This card shows you Joseph's narrow escape."

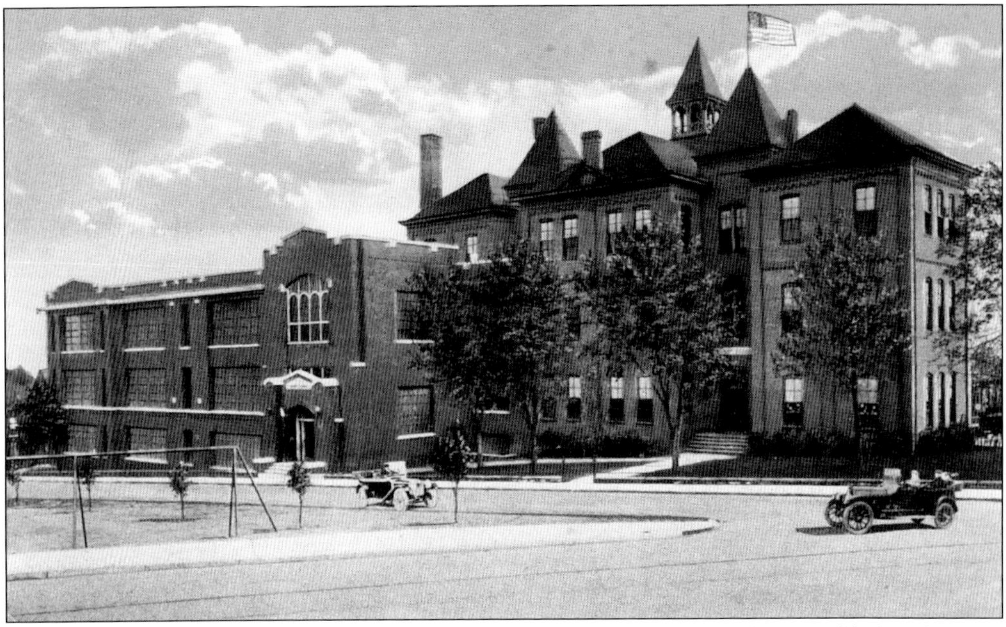

The Moses School. (Published by CC&C Co.) In 1883 Mechanicsville was added to the city, and the Moses School was opened on Deaderick Avenue. A playground was added in 1915, and in 1928, Moses pioneered a new method of instruction called "the platoon system," but by 1941 this innovation was discarded. In 1933 Moses also initiated one of the first nursery schools in the state.

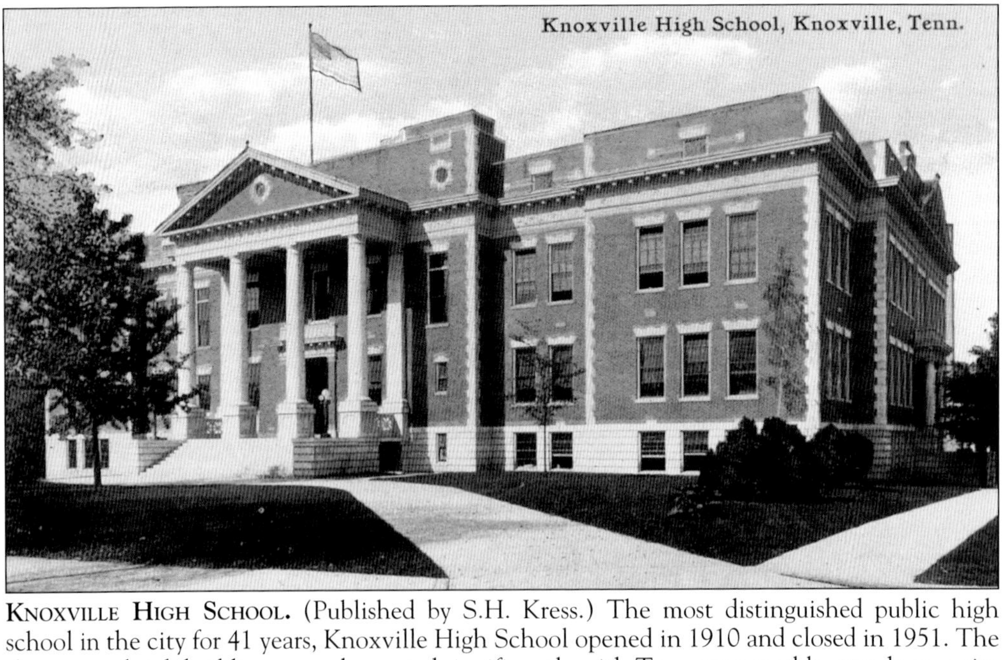

Knoxville High School. (Published by S.H. Kress.) The most distinguished public high school in the city for 41 years, Knoxville High School opened in 1910 and closed in 1951. The three-story brick building, complemented significantly with Tennessee marble, stands on a city block facing East Fifth Avenue. Known as a "college entrance" school, it offered a wide-ranging variety in its selection of courses. Since 1951, the building has been the headquarters of the city schools administration.

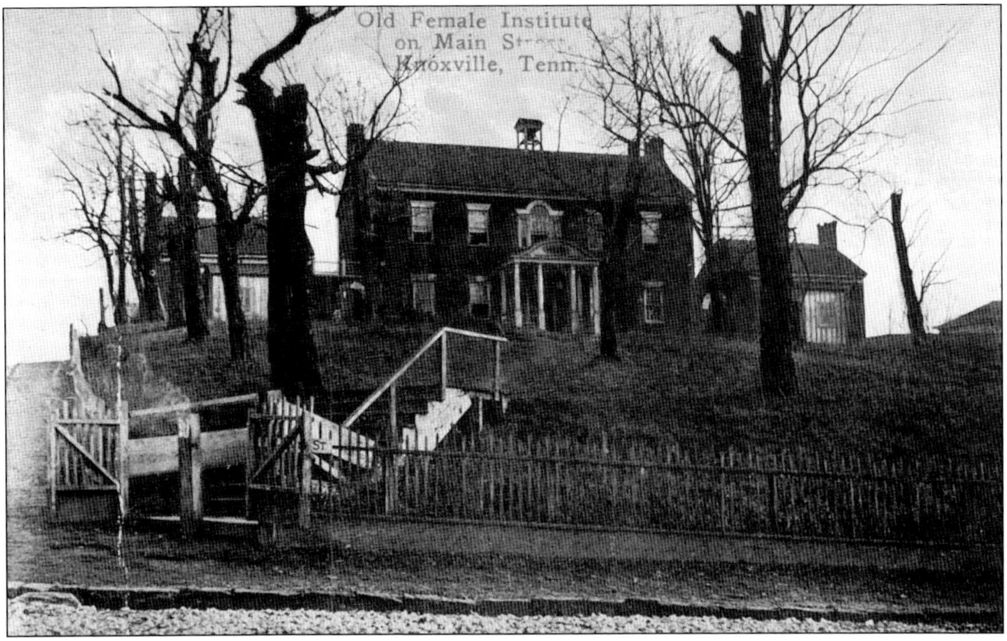

THE OLD FEMALE INSTITUTE ON MAIN STREET. (No publication data.) The East Tennessee Female Institute opened in these buildings at what is now Main and Henley Streets in 1829. It served young women as a school throughout most of the nineteenth century, being demolished in 1889 for private residences. The Church Street Methodist Church, built in 1930, now occupies the site.

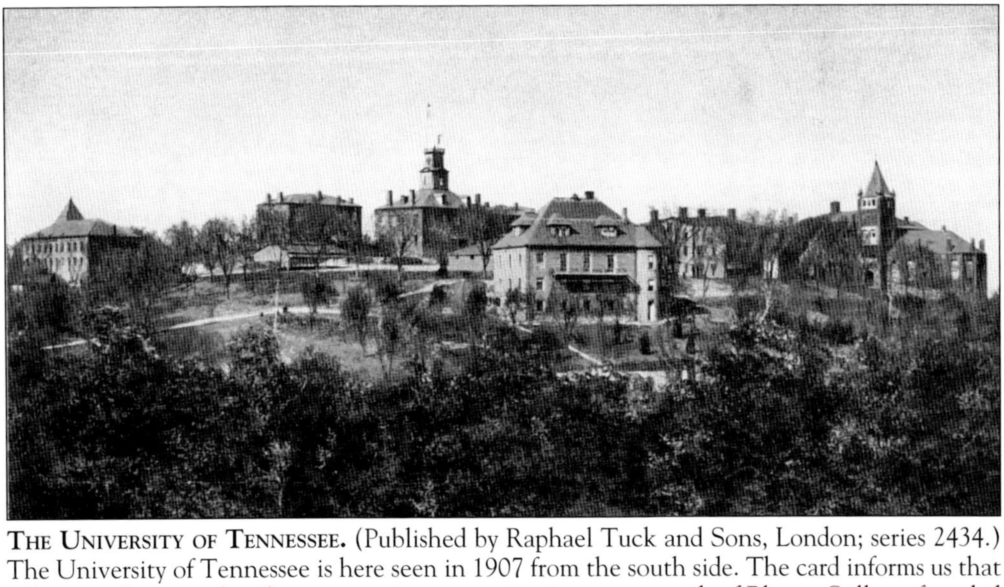

THE UNIVERSITY OF TENNESSEE. (Published by Raphael Tuck and Sons, London; series 2434.) The University of Tennessee is here seen in 1907 from the south side. The card informs us that "This co-educational and non-sectarian institution is an outgrowth of Blount College, founded in 1794. It became East Tennessee College in 1807, Tennessee University in 1840, and the University of Tennessee in 1879. It has 100 instructors and 800 students."

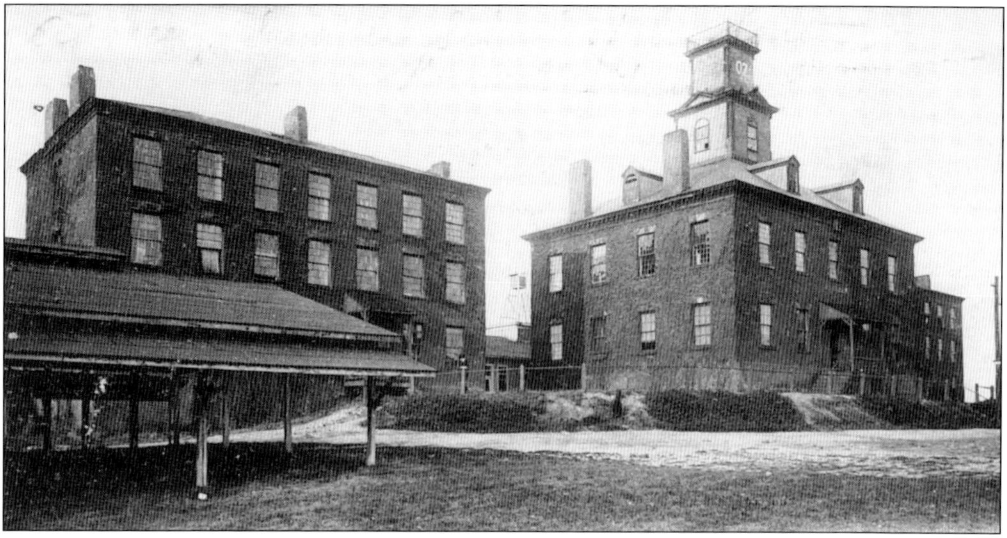

West College, Old College, University of Tennessee. (Published by Rotograph Co. New York; card sent 1907.) Old College, on the site of the present Ayres Hall, was the first building constructed on the University of Tennessee campus. Dating from 1828, it cost $13,000. West College and East College flanked it on either side. After 1906 the cupola of the Old College displayed class dates on the tower. It was razed in 1919.

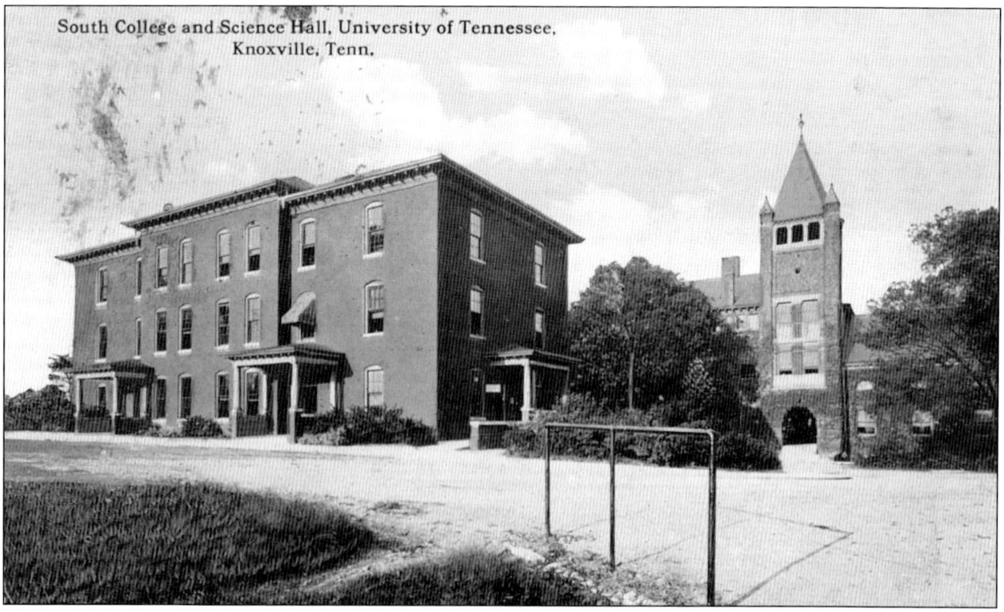

South College and Science Hall. (Published by S.H. Kress; card sent 1914.) South College, built in 1872 at a cost of about $10,500, is the oldest building on "the Hill" still in use. Originally a men's dormitory, it was later a classroom building and an administration building. Most recently it has become the home of the university's Science Alliance, which promotes research and collaboration with the Oak Ridge National Laboratory.

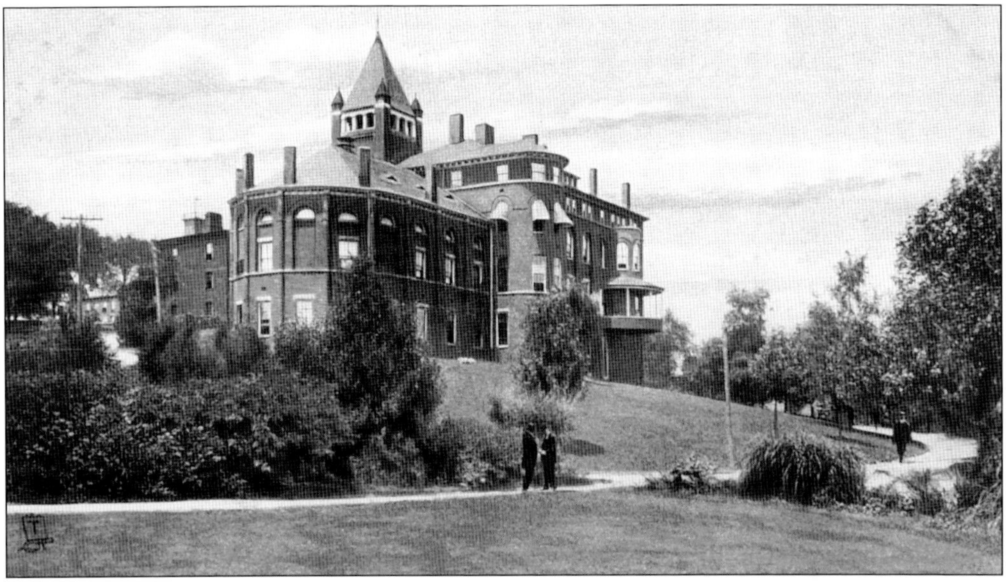

Science Hall, University of Tennessee. (Published by Raphael Tuck and Sons, London; series 2722.) Science Hall was built in 1892 at a cost of $40,000. It was a beautiful and graceful building which contained a small auditorium used for a chapel and for dramatic and musical performances. One of the prides of the campus, it had high ceilings and wainscotted rooms. In the auditorium there was a small organ on the balcony. The structure was demolished in 1967.

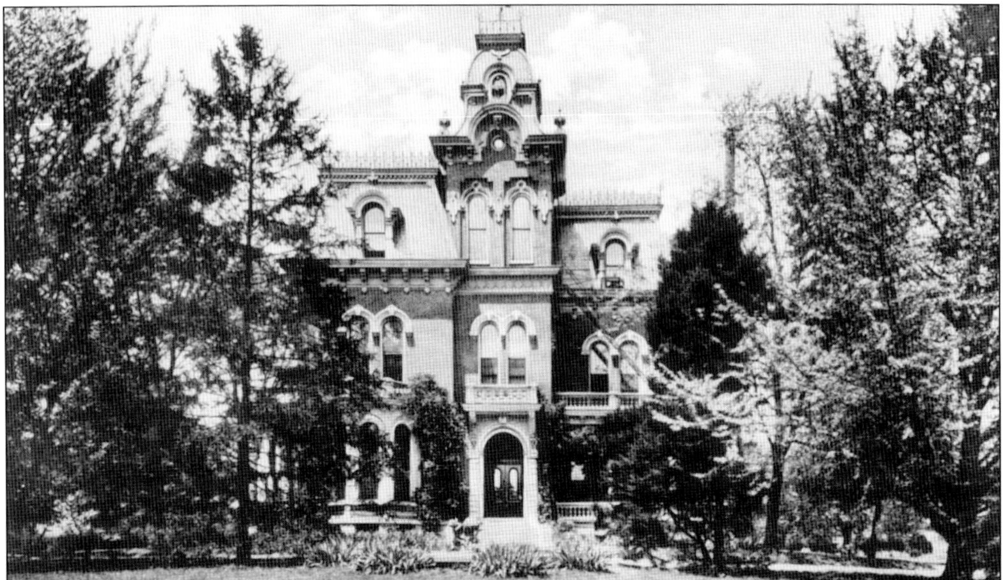

The Old Sophronia Strong Hall. (Published by University of Tennessee Co-operative Bookstore.) This building was the home of Daniel Briscoe Sr., whose family lived in it from 1900 to 1920, at which time it was sold to the University of Tennessee. The present Sophronia Strong Hall was built on this site in 1925 at a cost of $143,000. It is a residential hall for women and includes a large cafeteria patronized not only by students, but also by the public.

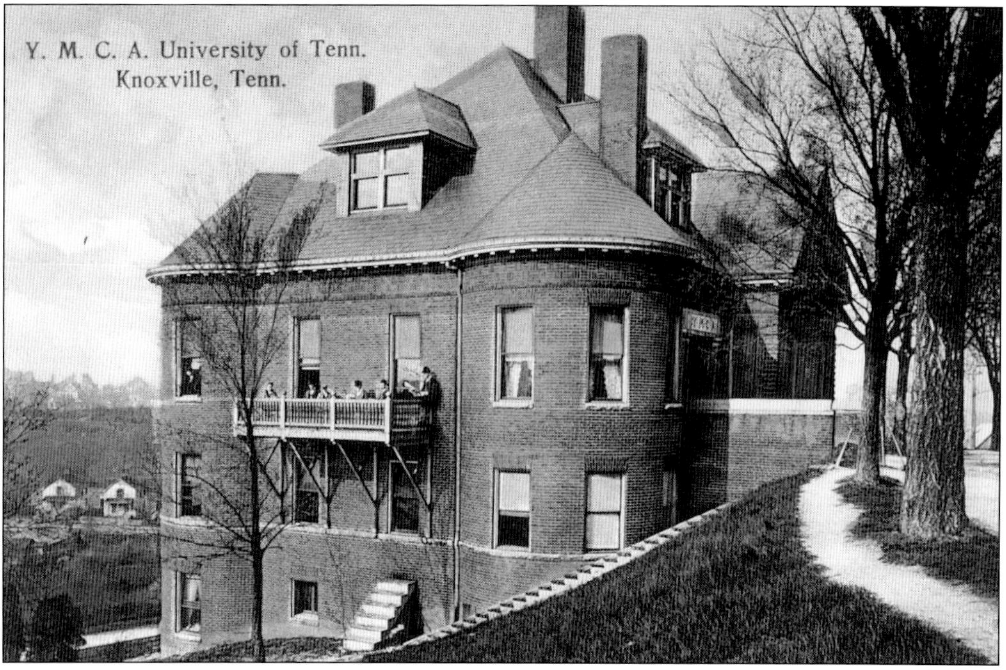

YMCA, University of Tennessee. (Published by S.H. Kress.) The YMCA chapter at the University of Tennessee was organized in 1876, one of the first in a Southern college. The building pictured came about in 1891; it contained a bowling alley, gymnasium, race track, lockers, and baths. It was the only physical education facility on campus until the Alumni Gymnasium was built in 1934. The building was destroyed by fire in 1943.

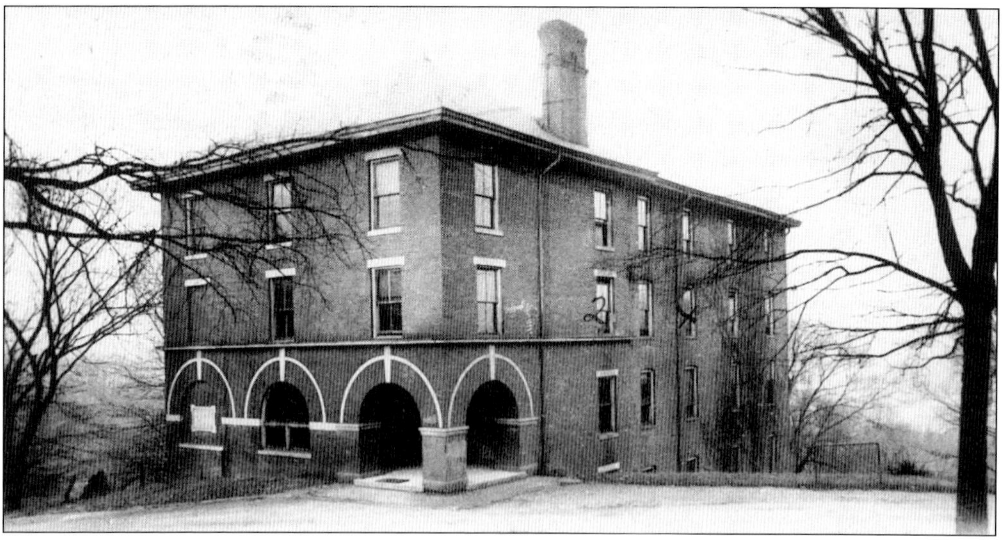

Humes Hall, University of Tennessee. (Published by Rotograph Co., New York; card sent 1908.) North College, built in 1874, was renamed Humes Hall in 1896, to honor Thomas William Humes (1815–1892), clergyman, journalist, and university president (1865–1883). He was instrumental in bringing order to the campus after the Civil War. Between 1877 and 1883 he was also the librarian of the Lawson McGhee Library. Humes Hall was demolished in 1950.

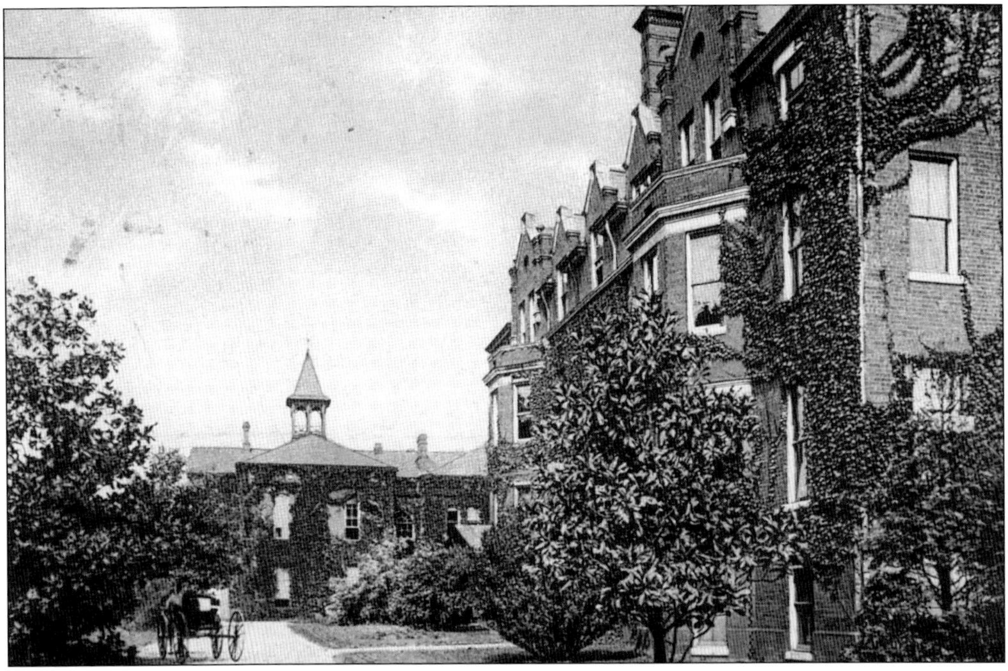

THE BARBARA BLOUNT AND AGRICULTURAL HALLS. (Published by Monroe Howard.) Barbara Blount Hall, built about 1901 to accommodate the newly readmitted coeds, was named for William Blount's daughter, who was one of the first women to enter the university in 1794. The building was razed in 1979. Agricultural Hall was built in 1903 and was destroyed by fire in 1934.

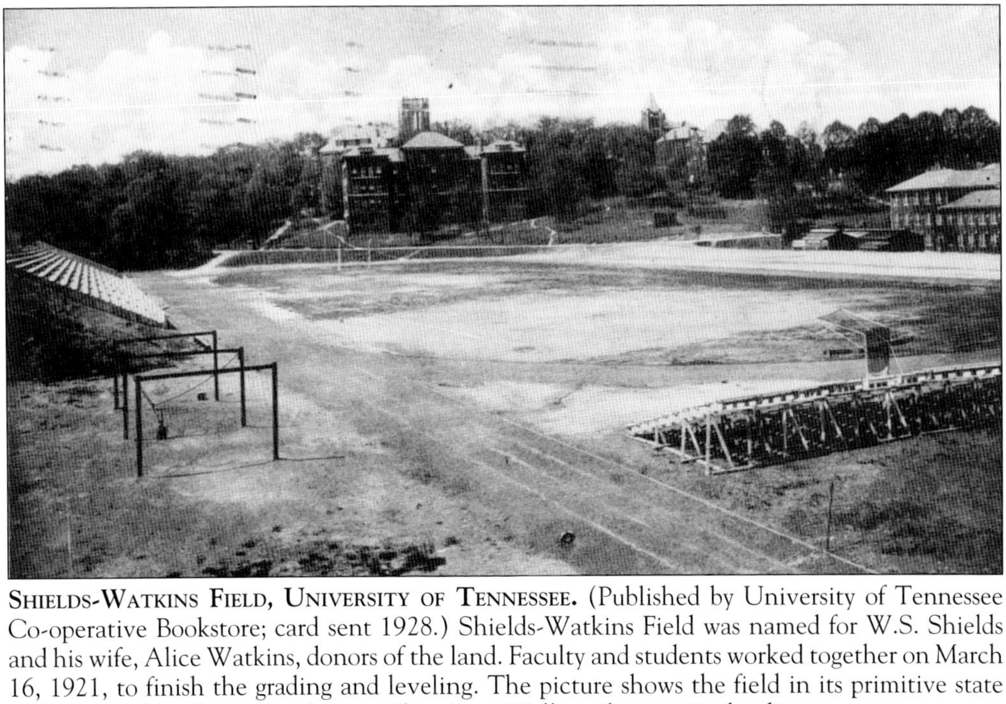

SHIELDS-WATKINS FIELD, UNIVERSITY OF TENNESSEE. (Published by University of Tennessee Co-operative Bookstore; card sent 1928.) Shields-Watkins Field was named for W.S. Shields and his wife, Alice Watkins, donors of the land. Faculty and students worked together on March 16, 1921, to finish the grading and leveling. The picture shows the field in its primitive state with skimpy bleachers on only two sides. Ayres Hall can be seen in the distance.

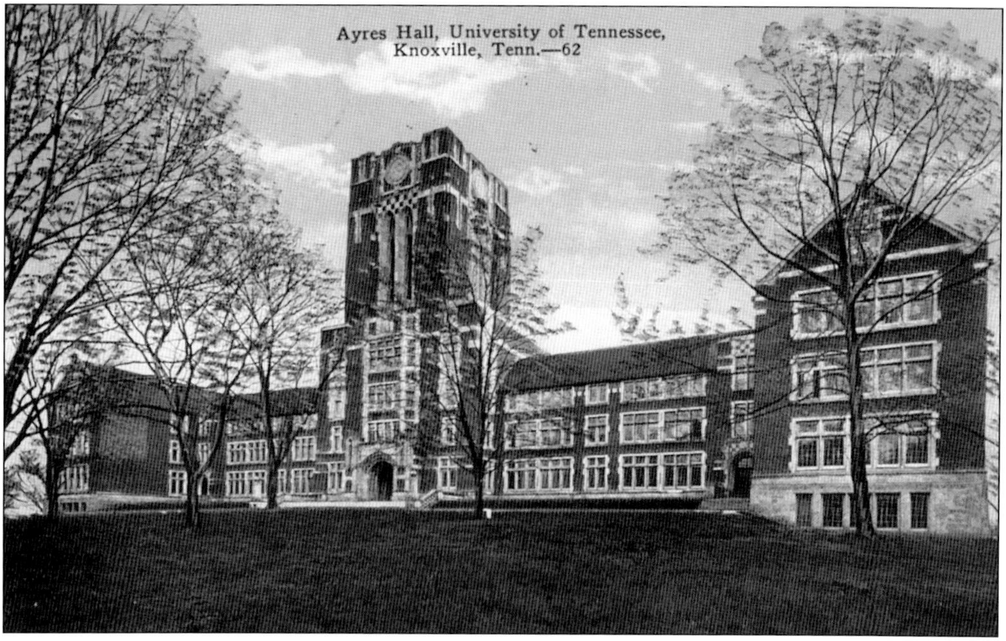

AYRES HALL, UNIVERSITY OF TENNESSEE. (Published by E.C. Kropp, Milwaukee; card sent 1931.) This impressive building became the centerpiece of the Knoxville campus in 1922, replacing Old College, East College, and West College at the top of "the Hill." The result of the successful lobbying of Present Brown Ayres, the building cost about $300,000. Dr. Ayres served the university as its president from 1904 to 1919.

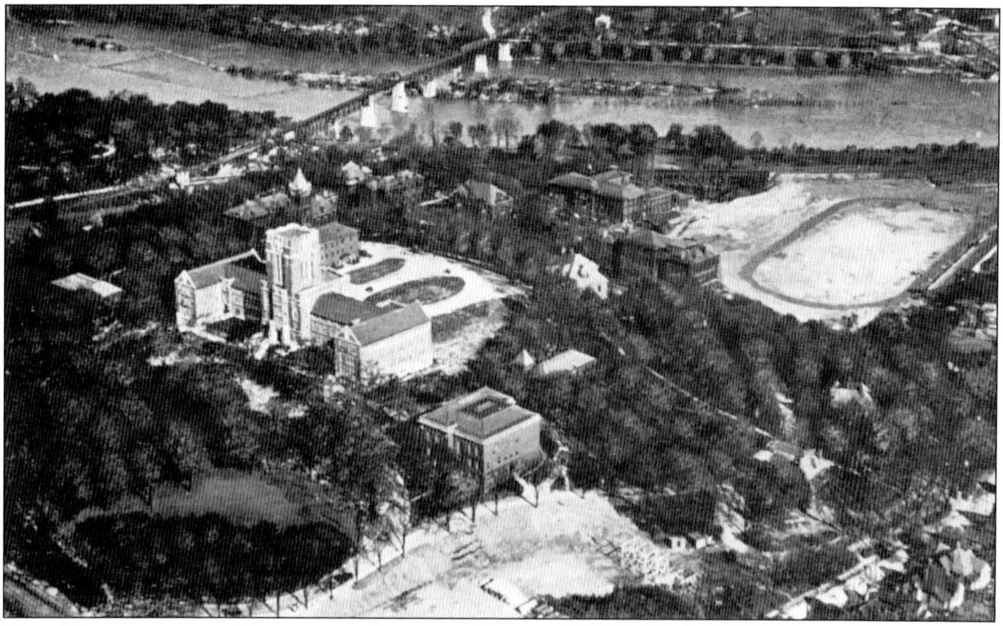

THE UNIVERSITY OF TENNESSEE CAMPUS, KNOXVILLE. (Published by Knoxville Engraving Company.) This splendid overview of the University of Tennessee campus shows the commanding presence of Ayres Hall in the center with the parade ground just behind it. The undeveloped athletic field is at right, with the Tennessee River beyond.

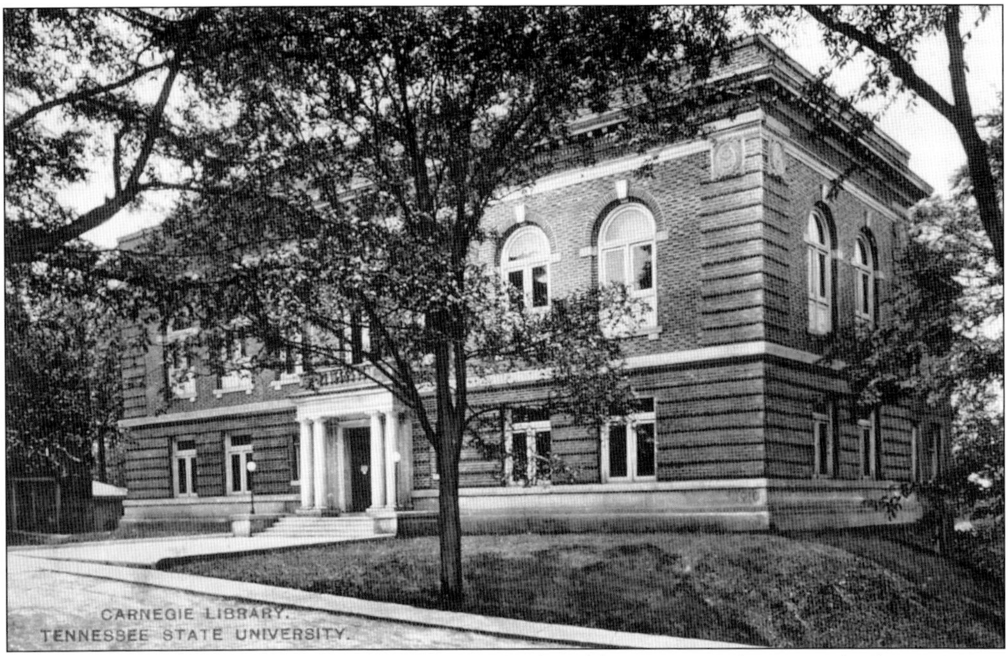

THE CARNEGIE LIBRARY. (No publication data.) The old Carnegie Library was built in 1911 to the designs of Patton and Miller of Chicago. It was no longer used as a library after the Hoskins Library was built across Cumberland Avenue, but was remodeled to serve as an administration building in 1934.

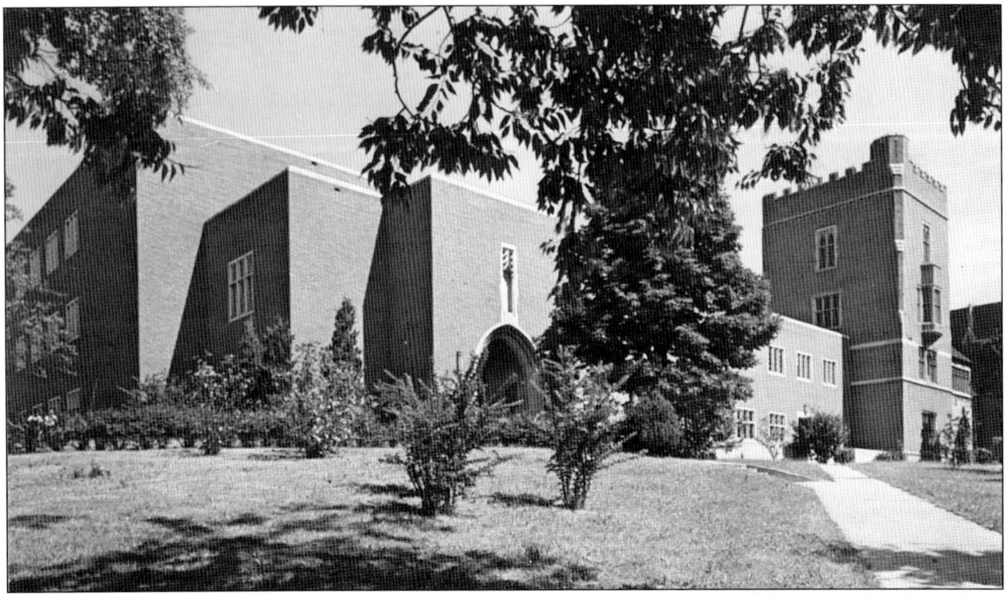

THE JAMES D. HOSKINS LIBRARY, UNIVERSITY OF TENNESSEE. (No publication data.) Built in 1931, the James D. Hoskins Library was the principal library on campus until 1969, containing both undergraduate and graduate collections, as well as rare books and manuscripts. Located on Cumberland Avenue across from "the Hill," it is still the repository for books and archival memorabilia needed by graduate students and historians. James D. Hoskins was president of the university between 1934 and 1946.

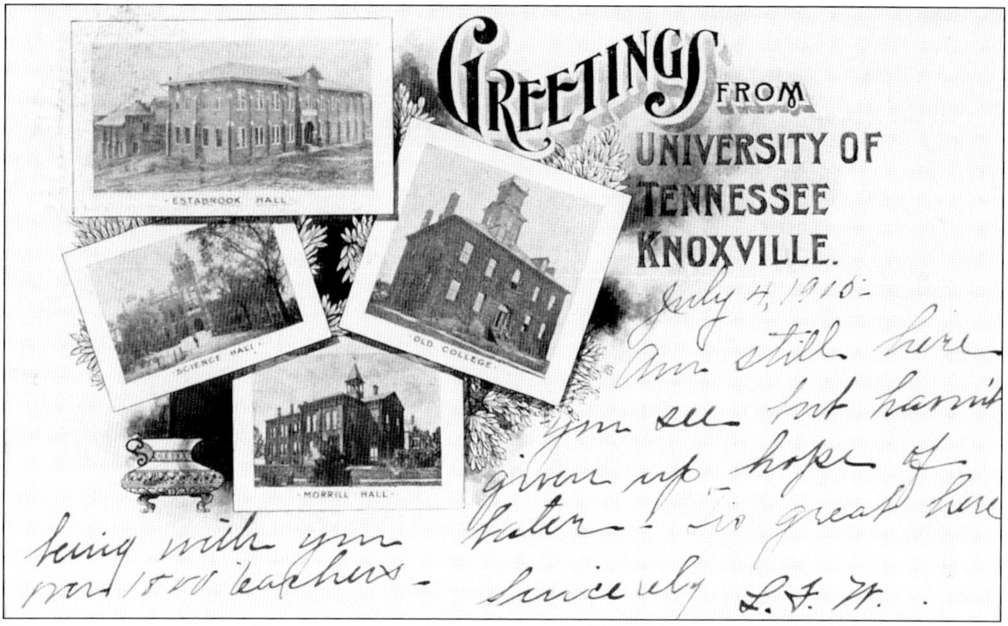

GREETINGS FROM THE **U**NIVERSITY OF **T**ENNESSEE. (No publication data; card sent 1910.) This type of "Greetings from . . ." card was very popular between 1900 and 1910. Before 1907 messages had to be written on the front of the card, and printers left ample room. Here we see four "vignette" pictures of University of Tennessee buildings.

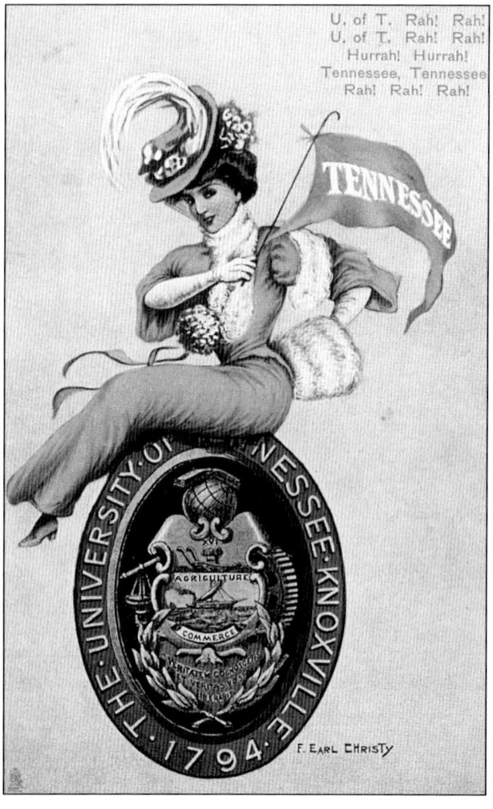

A UNIVERSITY OF **T**ENNESSEE **C**HEERLEADER. (Published by Raphael Tuck and Sons, London; series 2452.) This card is one in a series of university coed cheerleaders perched on her university's official seal. The artist was F. Earl Christy, a prominent postcard artist of the early 1900s. By the girl's attire we can assume the date is around 1907. The whole series of Christy girls is much sought after by postcard collectors.

Five

Streets

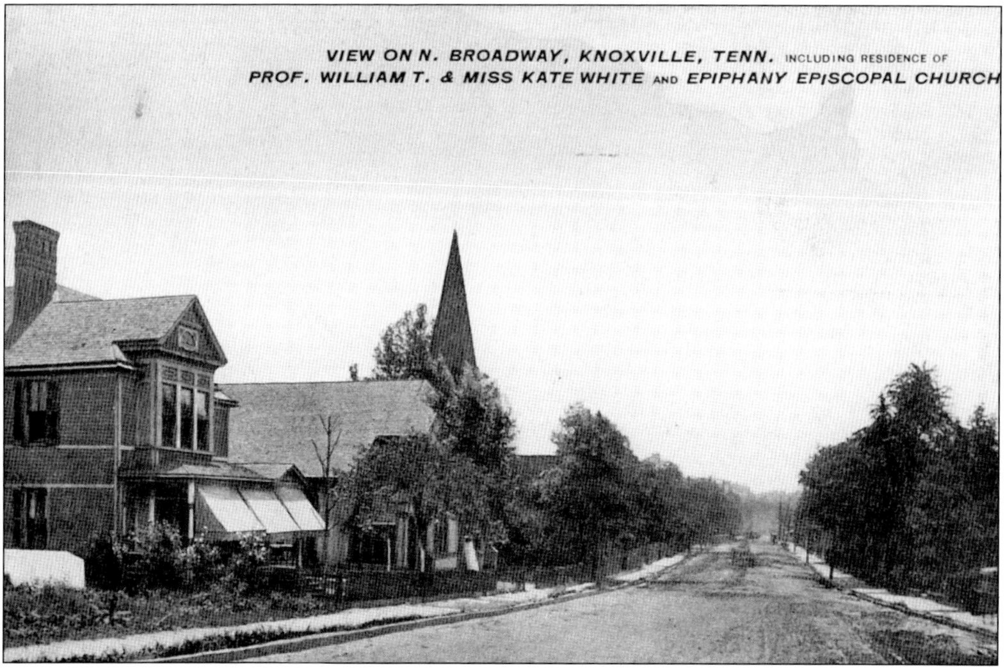

A View on North Broadway, Knoxville. (Published by M. Howard, Knoxville.) Broadway was first called Tazewell Pike and later Broad Street. The Epiphany Episcopal Church, located near Broadway and Central, closed in 1920; its congregation moved to 1101 North Broadway, where it founded the St. James Episcopal Church. Professor William T. White was the principal at Girls' High School early in the century. Miss Kate White was president of the Ossoli Circle in 1908–1909.

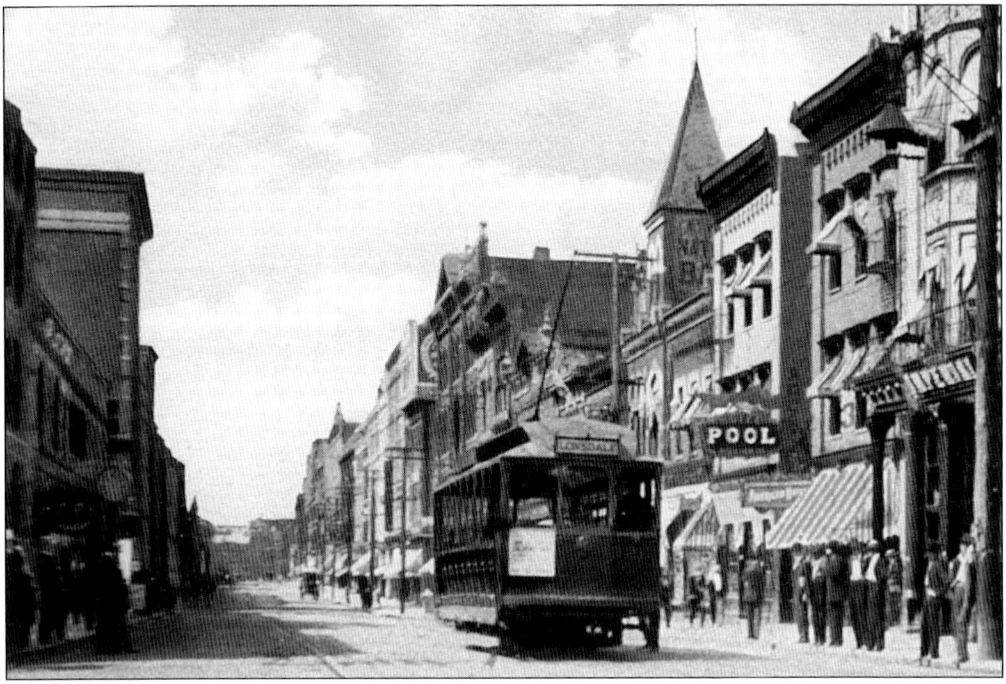

GAY STREET, KNOXVILLE. (Published by Souvenir Post Card Co., New York.) Gay Street is seen here about 1910 at the corner of Clinch Avenue. The Imperial Hotel is at right; the Lonsdale trolley pauses to pick up passengers. Most buildings at this time were less than four stories high.

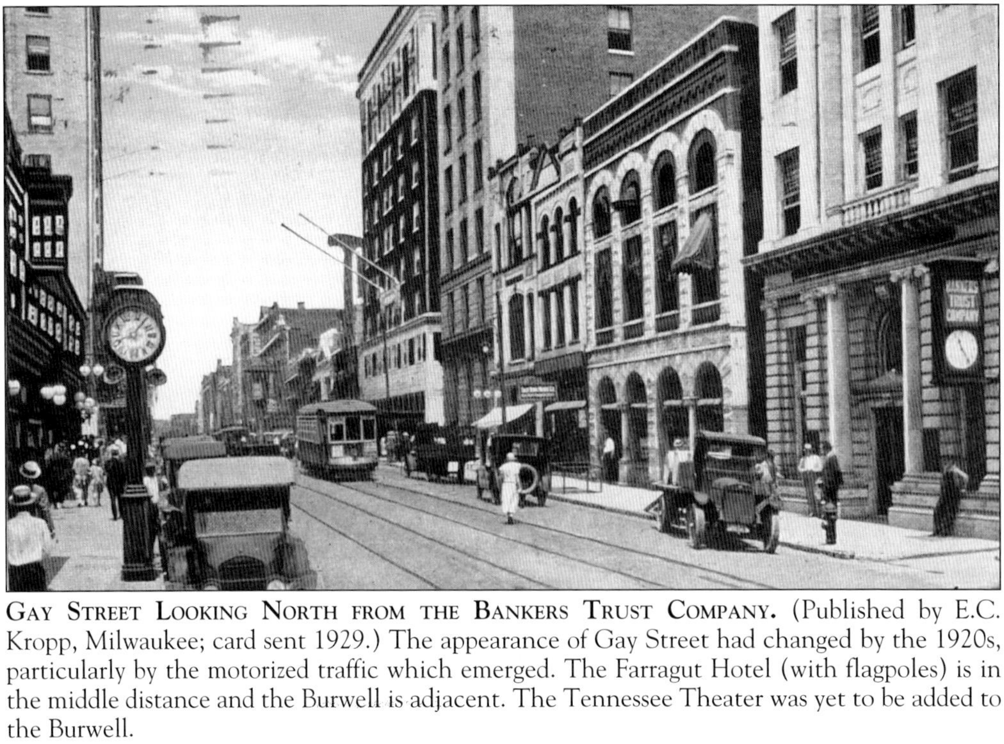

GAY STREET LOOKING NORTH FROM THE BANKERS TRUST COMPANY. (Published by E.C. Kropp, Milwaukee; card sent 1929.) The appearance of Gay Street had changed by the 1920s, particularly by the motorized traffic which emerged. The Farragut Hotel (with flagpoles) is in the middle distance and the Burwell is adjacent. The Tennessee Theater was yet to be added to the Burwell.

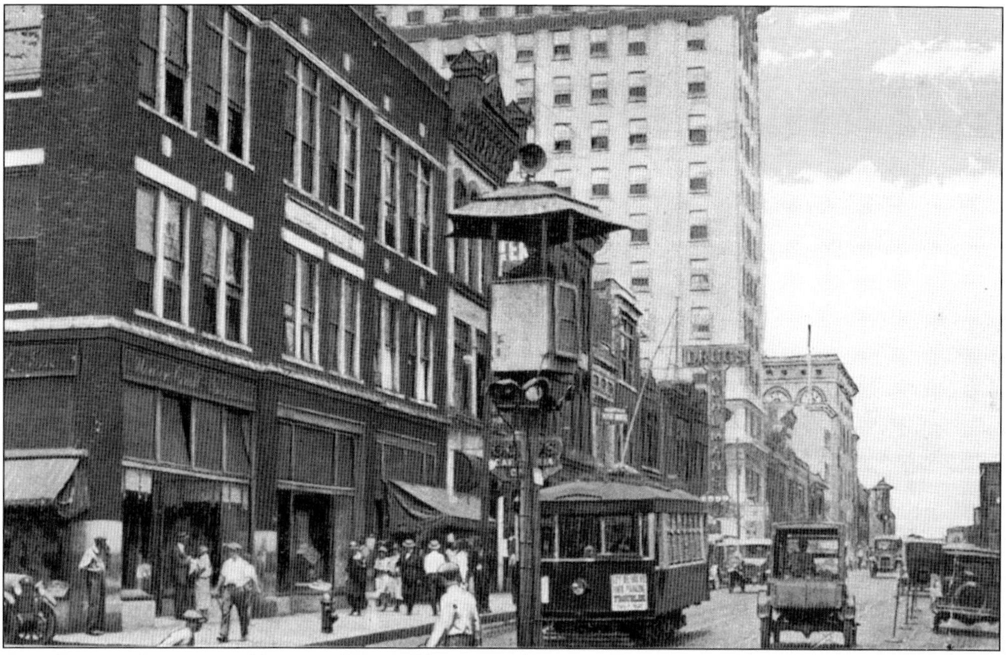

Gay Street Looking North. (No publication data; card sent 1927.) This view of 1920s Gay Street shows a now-abandoned reminder of the times—the traffic policeman's elevated station on his pole at the intersection of Gay and Church. Flower Craft, Inc.'s sign is visible on the store at left. Farther up the block we can see the signs of Good's Cafeteria (behind the policeman's pole) and Kuhlman's Drugs.

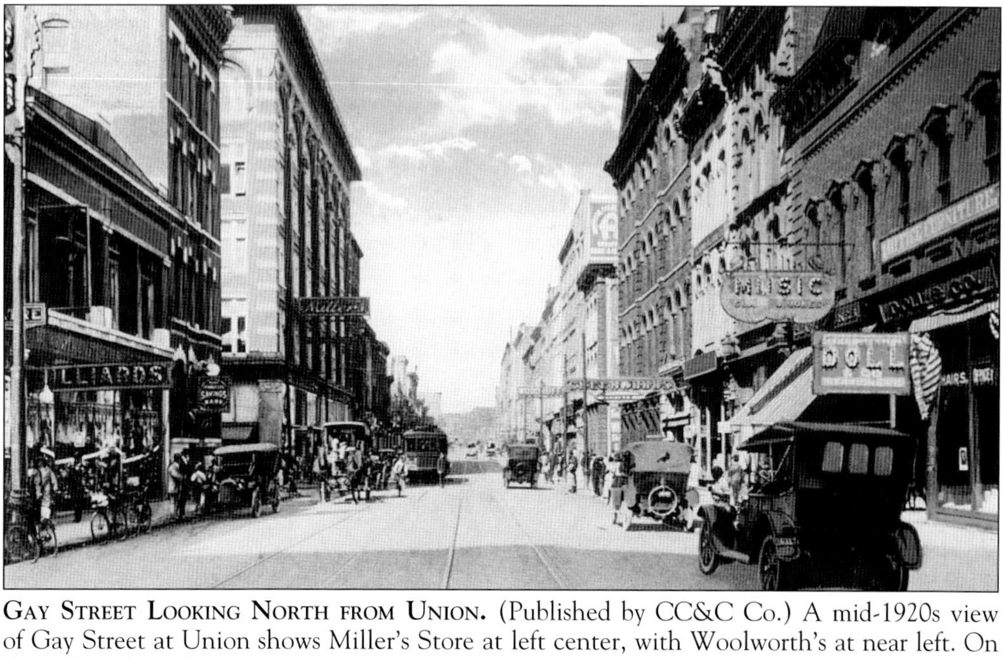

Gay Street Looking North from Union. (Published by CC&C Co.) A mid-1920s view of Gay Street at Union shows Miller's Store at left center, with Woolworth's at near left. On the right side of the street we see Clark and Jones Music Store and Woodruff's in the distance. The Doll Furniture Company, which sold office furniture, is at near right. Transportation is represented by both old and new; we see the horse and buggy, the automobile, and the trolley.

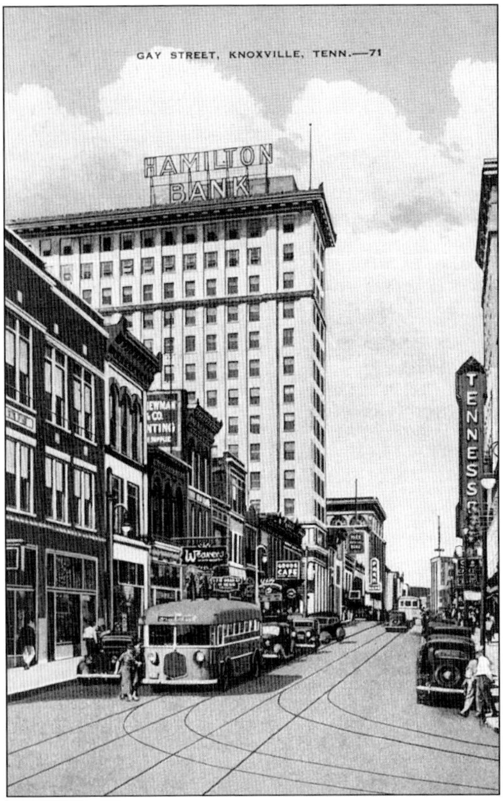

Gay Street. (Published by Standard News Agency, Knoxville; card sent 1937.) Interesting changes have come about in the 1930s decade. Busses have entered the scene, though trolleys have not vanished yet. The Tennessee Theater is at right with the S & W Cafeteria next door. On the left, we see the S.B. Newman Printing Company, Weaver's Cafeteria, Good's Café, the imposing Hamilton Bank Building, and, in the far distance, the Sterchi Brothers building with its perpendicular sign.

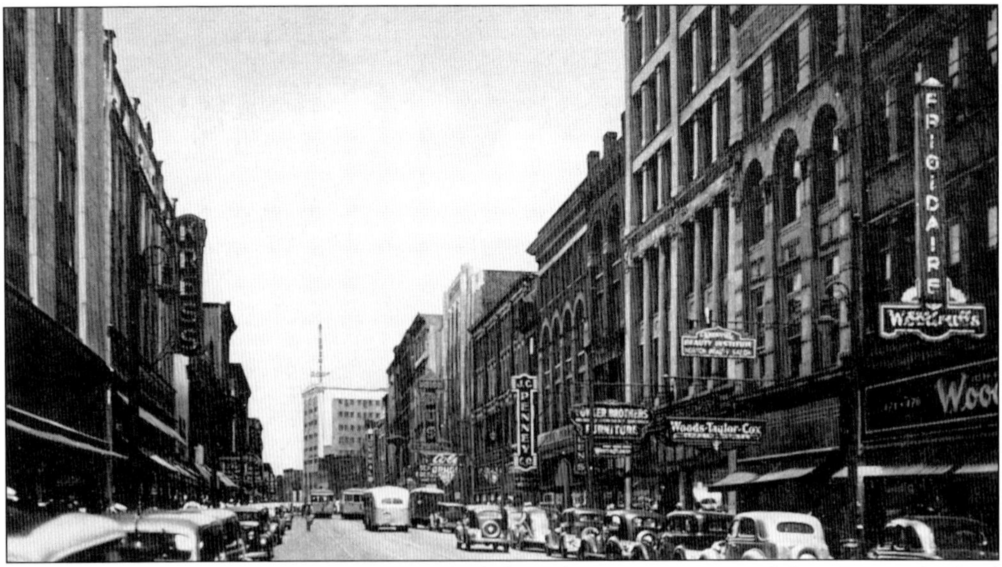

Gay Street Looking North. (Published by Thompson's; printed by Graycraft Card Co., Danville, Virginia.) Around 1940 on Gay Street's 400 block, we see, at left, S.H. Kress, the "Five and Ten-Cent Store," with the Strand Theater down the block; at right we see Woodruff's, Woods-Taylor-Cox, Fowler's, Penney's, Cole Drugs, the Union Bus Terminal, the Journal Building, and Sterchi's at center distance. The parking problem was already in evidence.

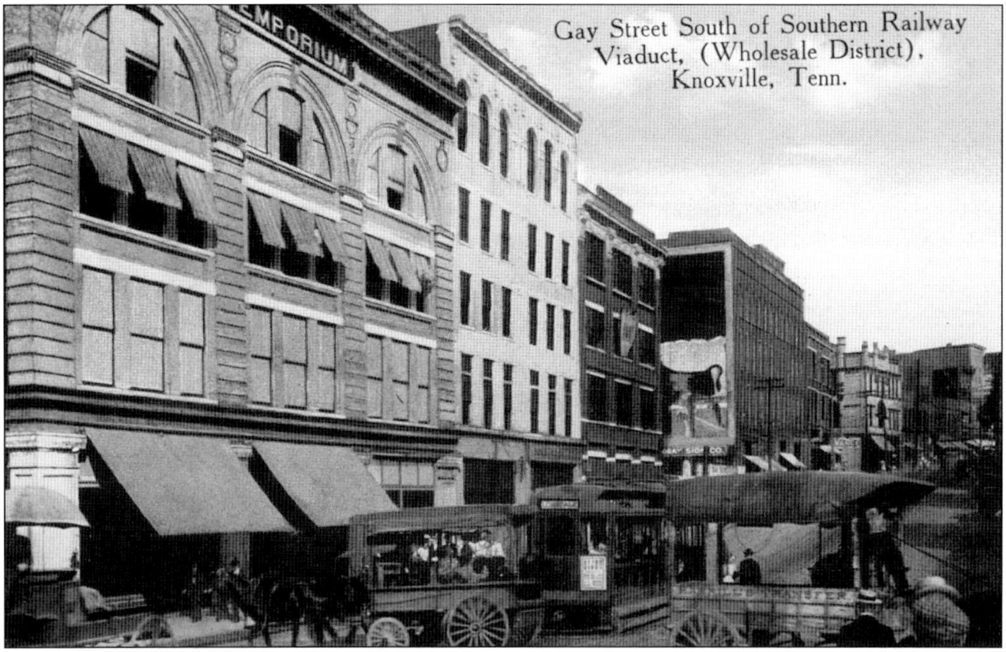

GAY STREET SOUTH OF THE SOUTHERN RAILWAY VIADUCT. (No publication data.) At Gay Street and Jackson Avenue we see part of the warehouse district adjacent to the Southern Railway. The horse-and-buggy transport indicates that the scene took place about 1910. The trolley has a Bijou Theatre advertisement on its front. The Emporium, still standing at 100 South Gay Street, was built in 1898. Its three Romanesque arches continue to provide an impressive appearance.

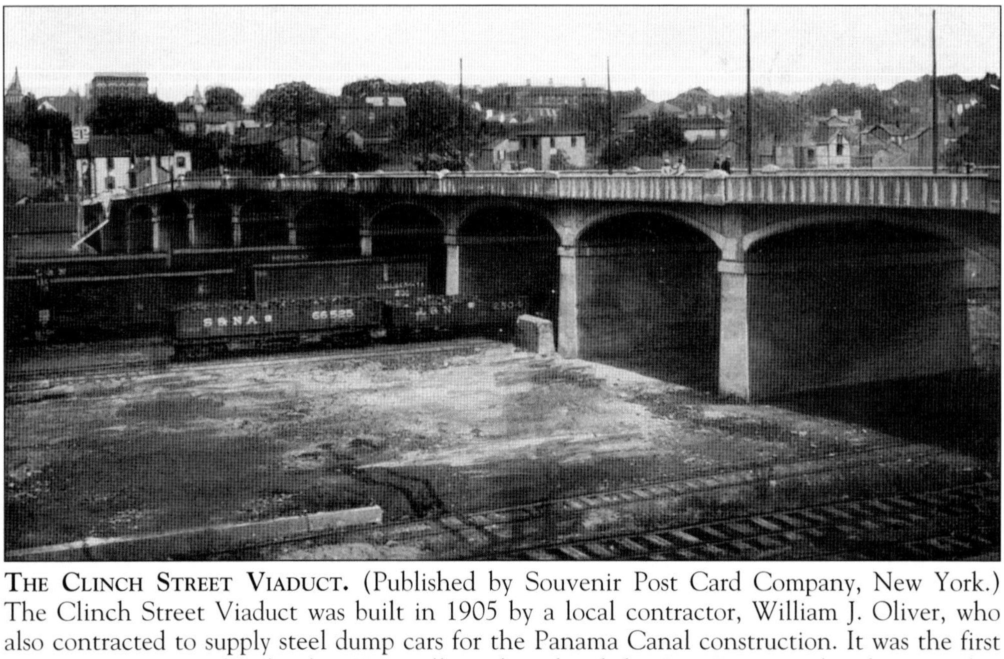

THE CLINCH STREET VIADUCT. (Published by Souvenir Post Card Company, New York.) The Clinch Street Viaduct was built in 1905 by a local contractor, William J. Oliver, who also contracted to supply steel dump cars for the Panama Canal construction. It was the first concrete structure of its kind in Knoxville and predated the Gay Street viaduct by a number of years.

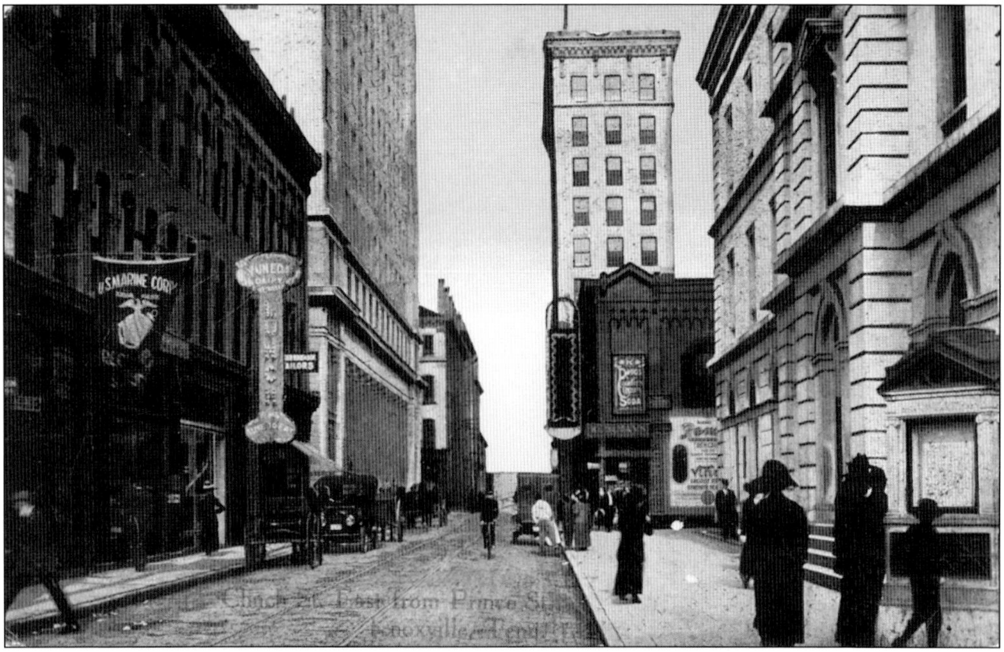

CLINCH STREET EAST FROM PRINCE. (Published by S.H. Kress.) This picture looks toward Gay Street along Clinch from Market (formerly called Prince). In the right distance we see the Burwell Building, and on the left, the Holston Bank Building. Just beyond the Holston, the Imperial Hotel is barely visible. At right is the U.S. Custom House, now the East Tennessee Historical Center. The year is about 1916.

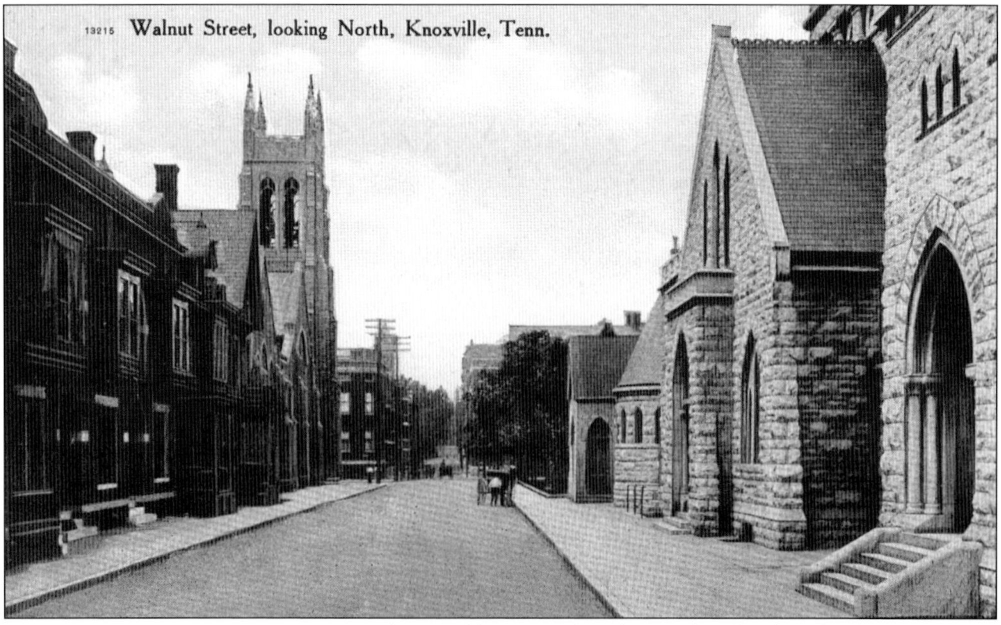

WALNUT STREET LOOKING NORTH. (No publication data.) Familiar landmarks dominate this postcard scene. In the foreground we see St. John's Episcopal Church (built 1892) at Walnut and Cumberland; and in the left background we see the Second Presbyterian Church at Walnut and Church (at this site from 1906 to 1957).

Six

Parks and Expositions

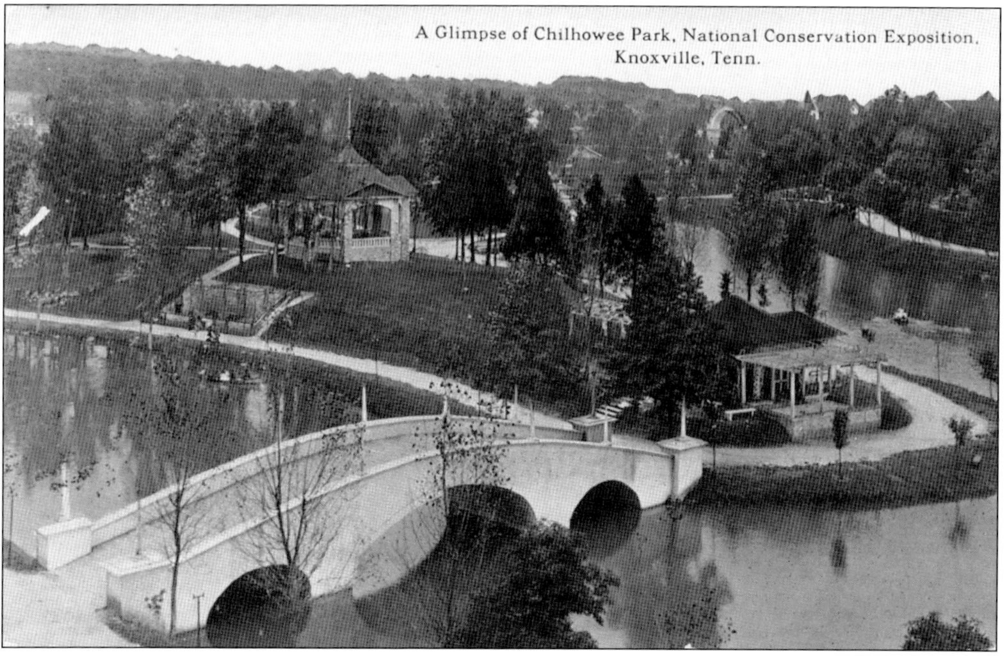

A GLIMPSE OF CHILHOWEE PARK, NATIONAL CONSERVATION EXPOSITION. (No publication data; card sent 1913.) The viewer of this scene is apparently standing on the steps of the Administration Building; coming into the park, one crossed this graceful bridge to approach the building. The lake was a significant part of the park and provided many activities such as swimming and boating. The bandstand is seen here at left center.

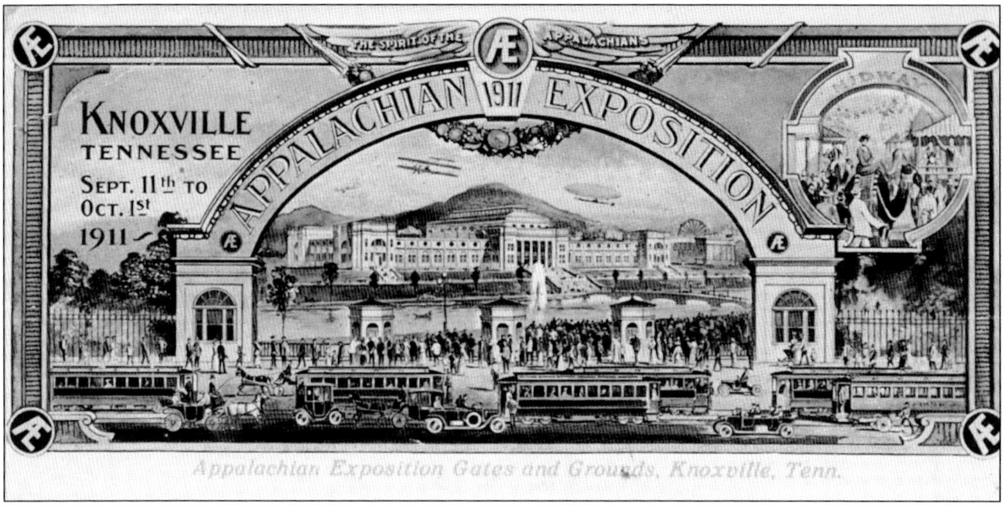

THE APPALACHIAN EXPOSITION GATES AND GROUNDS. (Published by Charles C. Cullen.) This card was published in 1911 to announce the second Appalachian Expo. The artist records the main gate with the lake, bridges, and the Administration Building in the background. A vignette at right illustrates the "Midway" showing a woman riding a camel. Crowds of people are on the grounds, and others are arriving by horse-drawn buggies, automobiles, and trolleys.

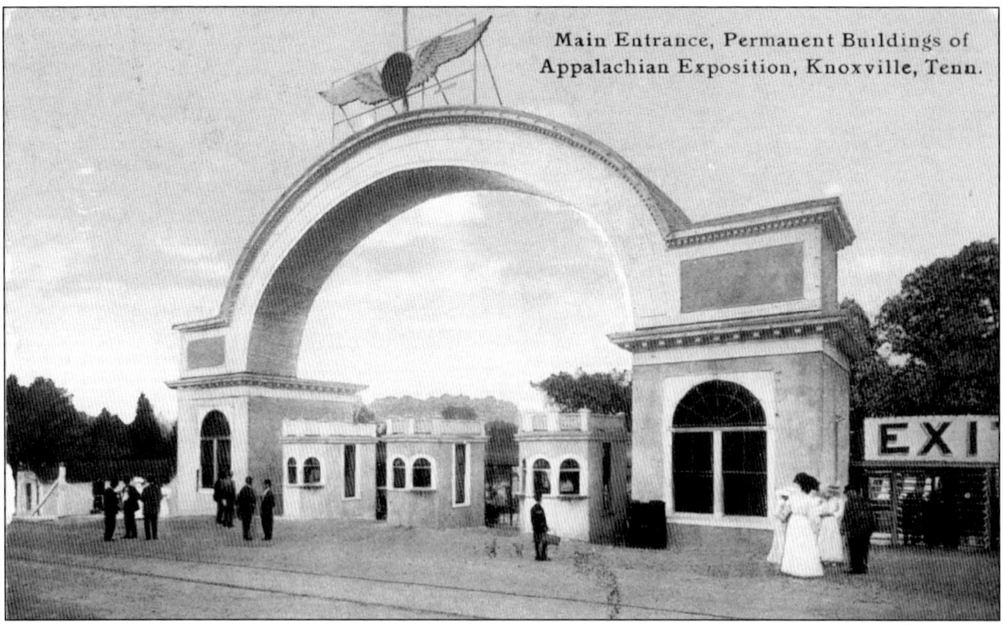

THE MAIN ENTRANCE, PERMANENT BUILDINGS OF THE APPALACHIAN EXPOSITION. (Published by S.H. Kress; card sent 1911.) A close-up of the main gate shows the ticket booths and several patrons. The lady prominent at right wears the typical long white dress and big fussy hat; the others in the group wear the popular "boater" hats. The wings above the arch with the large AE in the center medallion formed the symbol of the exposition.

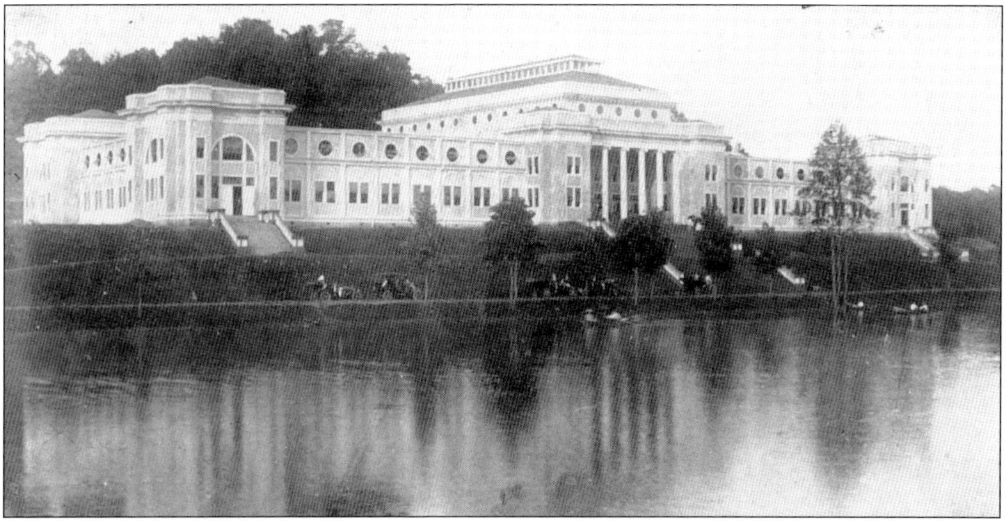

THE CENTRAL ADMINISTRATION BUILDING, APPALACHIAN EXPOSITION. (No publication data; card sent 1910.) On the advertising card put out by Bickley, McClure, and Co., we see the central building of the exposition, designed by Knoxville architect John R. Graf. For the 1913 expo the building was expanded to 84,000 square feet of floor space, and the bridge leading to it (absent here) was also built. Its name was changed to the Machinery and Liberal Arts Building.

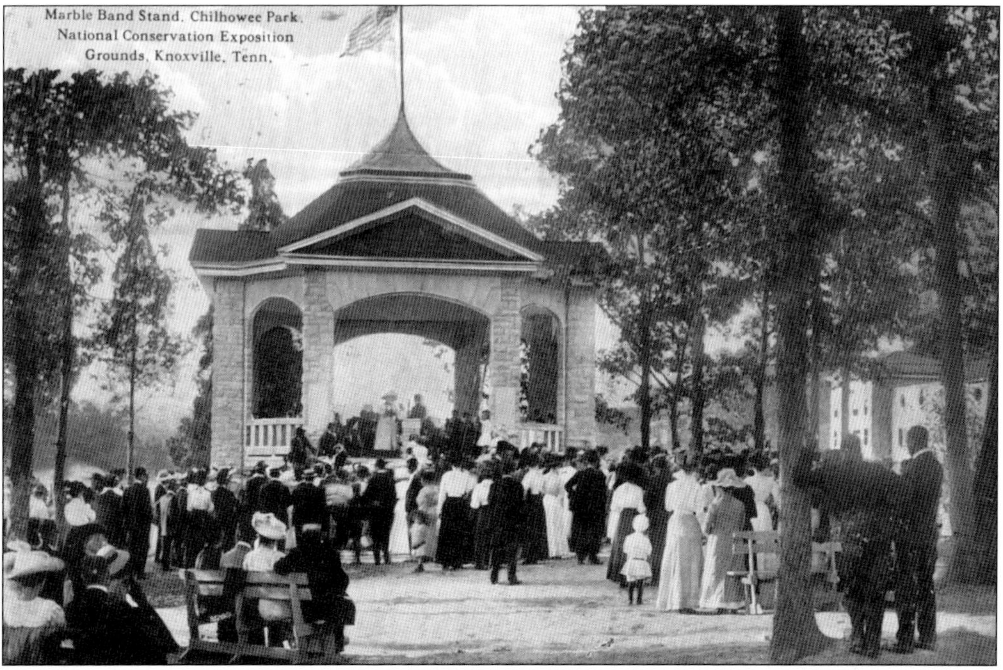

THE MARBLE BANDSTAND, CHILHOWEE PARK, NATIONAL CONSERVATION EXPOSITION GROUNDS. (Published by S.H. Kress; card sent 1913.) One by one the exhibit halls of the three expositions were destroyed by fire. The sole survivor today is the bandstand given by Knox County's marble producers to the Appalachian Expo of 1910 at a cost of $20,000. It was restored in 1976 by the Greater Knoxville American Revolution Bicentennial Commission.

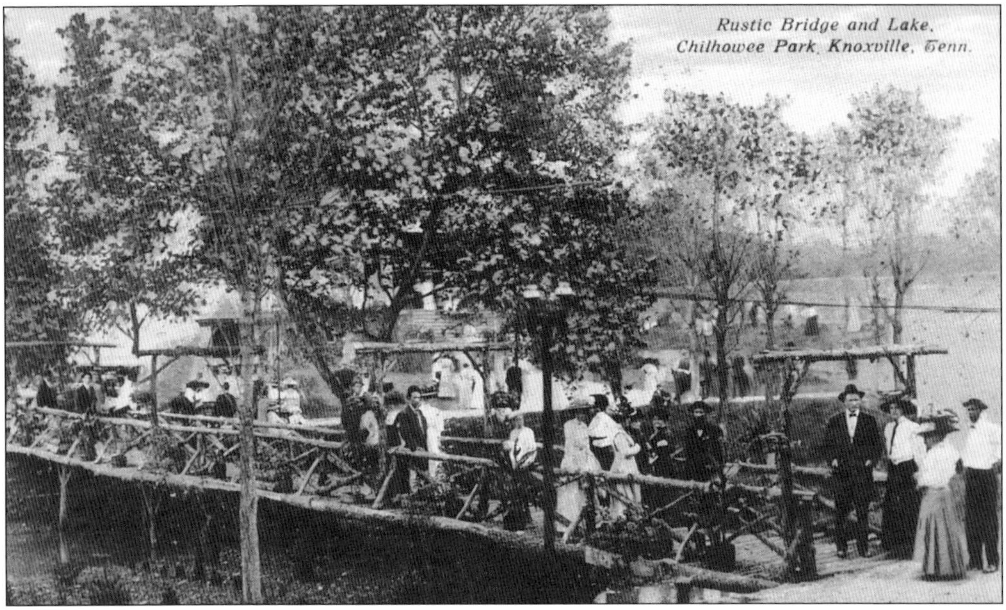

THE RUSTIC BRIDGE AND LAKE, CHILHOWEE PARK. (Published by Chapman Drug Co., Knoxville; card sent 1911.) The rustic bridge seen here and the buildings behind it were constructed for the first Appalachian Exposition in 1910. The expo attracted numerous visitors from many states, the largest crowd attending when former President Theodore Roosevelt made an appearance. The 1911 expo, under the leadership of Lawrence D. Tyson, was also enormously successful.

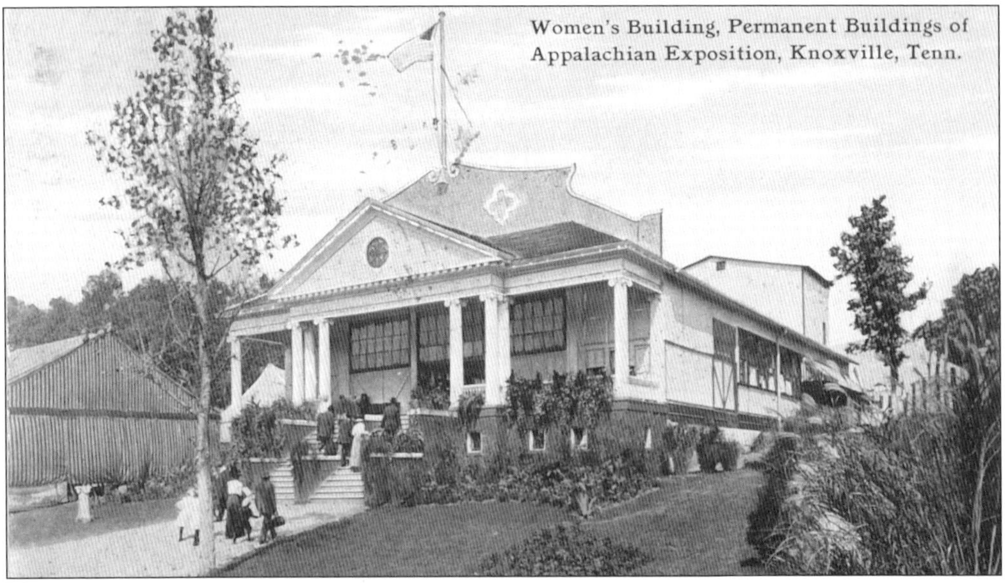

THE WOMEN'S BUILDING, APPALACHIAN EXPOSITION. (Published by S.H. Kress; card sent 1911.) Located just inside the main entrance of the exposition, the Women's Building exhibited arts and crafts typical of women worldwide. Included were blankets, basketry, hand-carved furniture, pottery, and needlework. Professions such as nursing, librarianship, and homemaking were given detailed exhibits as well. The feminine touch was enhanced by blooming plants throughout.

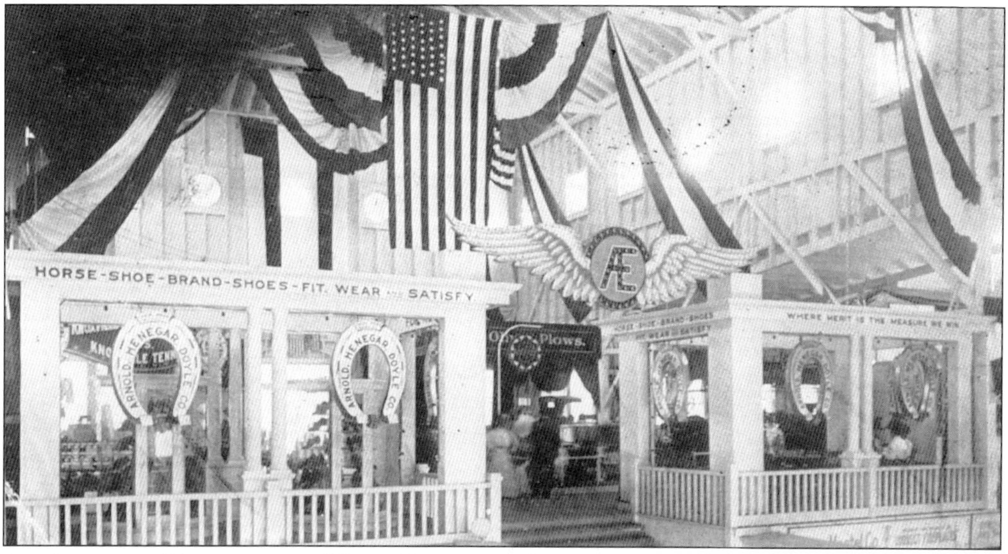

AN INTERIOR VIEW OF THE MAIN BUILDING, APPALACHIAN EXPOSITION. (No publication data; card sent 1910.) A suggestion of the size and detail of some of the exhibits is shown here. The Arnold, Henegar, & Doyle Company's exhibit is replete with columns, horseshoe brand symbols, AE logo, mottoes, flag, and banners. Its size overshadows the two dim figures in the entrance.

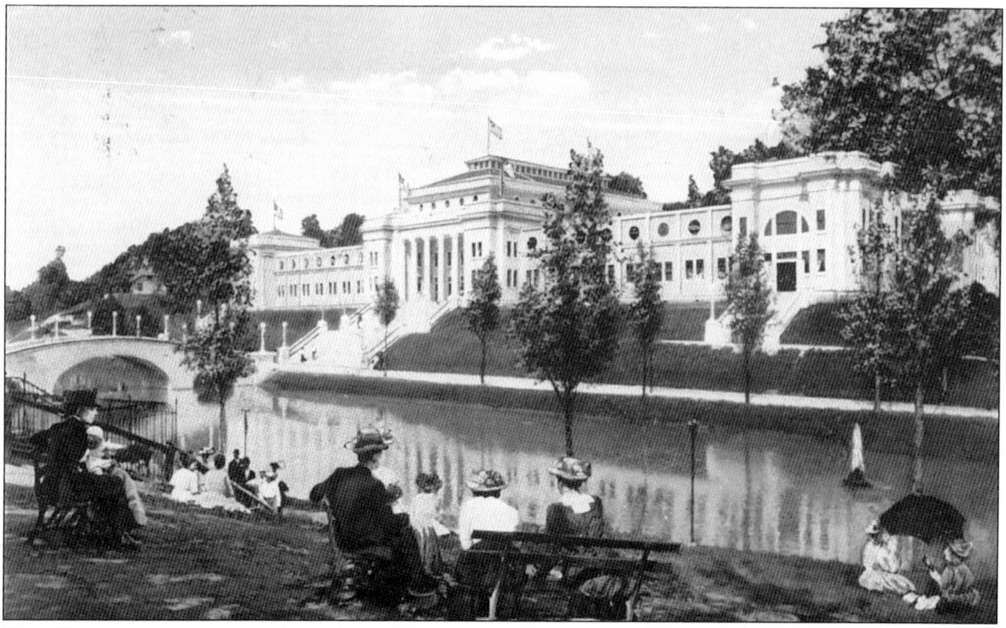

THE BRIDGE, LAKE, AND FINE ARTS BUILDING, CHILHOWEE PARK. (No publication data; card sent 1914.) A serene view of the Main Building (now called Fine Arts) and the lake shows people resting on the grass, as many did when coming to Chilhowee Park. The sender of the card says, "How would you like to swim in this pretty lake? It looks cooler than it really is. This is a pretty city, but I believe I prefer Wilmington where all you dear ones are."

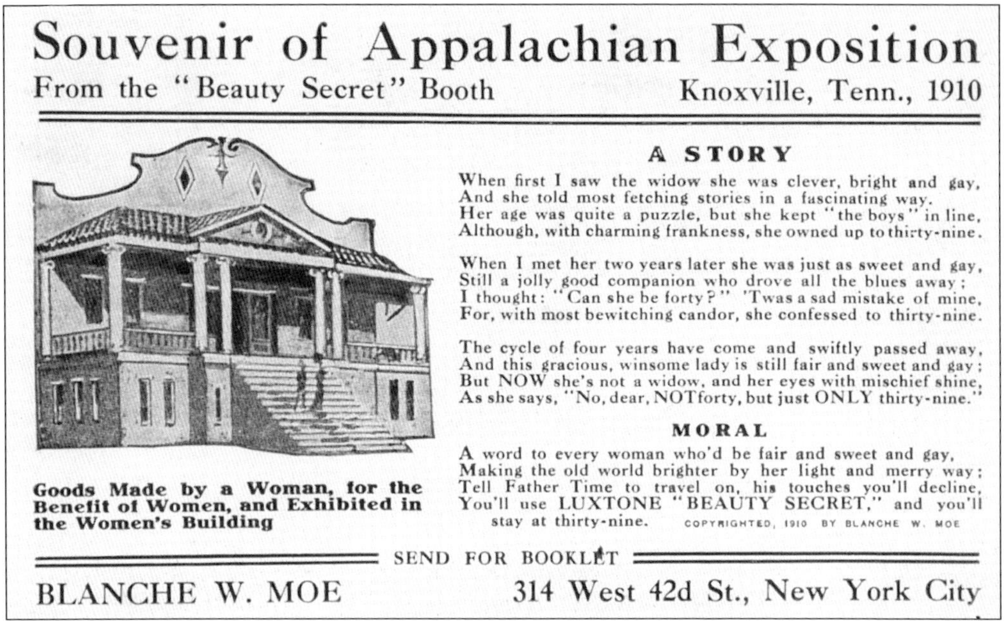

A SOUVENIR OF THE APPALACHIAN EXPOSITION, KNOXVILLE, 1910. (No publication data; card sent 1911.) Exhibiting her beauty products in the Women's Building, Blanche W. Moe of New York City reminds her "fortyish" female visitors to "use Luxtone Beauty Secret and you'll stay at thirty-nine." Many exhibitors distributed such souvenirs at the exhibition.

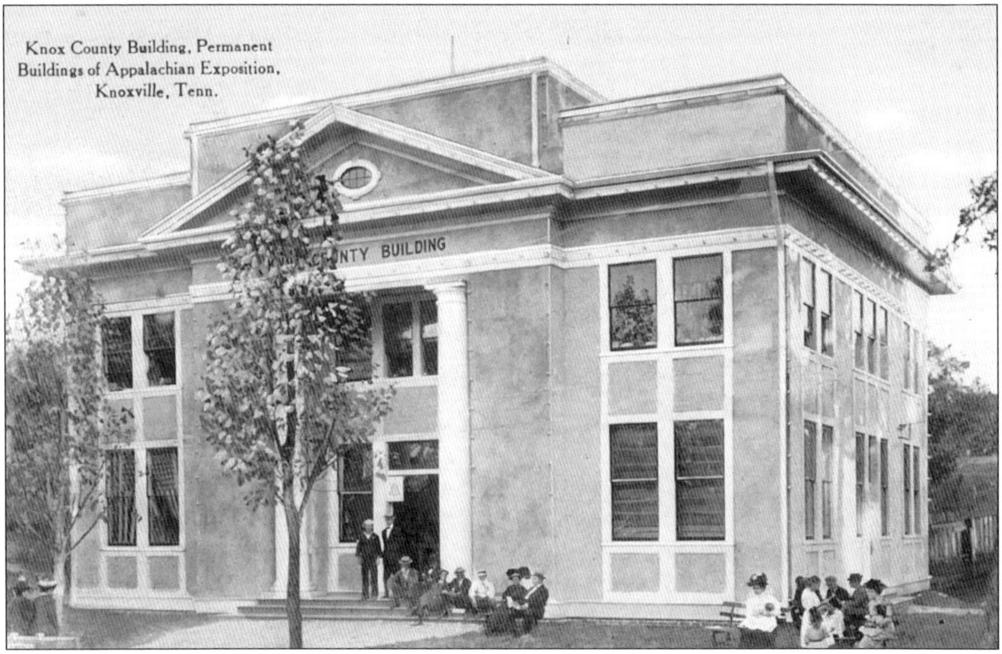

THE KNOX COUNTY BUILDING, APPALACHIAN EXPOSITION. (No publication data.) Devoted to the products and activities of Knox County, the Knox County Building was one of the six original buildings constructed for the exposition. Most of the exhibits there concerned farms and farming.

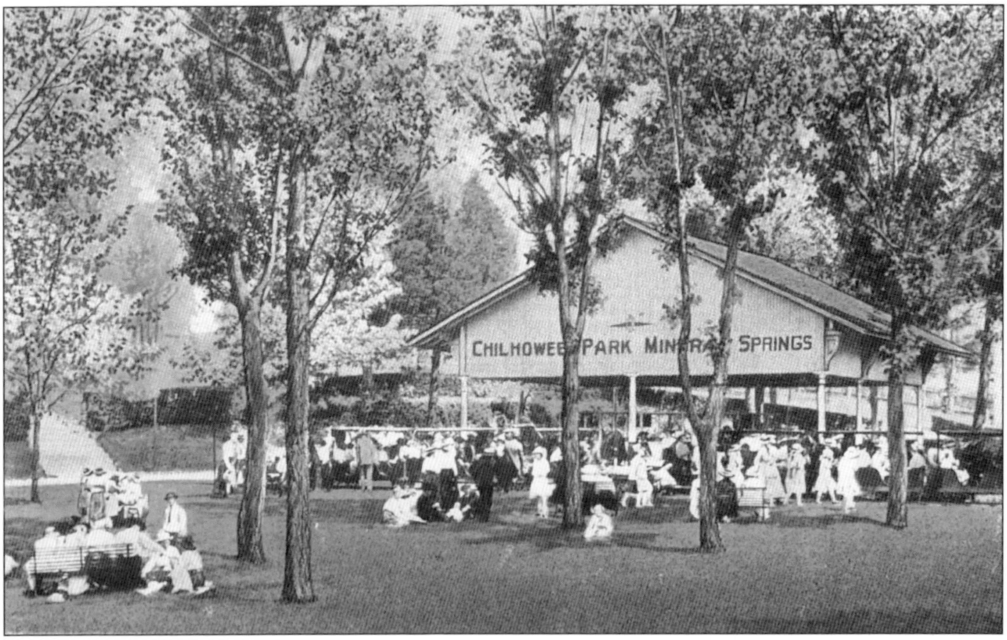

Chilhowee Park Mineral Springs. (Published by CC&C Co.) Mineral springs were popular gathering places in the first decades of the century. The spring in Chilhowee Park was a competitor of the well-known Fountain City spring. Families enjoyed having picnics at these locations; belief in the medicinal properties of spring waters was widespread.

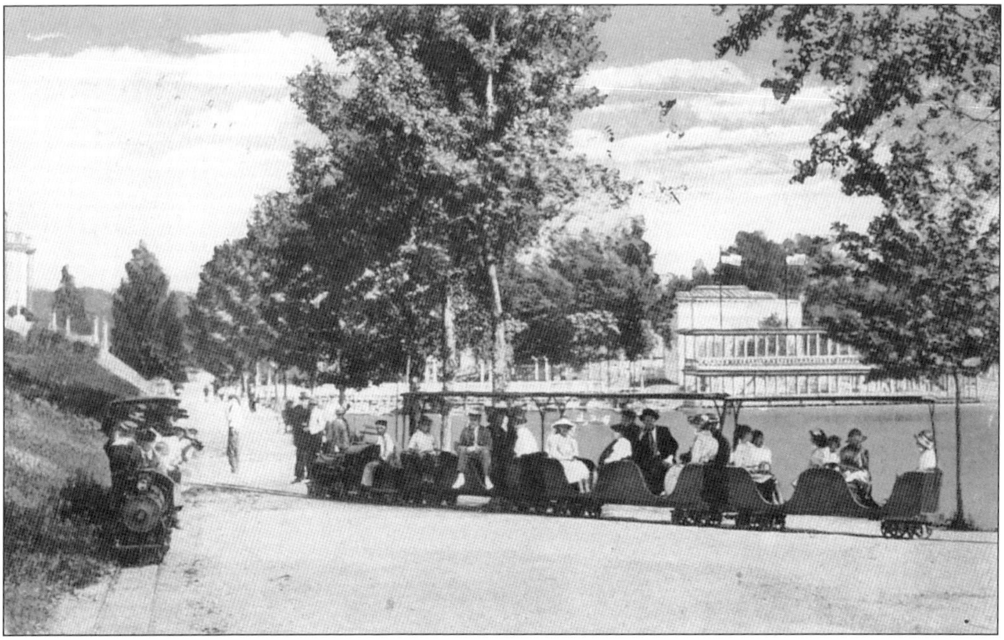

A View of Chilhowee Park and the Miniature Railway. (Published by CC&C Co; card sent 1920.) Before and after the expositions took place, Chilhowee Park offered several kinds of family recreation. The miniature railway which carried "sightseers" around the lake was especially popular.

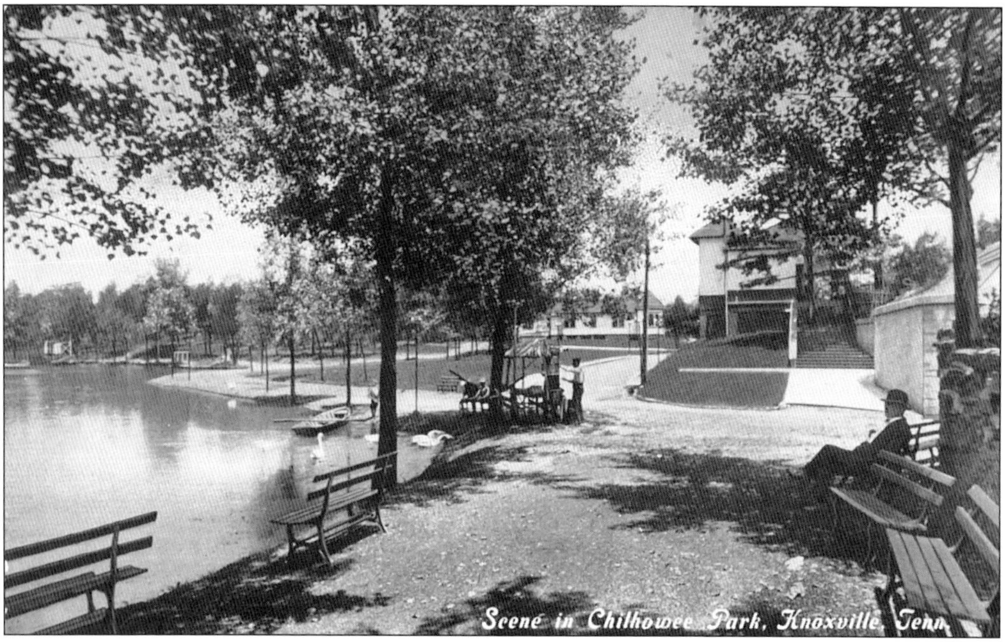

A Scene in Chilhowee Park, Knoxville. (Published by S.H. Kress.) Perhaps a quiet Sunday afternoon is illustrated here. After the advent of streetcars in 1890, many families rode the trolley out to the park for recreation of choice. In addition to reflective places along the lake, there were also a roller coaster and a splendid merry-go-round, both in operation until the 1940s.

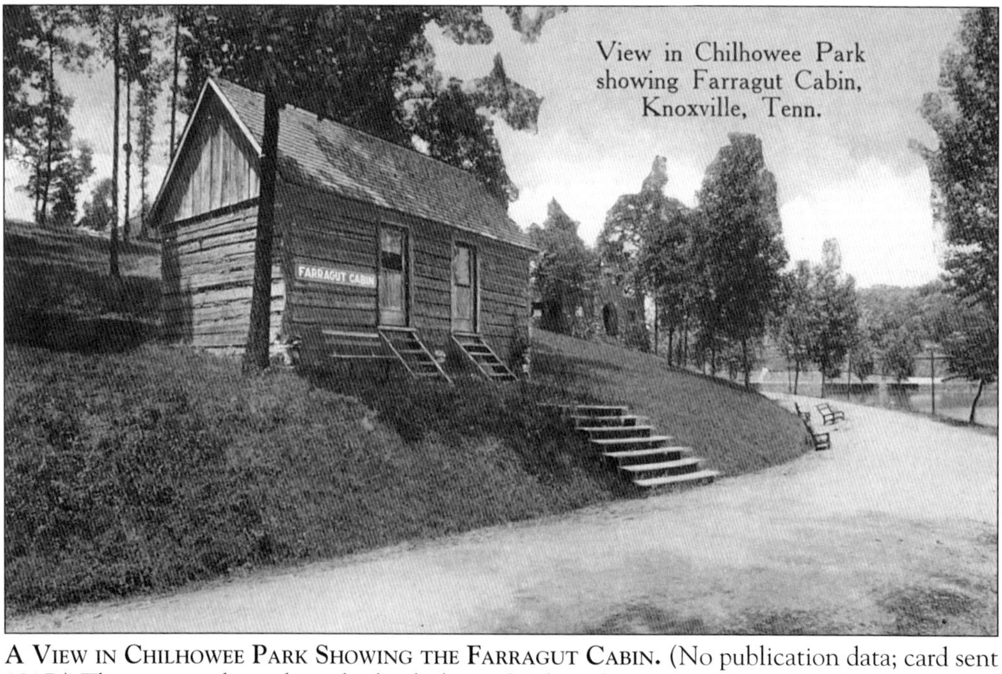

A View in Chilhowee Park Showing the Farragut Cabin. (No publication data; card sent 1917.) This pioneer log cabin, the birthplace of Admiral David Farragut, was dismantled and moved from its West Knox County location in 1910 to be reassembled in Chilhowee Park for the Appalachian Exposition. It was later destroyed by fire.

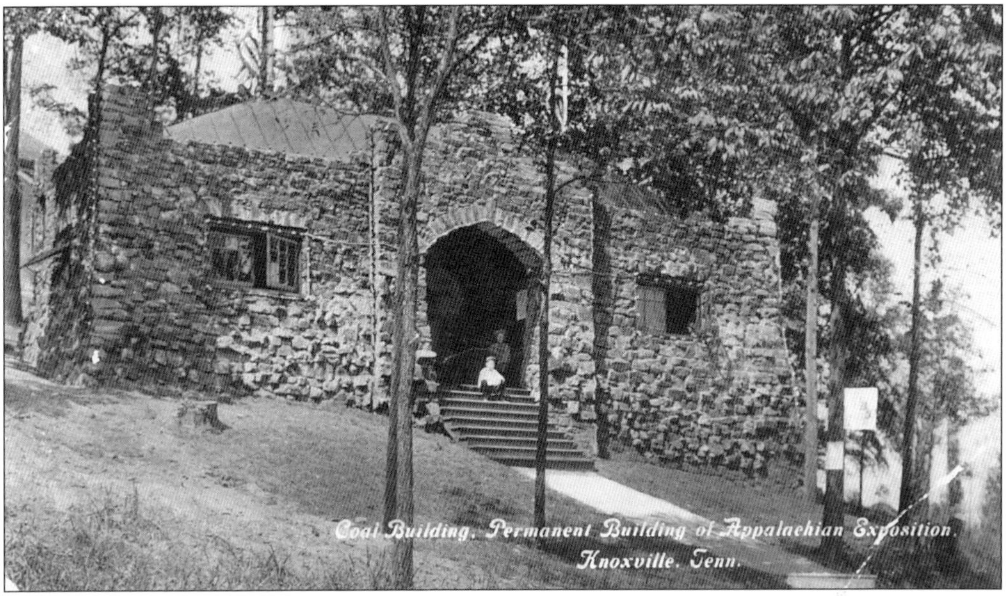

THE COAL BUILDING, APPALACHIAN EXPOSITION. (Published by S.H. Kress.) One of the most unusual buildings of the 1911 Appalachian Exposition was the Coal Building, which represented the mining interests of the Southern states. Its exterior was faced with large lumps of iridescent black coal.

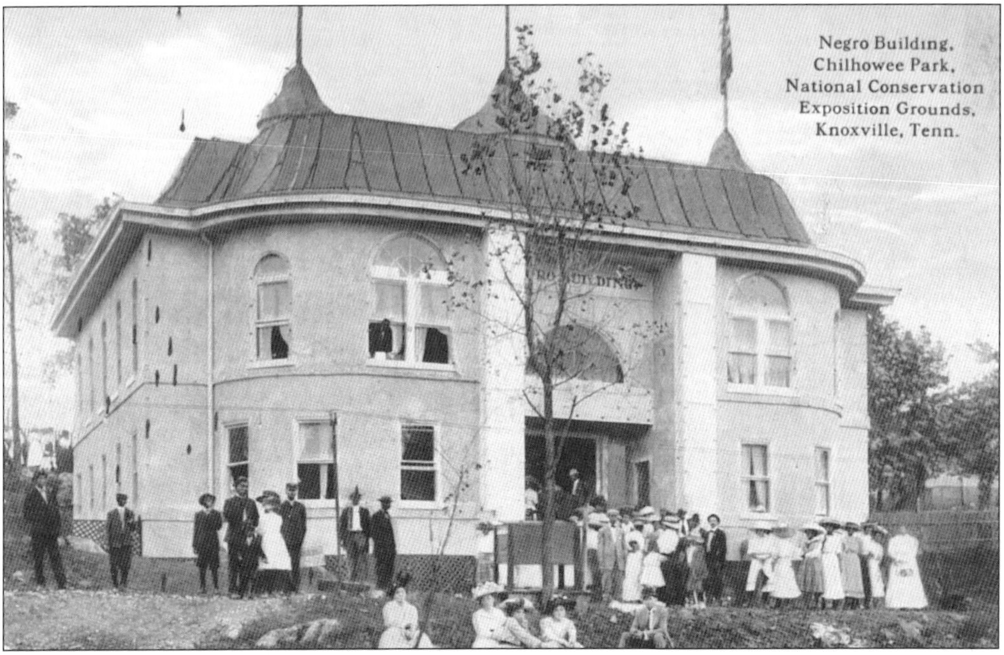

THE NEGRO BUILDING, CHILHOWEE PARK, NATIONAL CONSERVATION EXPOSITION. (Published by S.H. Kress.) Although the black population numbered less than 10% of Knox County citizens, the 1913 Exposition put forth a memorable Negro Building. The official report of the 1913 expo indicates that "it was designed by a Negro architect, built by a Negro contractor and Negro workmen, with money subscribed by Negro citizens of Knoxville." The project was directed by Dr. H.M. Green.

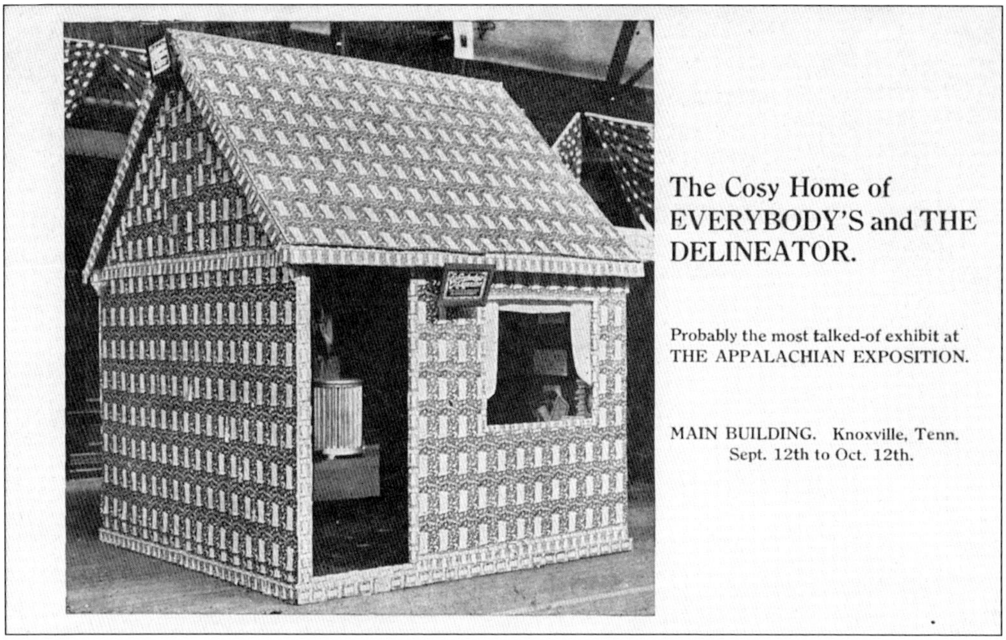

THE COSY HOME OF *EVERYBODY'S* AND THE *DELINEATOR*. (No publication data.) This souvenir card from the Appalachian Exposition of 1910 indicates that two magazines, *Everybody's* and the *Delineator*, were exhibited in their "Cosy Home" in the Main Building. The *Delineator* was a popular homemaker's magazine which featured articles and advice for women.

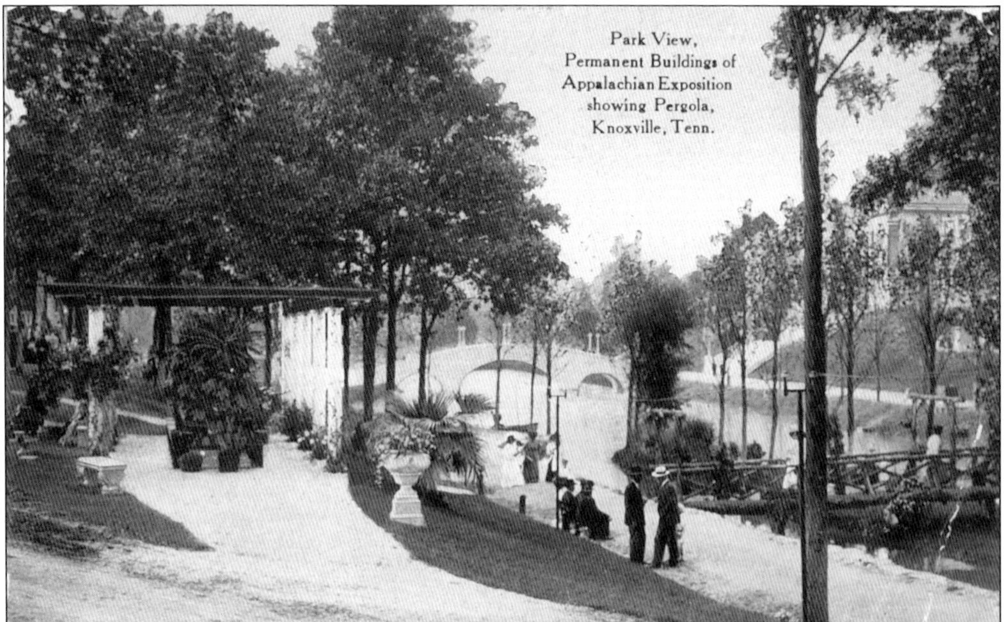

PARK VIEW, THE PERMANENT BUILDINGS OF THE APPALACHIAN EXPOSITION, SHOWING PERGOLA. (Published by S.H. Kress; card sent 1911.) In this broad view of one side of Chilhowee Park, we see the main building almost hidden in the trees at right, a portion of the lake, two bridges, and the attractive pergola at left.

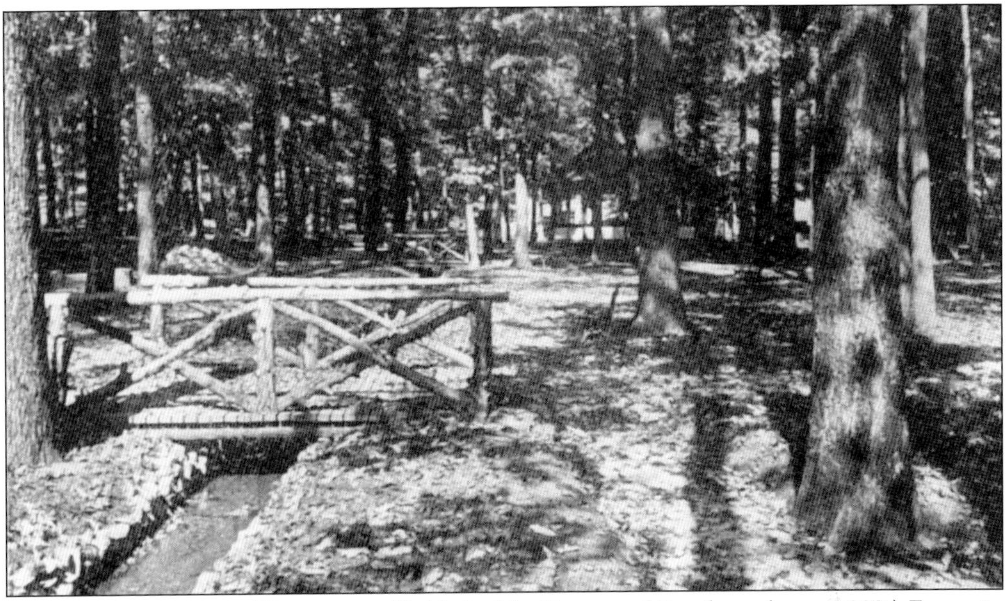

FOUNTAIN CITY PARK, KNOXVILLE. (Published by Reese and Reed; card sent 1908.) Fountain City is an old suburb of Knoxville dating back to 1791 and is the site of many religious camp meetings held in subsequent decades. The park originated about 1830 from the campground. The spring there, known as Fountain Head, inspired the community to grow up around it.

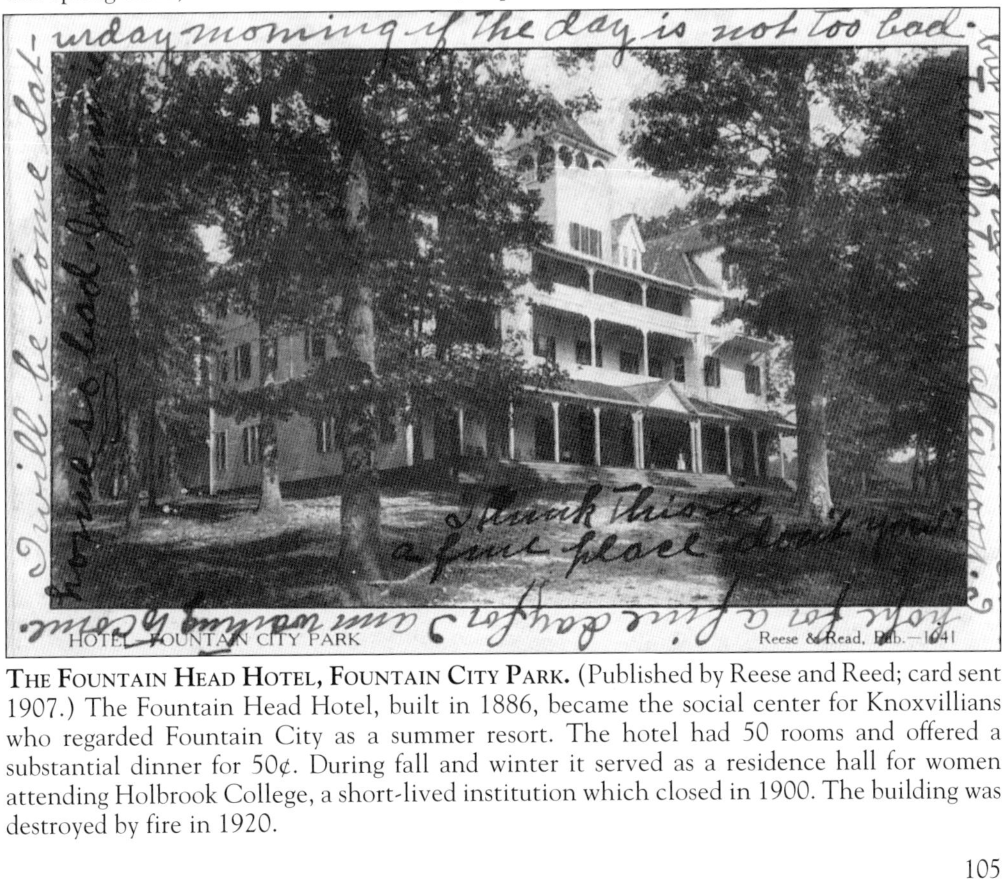

THE FOUNTAIN HEAD HOTEL, FOUNTAIN CITY PARK. (Published by Reese and Reed; card sent 1907.) The Fountain Head Hotel, built in 1886, became the social center for Knoxvillians who regarded Fountain City as a summer resort. The hotel had 50 rooms and offered a substantial dinner for 50¢. During fall and winter it served as a residence hall for women attending Holbrook College, a short-lived institution which closed in 1900. The building was destroyed by fire in 1920.

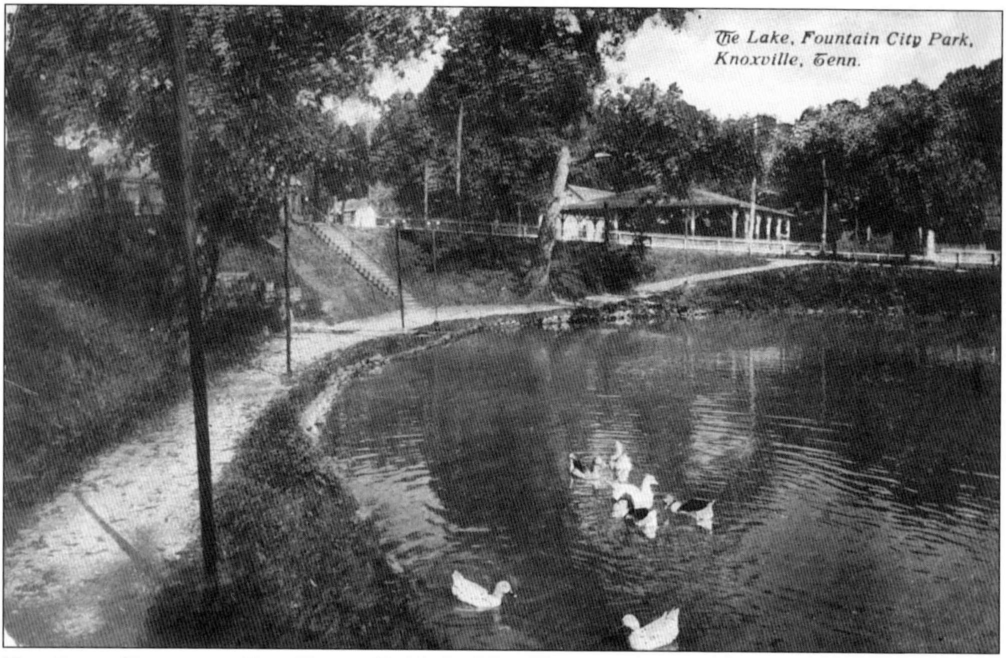

The Lake, Fountain City Park. (Published by Chapman Drug Co; card sent 1911.) In 1890 a steam railway began operating between Knoxville and the park. Its open-sided passenger cars were pulled by a noiseless ("dummy") engine. Then, as now, Fountain City Lake was a pleasant place to visit. In recent years, the Fountain City Garden Club has added shrubs and flowers and the Lions Club has added other improvements.

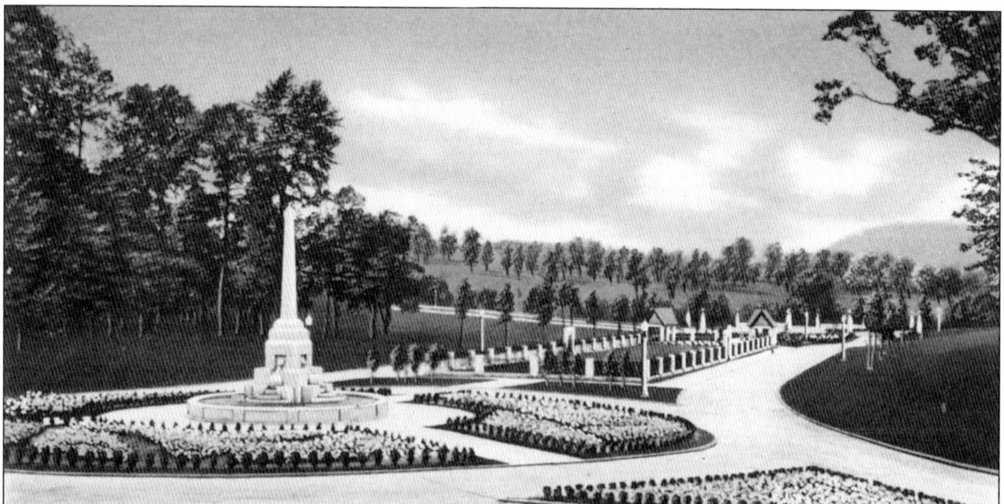

Talahi Park, Sequoyah Hills, Knoxville. (Published by Standard Souvenirs and Novelties, Knoxville.) Knoxville's first planned subdivision was Sequoyah Hills, named for Sequoyah, the Cherokee Indian who invented a phonetic alphabet. The entrance to the planned mall and park is here idealized; no homes are seen. The Sequoyah Hills area was annexed to the City of Knoxville in 1917 and now contains many beautiful homes.

Seven

The Black Community

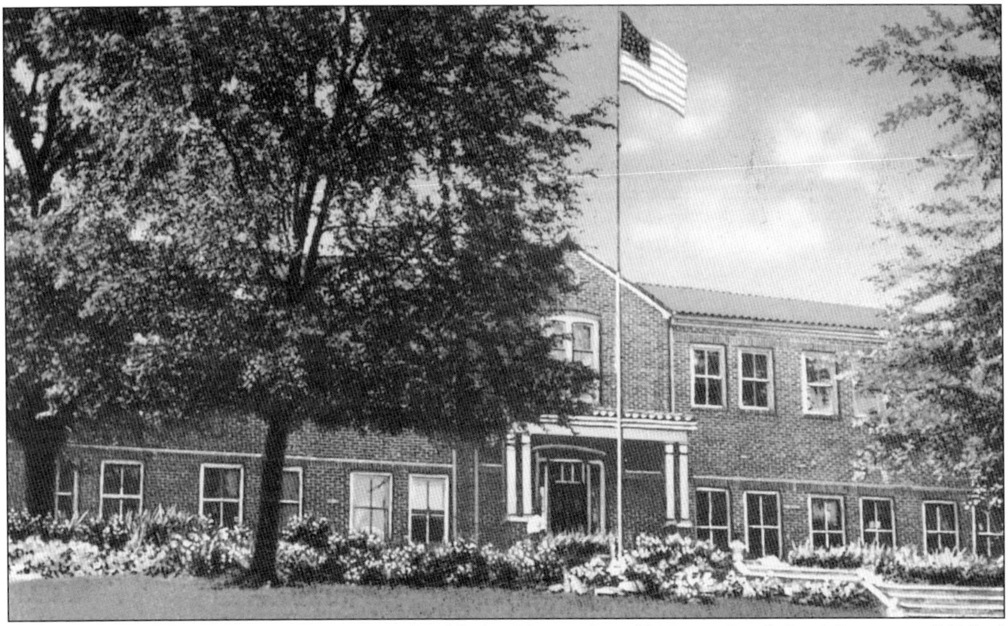

The Ethel Beck Home, Knoxville. (Published by Asheville Post Card Co.) James and Ethel Beck, lifelong participants in black community betterment, founded the Knoxville Colored Orphanage in 1919, which became the Ethel Beck Home of Negro Boys and Girls in 1941. James Beck was a teacher and a political activist; Ethel Benson Beck served in numerous community activities. The Beck Home ceased operations in 1953. Currently a Seventh-Day Adventist Church stands on the site.

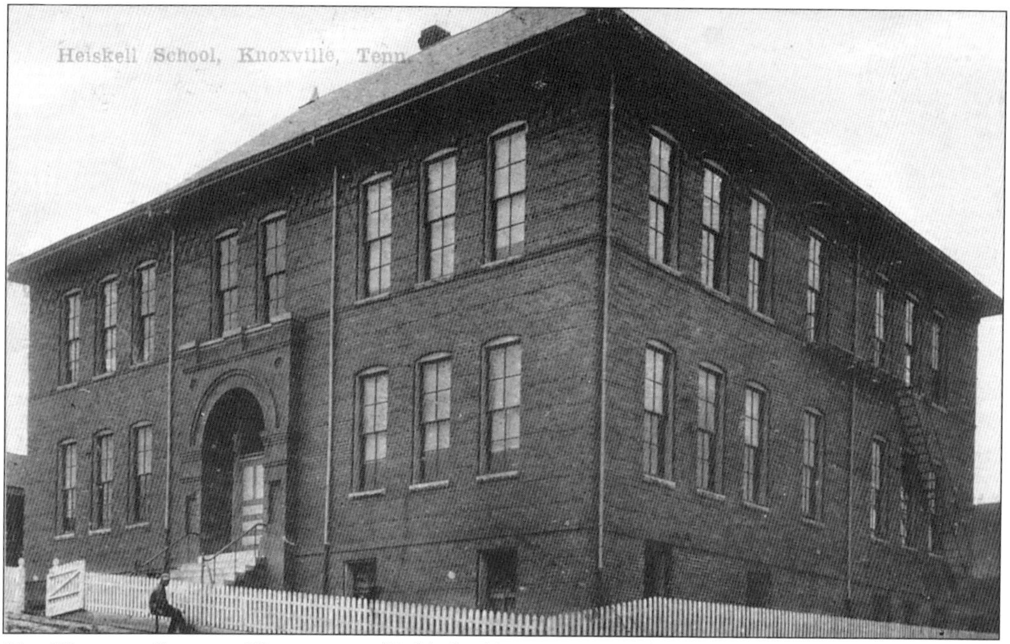

THE HEISKELL SCHOOL, KNOXVILLE. (Published by F.G. Asquith; card sent 1912.) Located at 903 Campbell Street, Heiskell Elementary School was dedicated in 1897. It was the first new school for blacks in Knoxville, named for Mayor Samuel G. Heiskell, under whose administration it was built. Mayor Heiskell was elected five different times; he was known for his personal integrity and his liberal views toward blacks.

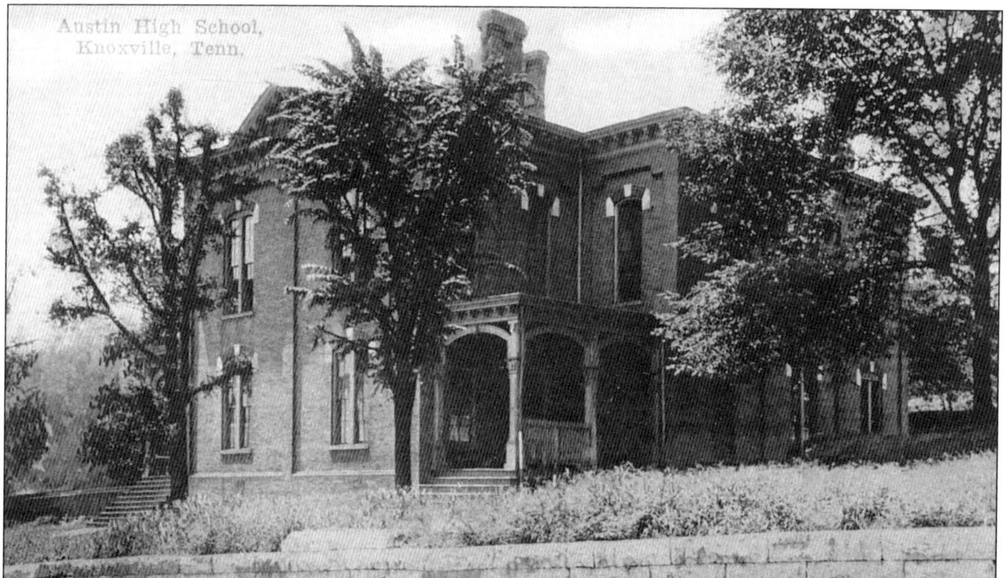

AUSTIN HIGH SCHOOL, KNOXVILLE. (Published by F.G. Asquith, Knoxville.) Austin High School, established at 327 South Central in 1879, was named for Miss Emily Austin, a white lady from Philadelphia who came to Knoxville in 1870 as a teacher of black children. Austin High has moved several times through the years. In 1968 the school merged with East High School and became Austin-East, now located on Martin Luther King Avenue.

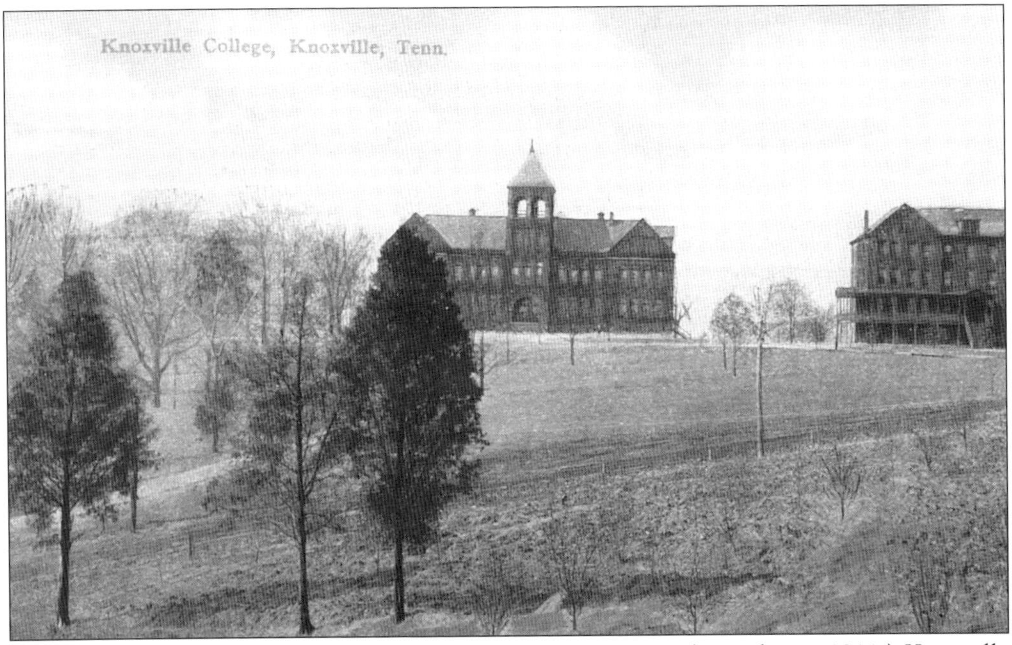

Knoxville College. (Published by A.C. Bosselman, New York; card sent 1911.) Knoxville College was founded in 1875 by the United Presbyterian Church as a grade and normal school for blacks. For many years it contained all the grades below college level; however, in 1930 the academy was closed. The college regularly grants B.A., B.S., and B.Mus. degrees.

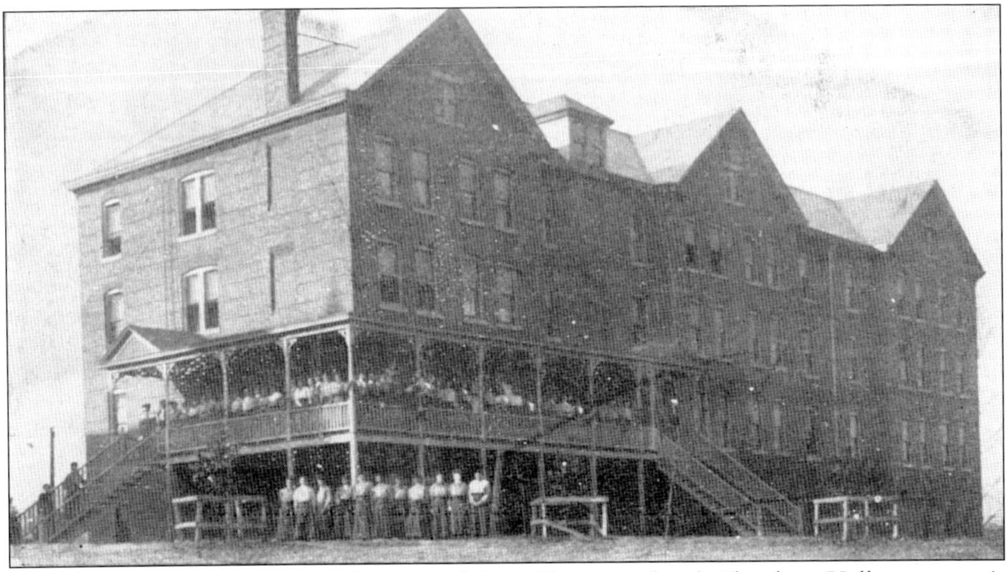

Elnathan Hall, Knoxville College. (No publication data.) Elnathan Hall, a women's dormitory, was built in 1893. It accommodated 100 students, and it had its own kitchen and dining room. In 1896 it was destroyed by fire but was rebuilt with improvements in 1898. The attire of the young women in the picture indicates that the photo was taken about 1910.

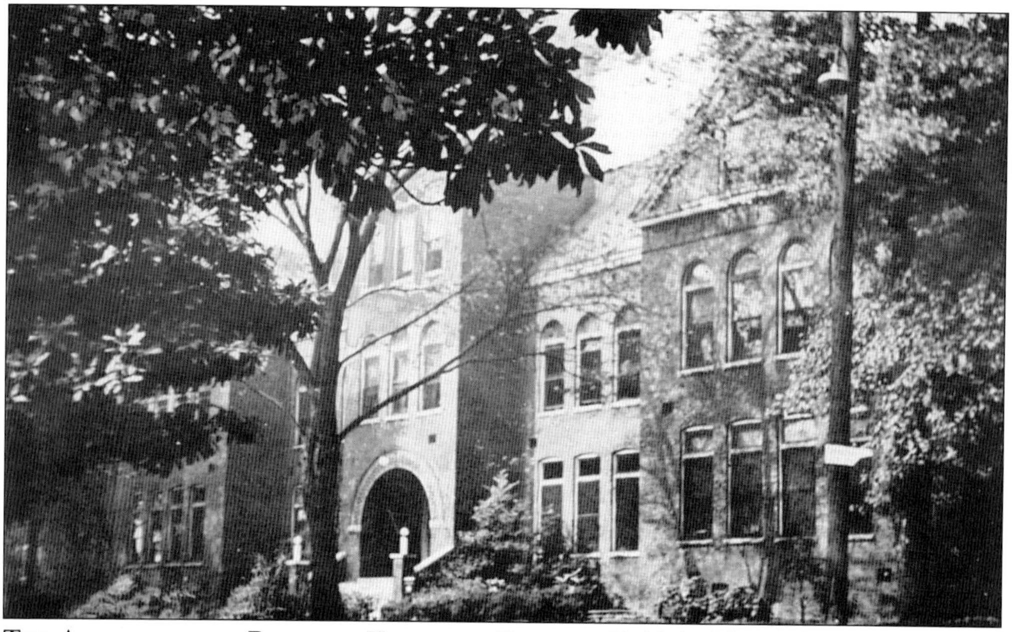

THE ADMINISTRATION BUILDING, KNOXVILLE COLLEGE. (Published by Eagle Post Card View Company, New York.) McKee Hall, the Administration Building, was erected in 1876, one of the first buildings on the campus. It housed not only the president's office, but also the chapel, kitchen, laundry room, dining room, classrooms, and dormitory rooms. Destroyed by fire in 1894, it was rebuilt on its original site in 1898 alongside a new dormitory for men.

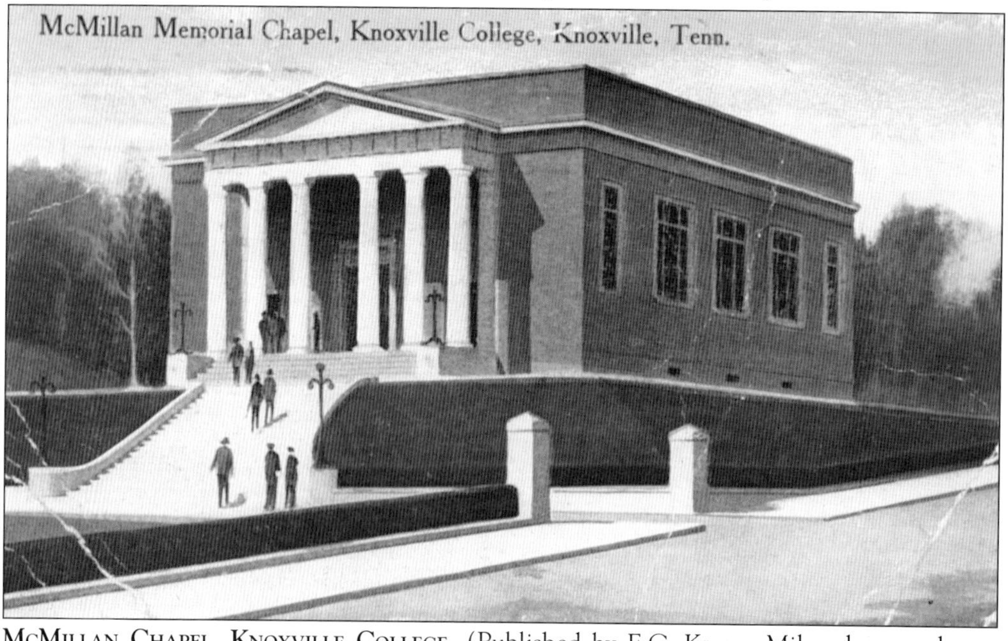

MCMILLAN CHAPEL, KNOXVILLE COLLEGE. (Published by E.C. Kropp, Milwaukee; card sent 1919.) Built in 1913, McMillan Chapel was named for Rev. W.H. McMillan, pastor of the Second United Presbyterian Church of Pittsburgh and chairman of the Freedmen's Bureau. Designed by William Thomas Jones, a 1909 graduate of the college, the building was erected by the industrial department using bricks made in the college brickyard.

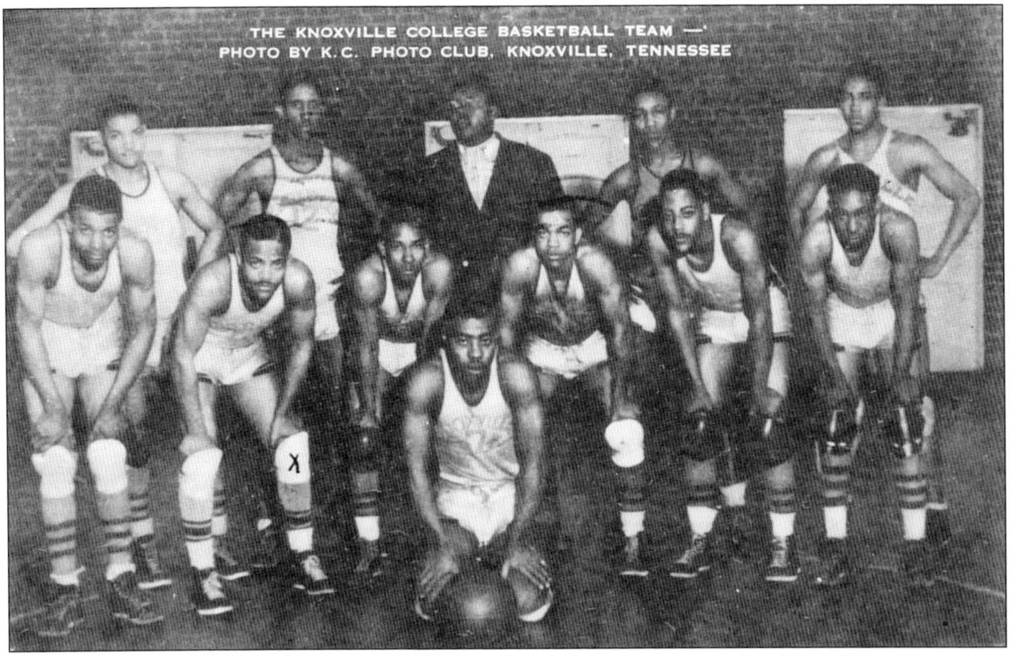

The Knoxville College Basketball Team. (Published by Artvue Card Co., New York; card sent 1946.) Knoxville College first formed a basketball team in 1927 when its gymnasium was built. After a slow start, the team improved substantially, and basketball has been a major sport since. This team, evidently from the early 1940s, seems stalwart and aggressive. The sender of the card, a woman, for a reason not revealed, put an "x" on the knee of one of the players in the picture.

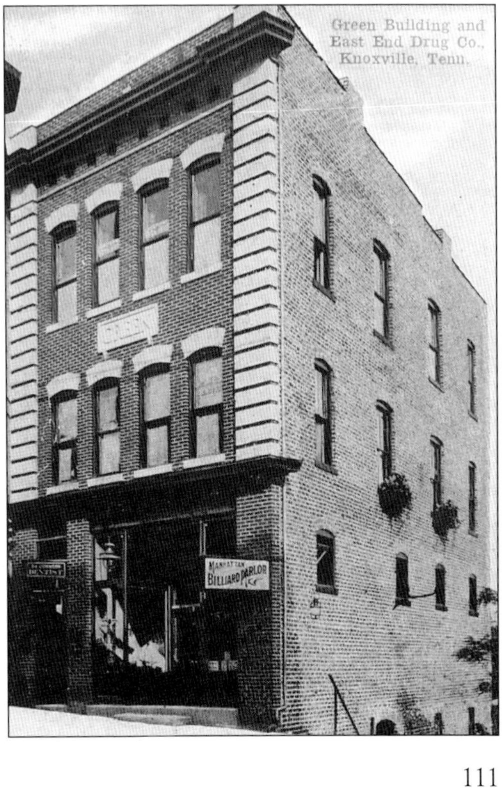

The Green Building and East End Drug Company. (Published by Gredig and Lynn, Architects, Knoxville.) During the first two decades of this century, the Green Building and East End Drug Company were located at 108 East Vine Avenue. The building was named for Dr. Henry Morgan Green, the esteemed local physician, who had an operating room upstairs. According to the signs, the building also housed Dr. Johnson, dentist, and the Manhattan Billiard Parlor.

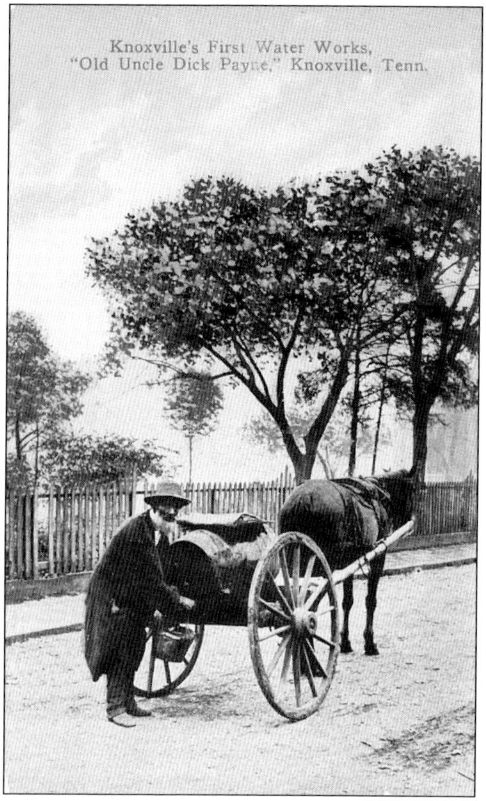

KNOXVILLE'S FIRST WATERWORKS, "OLD UNCLE DICK PAYNE." (No publication data.) Richard "Uncle Dick" Payne was probably Knoxville's first black businessman. He sold drinking water from nearby springs on the Knoxville streets between 1845 and 1885. There was no water purification plant in the city at that time. It is said that he sold more than a million buckets of drinking water. Payne Avenue was named for him.

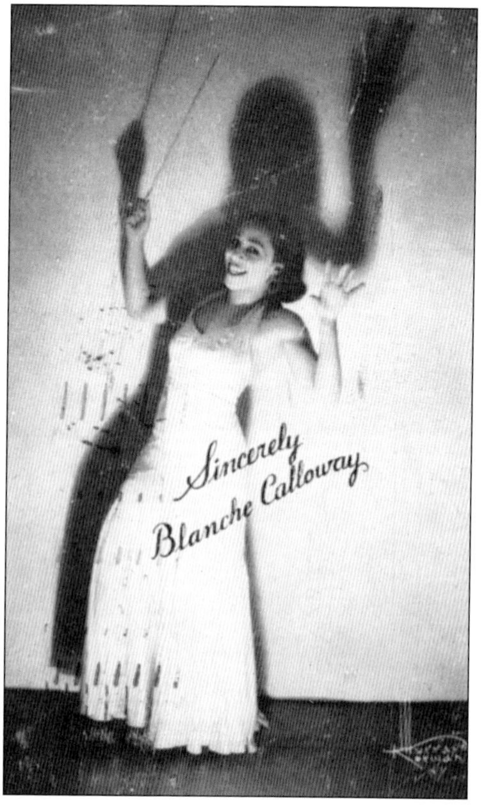

SINCERELY, BLANCHE CALLOWAY. (No publication data; card sent 1933.) Blanche Calloway, sister of the famous Cab Calloway, was a band leader and singer who traveled the entertainment circuits in the 1930s. Blanche had her own band and sang with it as featured performer. This card is her advance advertisement for an appearance at Sterchi Park on October 5, 1933. The imprint on the back of the card informs us that that there will be a "Dance for Colored. Admission 55¢. A section will be reserved for white people."

Eight

Potpourri

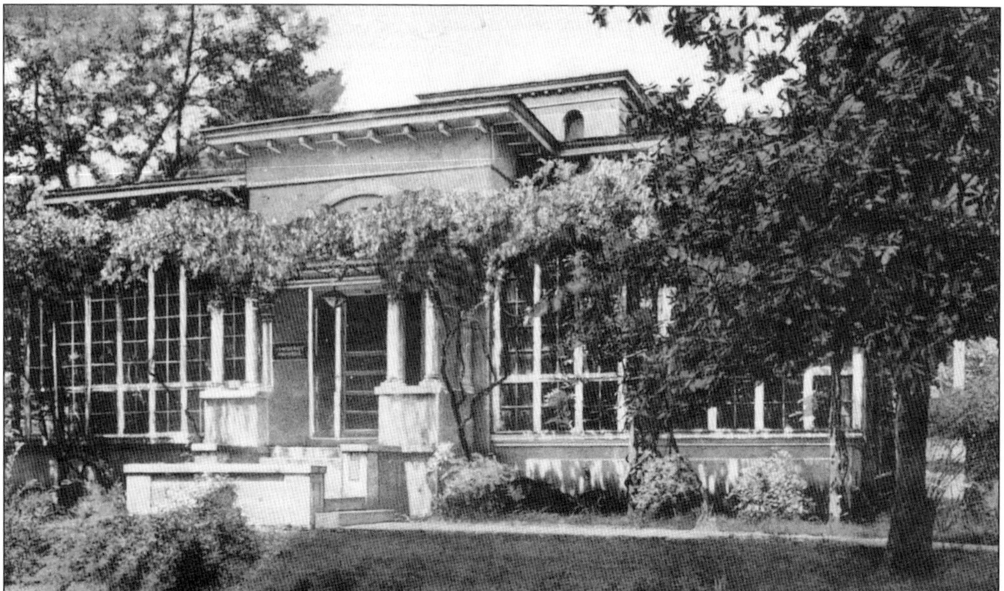

CONFEDERATE MEMORIAL HALL. (No publication data.) This building, now demolished, was the original Confederate Memorial Hall, built in 1862 and located at 803 Hill Avenue. The meetings and activities of the Knoxville Chapter of the United Daughters of the Confederacy (UDC) were held here. Since 1959 the UDC has administered Bleak House on Kingston Pike as a Confederate museum.

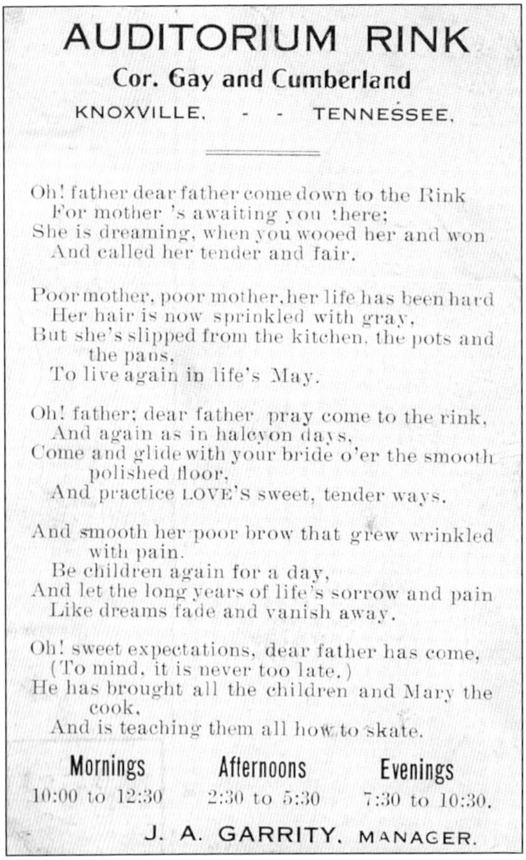

AUDITORIUM RINK

Cor. Gay and Cumberland

KNOXVILLE, - - TENNESSEE.

Oh! father dear father come down to the Rink
For mother 's awaiting you there;
She is dreaming, when you wooed her and won
And called her tender and fair.

Poor mother, poor mother, her life has been hard
Her hair is now sprinkled with gray,
But she's slipped from the kitchen, the pots and the pans,
To live again in life's May.

Oh! father; dear father pray come to the rink,
And again as in halcyon days,
Come and glide with your bride o'er the smooth polished floor,
And practice LOVE'S sweet, tender ways.

And smooth her poor brow that grew wrinkled with pain.
Be children again for a day,
And let the long years of life's sorrow and pain
Like dreams fade and vanish away.

Oh! sweet expectations, dear father has come,
(To mind, it is never too late.)
He has brought all the children and Mary the cook,
And is teaching them all how to skate.

Mornings	Afternoons	Evenings
10:00 to 12:30	2:30 to 5:30	7:30 to 10:30.

J. A. GARRITY, MANAGER.

The Auditorium Rink at the Corner of Gay and Cumberland. (No publication data.) Inside the huge round-roofed auditorium building at the corner of Gay and Cumberland, the skating rink was a popular place of family recreation. The quasi-humorous poem indicates that families are expected and that "father . . . is teaching them all to skate."

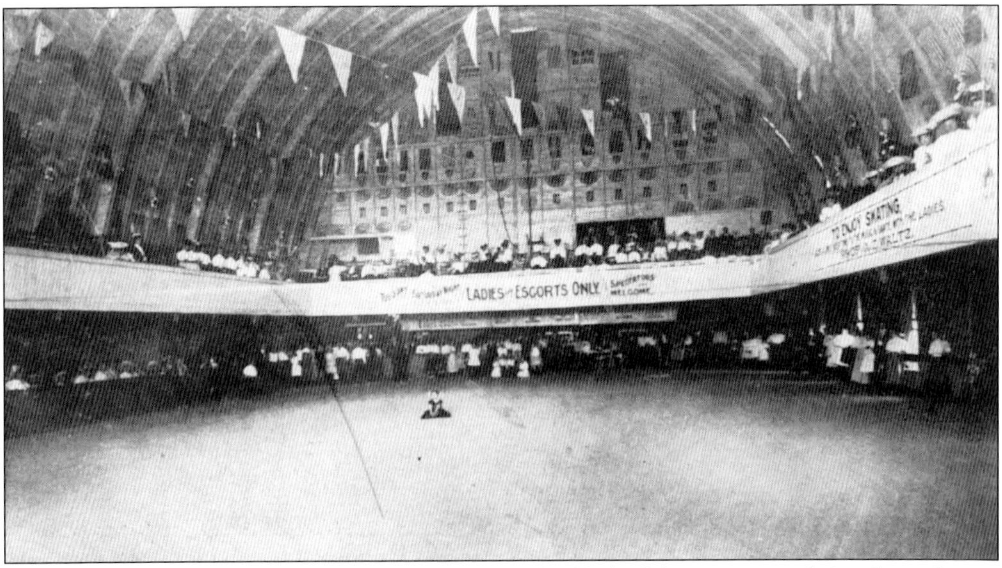

The Auditorium Skating Rink, Knoxville. (Published by Reese and Reed; card sent 1907.) The interior of the skating rink shows the cavernous dimensions of the building. The spectators in the balcony and the skaters on the sidelines appear to be watching a lone little girl in the center.

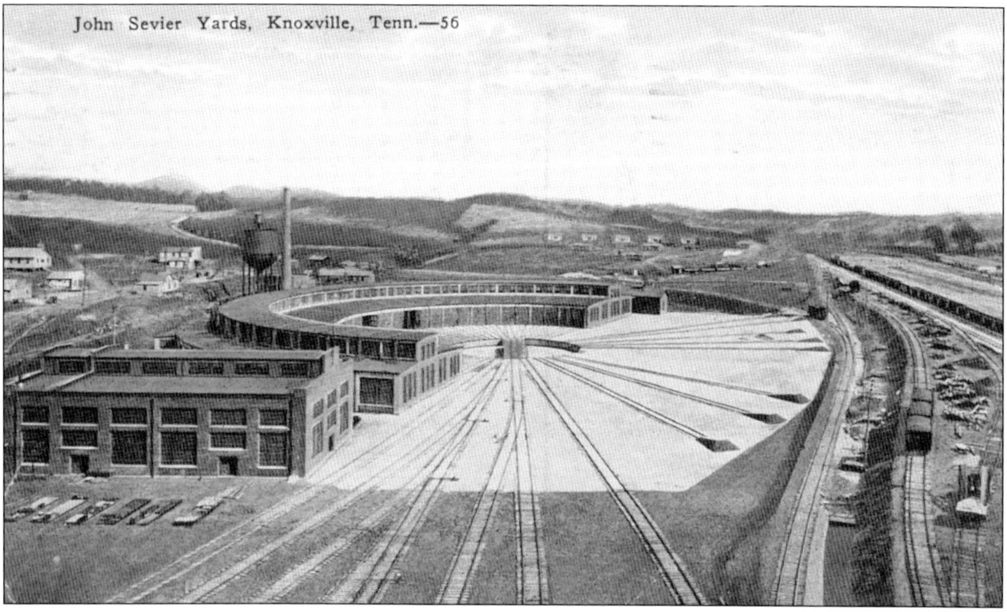

THE JOHN SEVIER YARDS, KNOXVILLE. (Published by E.C. Kropp, Milwaukee; card sent 1928.) Knoxville is the center of two railroad lines—the Southern Railway System and a north-south mainline of the Louisville and Nashville Railroad, both of which have contributed much to the city's economy through the years. Southern operates the John Sevier Yards north of the city, an important rail center that handles an average of 26 freight trains per day.

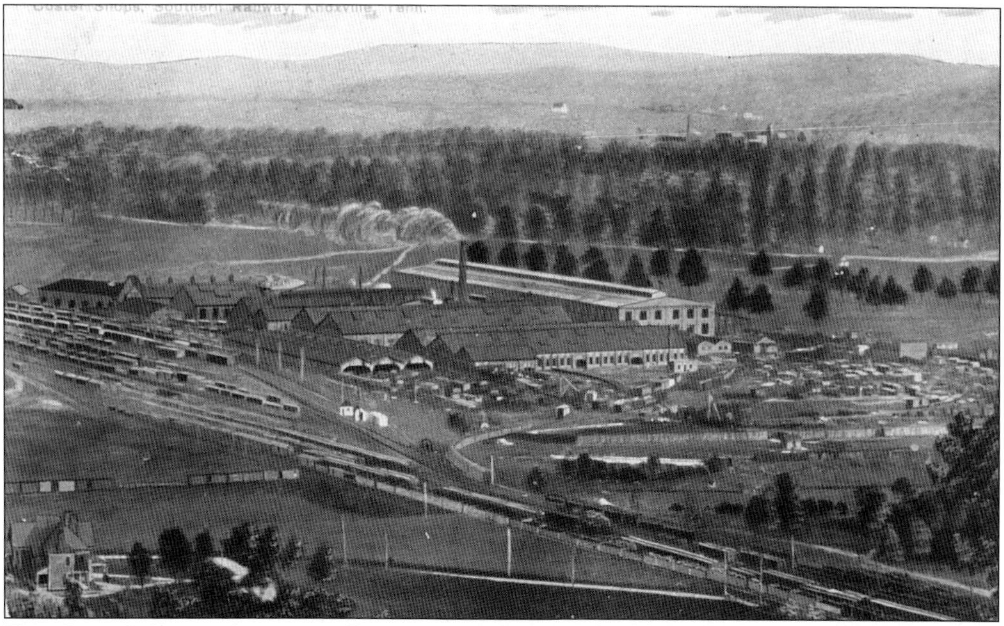

THE COSTER SHOPS, SOUTHERN RAILWAY, KNOXVILLE. (Published by Charles C. Cullen; card sent 1909.) An important car rebuilding facility of the Southern Railway, Coster Shops are located in north Knoxville. At one time Knoxville's largest employer of skilled mechanics and laborers, the shops have manufactured railroad cars, rails, car wheels, and virtually anything else needed by the railroad.

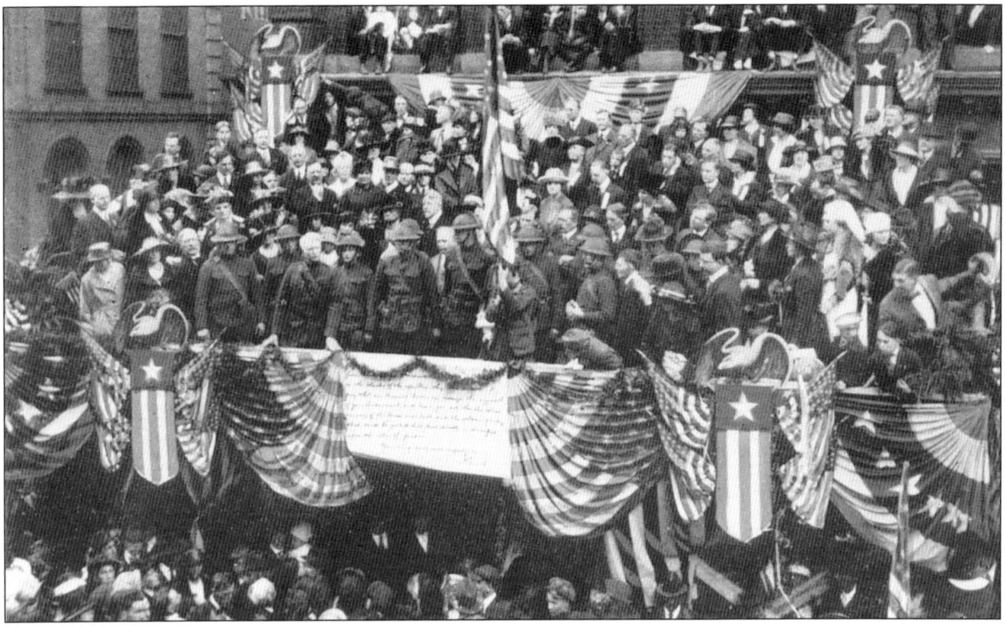

WELCOMING HOME THE 117TH INFANTRY, APRIL 5, 1919. (Published by CC&C Co.) East Tennessee sent many soldiers into World War I. Of particular note was the 117th Infantry, 30th Division, commanded by Brigadier General Lawrence D. Tyson. Here we see the reviewing stand on Gay Street on April 5, 1919, when General Tyson awarded medals for heroism to the 117th and welcomed them home.

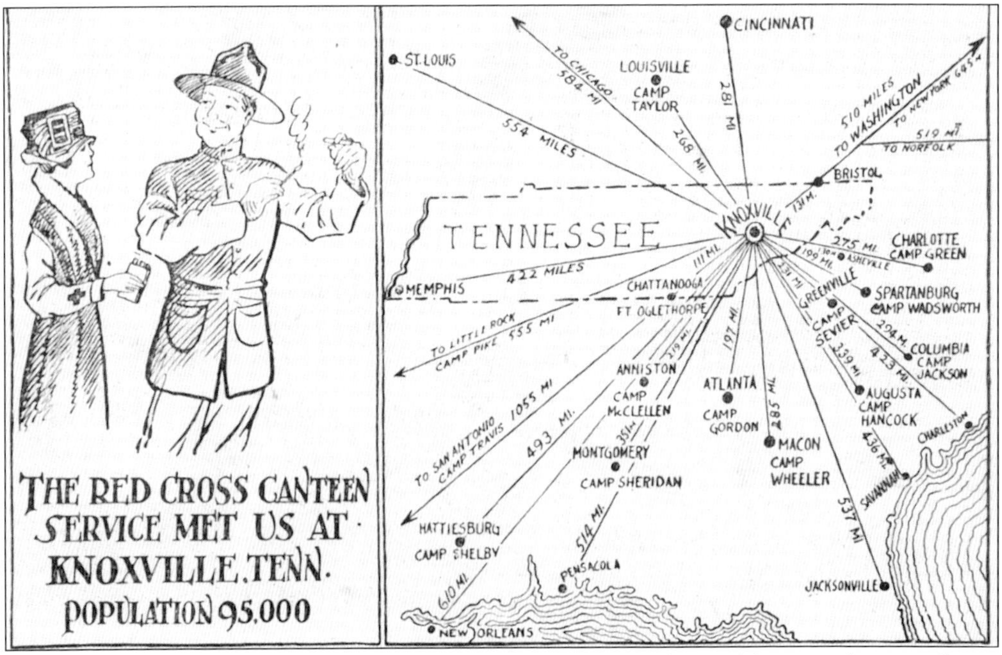

THE RED CROSS CANTEEN SERVICE MET US AT KNOXVILLE. (No publication data; card sent 1918.) During World War I, the Red Cross set up canteens for service men in railway stations all over the United States, and Knoxville was no exception. A map here pinpoints Knoxville and shows the locations of military camps in the near South.

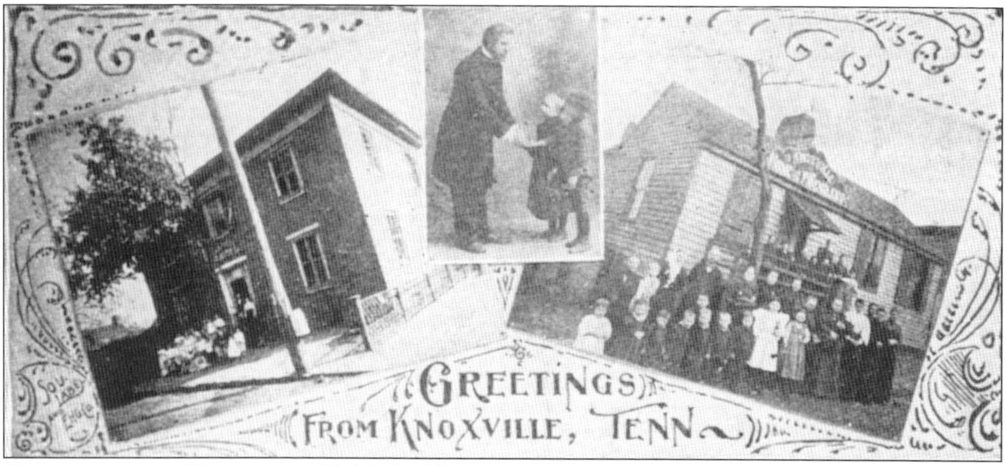

GREETINGS FROM KNOXVILLE. (Published by Reverend Lauritzen.) Early in the century Rev. J.R. Lauritzen, pastor of St. Peter's Evangelical Lutheran Church, operated a Children's Mission Home for orphans at 918 State Street. He published and sold a number of postcards showing Knoxville scenes or religious images to help finance his work. This card shows the reverend in the center vignette and two other pictures of orphans and their dwelling.

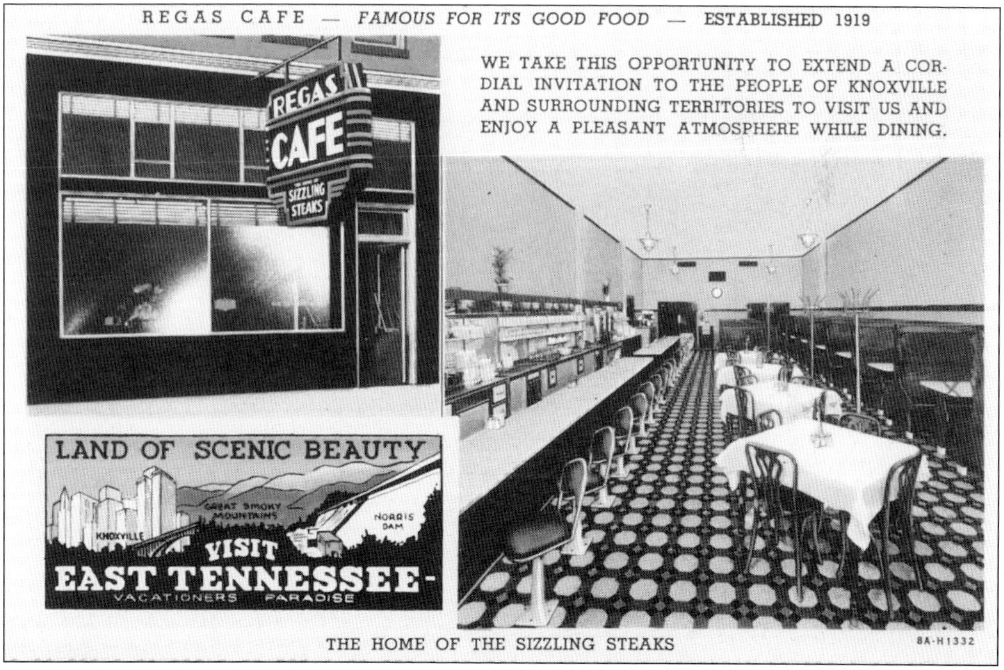

REGAS CAFE. (Published by Curt Teich, Chicago.) A long-lived and popular Knoxville restaurant, Regas Cafe at 318 North Gay Street was established in 1919. At first a 24-hour-a-day coffee shop, it is now much enlarged and elevated in ambience and is still at the same address. The postcard dates from the mid-1930s.

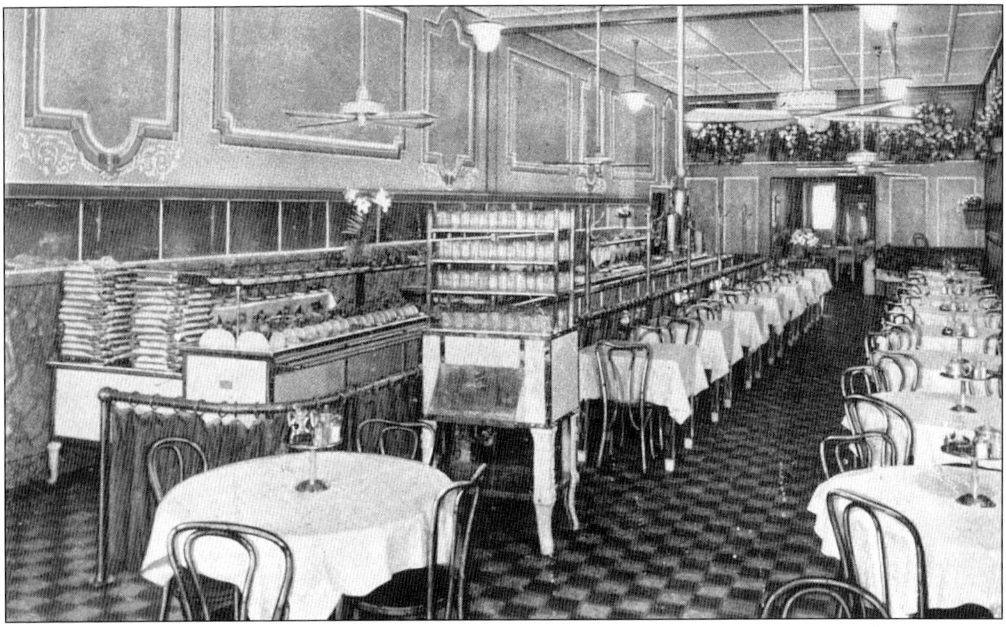

GOOD'S CAFETERIA-CAFE, KNOXVILLE. (Published by Harry G. Brown, Atlanta; card sent 1923.) Good's Cafeteria was located on Gay Street across from the Burwell Building and the Tennessee Theater. It endured for a number of years, as evidenced by many Gay Street scenes.

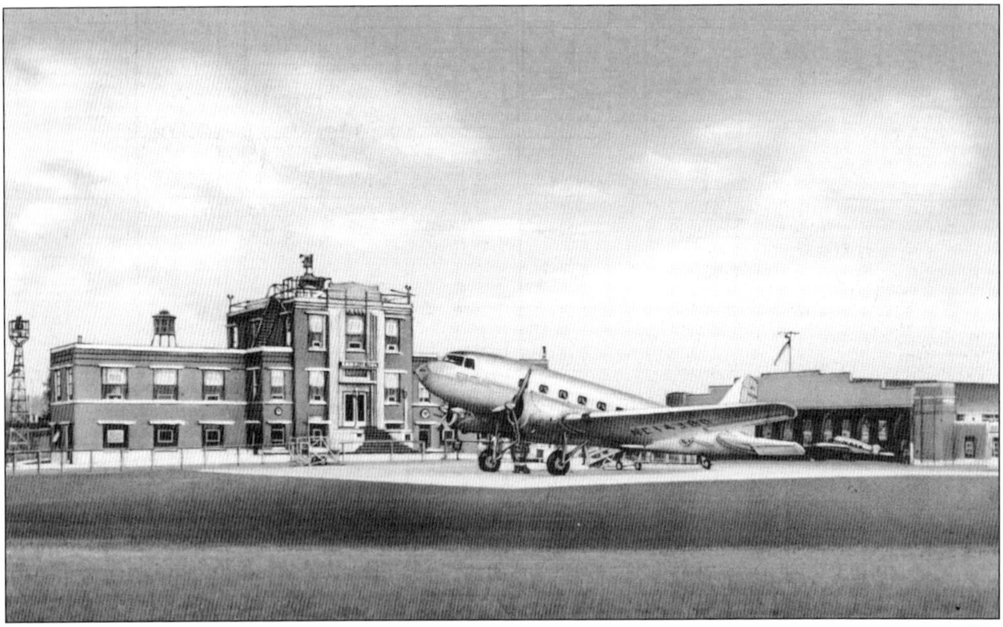

THE MUNICIPAL AIRPORT, KNOXVILLE. (Published by Standard News Agency, Knoxville; card sent 1943.) McGhee Tyson Municipal Airport was named for Naval Lieutenant McGhee Tyson, flyer son of Gen. L.D. Tyson, who was killed in World War I. First located on Sutherland Avenue, the airport was moved to Blount County 9 miles south of Knoxville in 1937. Constant growth and accelerated air traffic through the years have made it one of the country's principal airports.

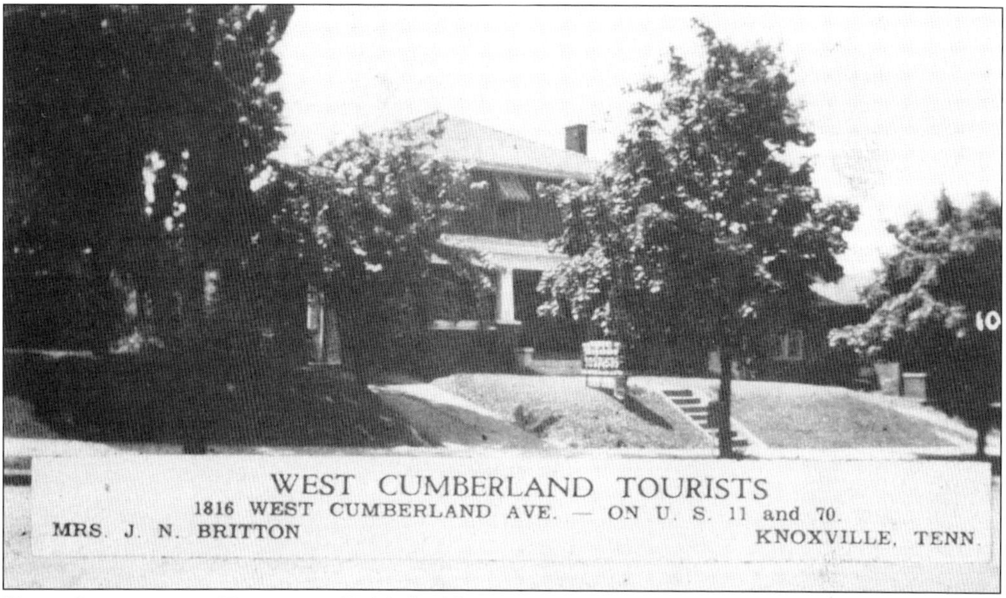

West Cumberland Tourists. (Published by National Press, Chicago; card sent 1939.) During the Depression years many larger homes were made into tourist hotels. This west Knoxville home on one of the major automobile routes undoubtedly provided a good night's rest at moderate rates.

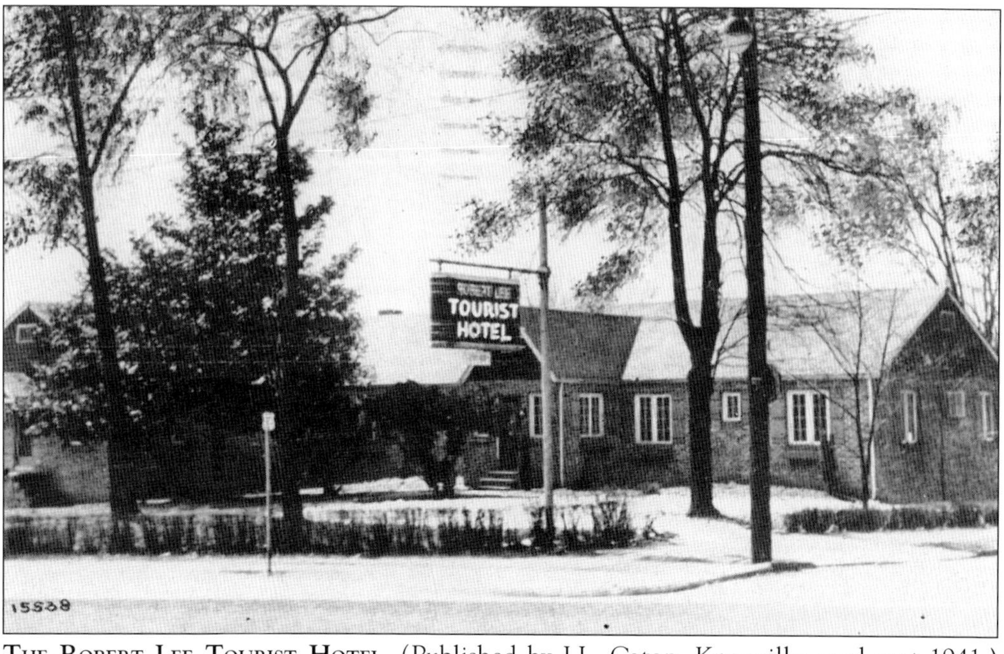

The Robert Lee Tourist Hotel. (Published by J.L. Caton, Knoxville; card sent 1941.) More commercially developed than many other tourist homes, the Robert Lee Tourist Hotel was on U.S. 25W at Scott and Central Streets in 1941. It was, according to its advertisement on the back of the card, "a unique hotel, Grade A, in a setting of fine old trees, reminiscent of the old South."

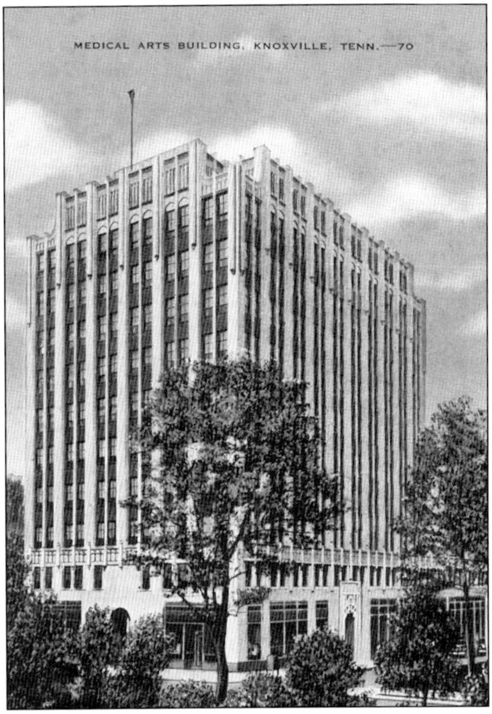

The Medical Arts Building. (Published by Standard News Agency, Knoxville.) Constructed in 1930 at the instigation of Dr. Herbert Acuff (1886–1951) and other local business and professional men, the Medical Arts Building stands at the corner of Main and Locust. Reflecting the Art Deco architecture of its time, it was tailor-made to meet the requirements of the medical profession. The architects were Manley and Young of Knoxville.

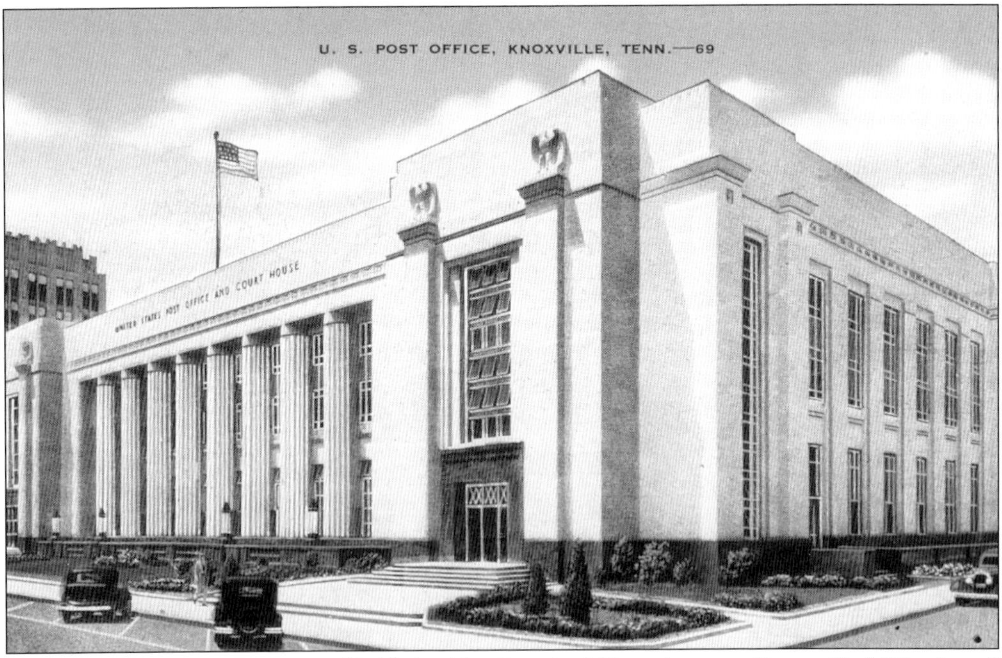

The Post Office, Knoxville. (Published by Standard New Agency, Knoxville.) The "new" post office, built in 1934 on Main Avenue, is made entirely from Tennessee marble quarried at Knoxville. The exterior is made of Craig pink, which appears white in sunny weather but turns rose pink on rainy days. The interior is constructed of assorted colors of marble. Baumann and Baumann, the architects, used a "stripped classical" style developed by Paul Cret in the 1920s, utilizing geometrical forms of cubes and cylinders.

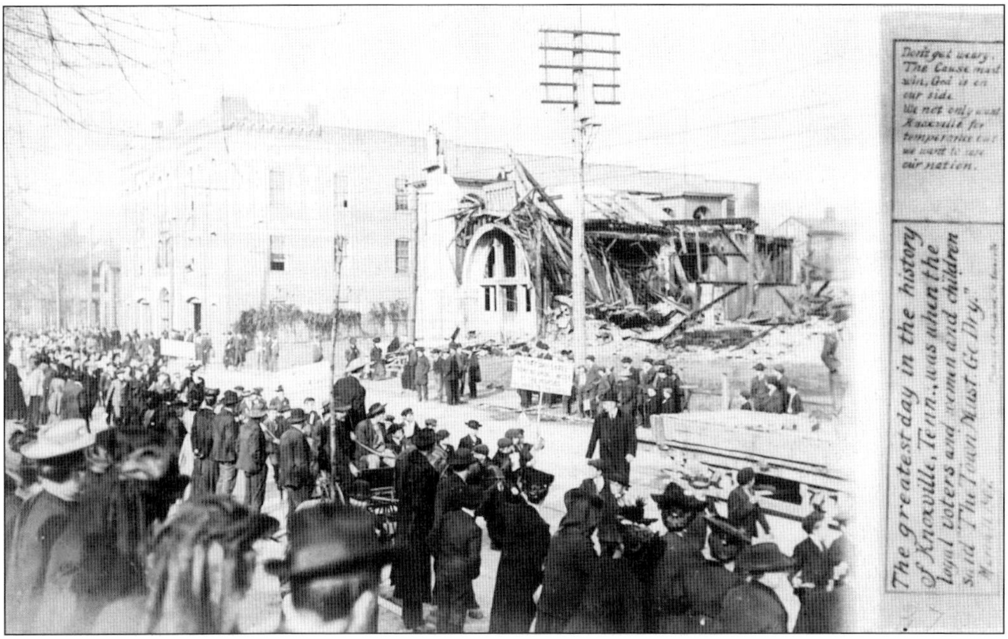

KNOXVILLE TEMPERANCE PARADE, 1907. (Real Photo; card unused.) Temperance was a major political issue in Knoxville in 1907. The voters overwhelmingly wished to prohibit the sale of liquor in the city, and many meetings and demonstrations took place. The picture shows a parade assembling on Main Avenue in front of the destroyed Woman's Building, which had only recently burned. The anti-liquor forces won the election, held March 11, 1907.

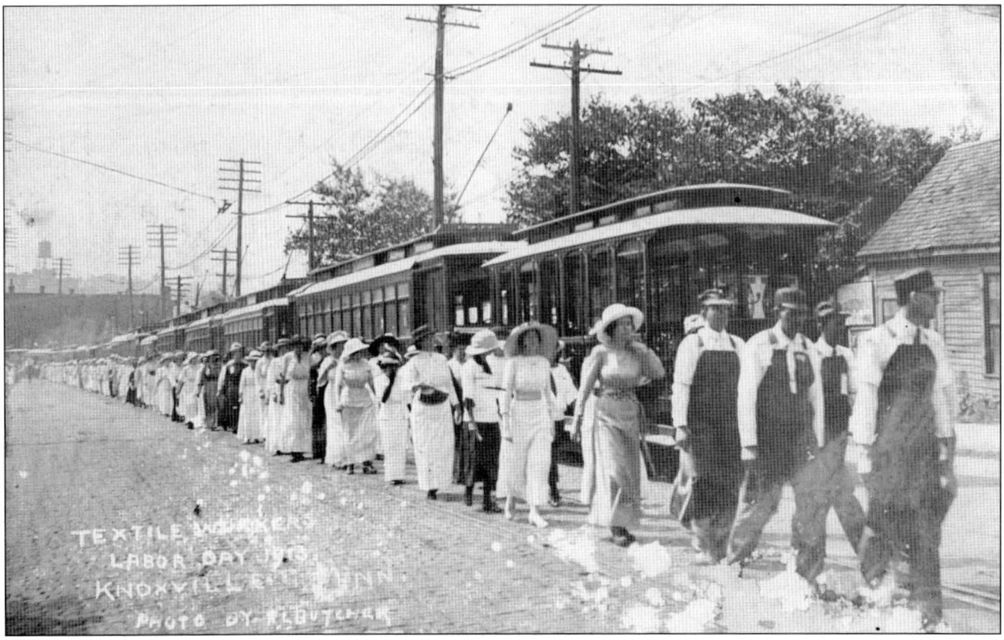

TEXTILE WORKERS, LABOR DAY, 1913, KNOXVILLE. (Real Photo; card unused.) Well-organized textile workers march from their trains or trolleys to begin a parade. The exact place is not identified here, nor is the textile plant from which the workers come.

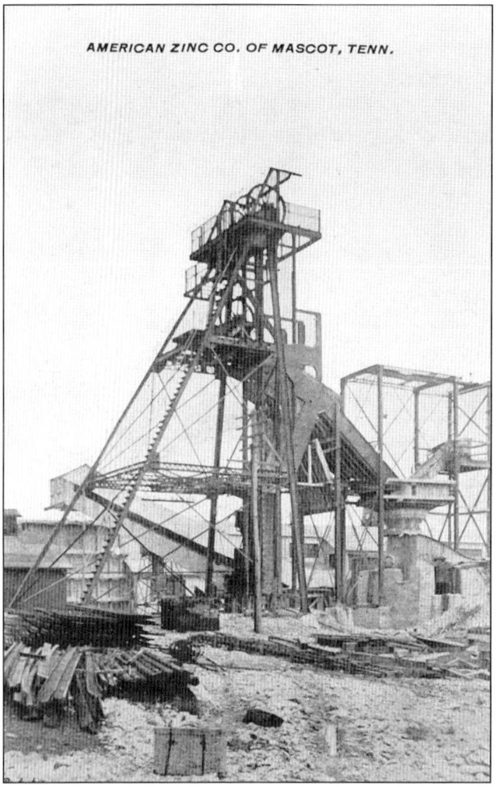

THE AMERICAN ZINC CO., MASCOT. (No publication data; card sent 1920.) Located about 8 miles northeast of Knoxville, Mascot was the home of the American Zinc Company of Tennessee in 1910. When American Zinc acquired the land, many farmers took up mining as a vocation and the town grew rapidly. After World War II the community declined, but it remains Knox County's principal mining center.

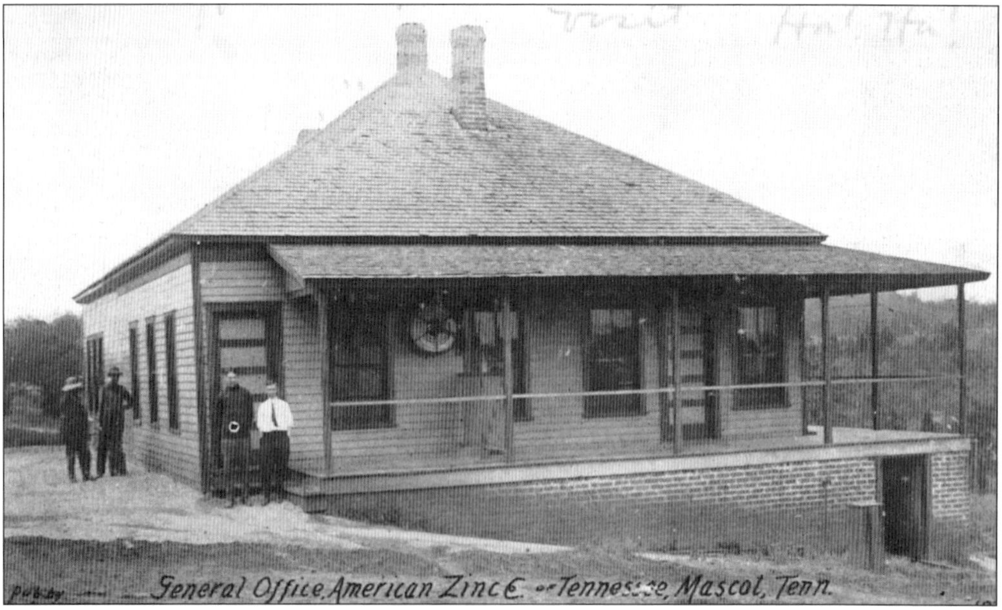

THE GENERAL OFFICE, AMERICAN ZINC, MASCOT, TENNESSEE. (No publication data; card sent 1914.) The village of Mascot originated in 1796, when various settlers acquired land here. In 1906 the Holston Mining Company arrived, selling out to American Zinc in 1910. In 1971 American Zinc sold to the American Smelting and Refining Company. The sender of this card says, "I am on #3 shift now as boss in the sludge room. All are doing well."

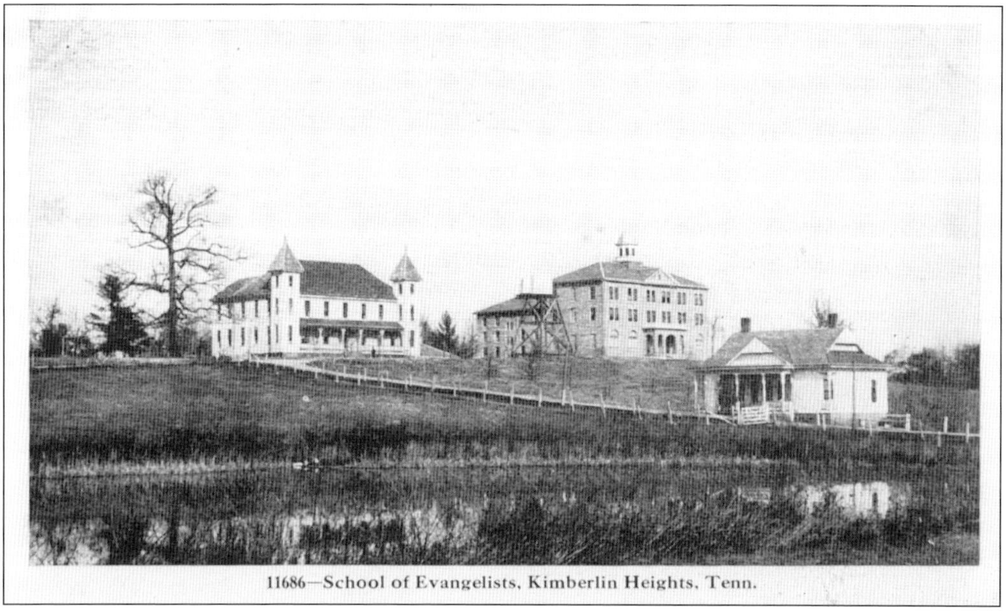

THE SCHOOL OF EVANGELISTS, KIMBERLIN HEIGHTS. (No publication data.) About 1887 the community of Gap Creek, located south of the French Broad, changed its name to Kimberlin Heights in memory of Jacob Kimberlin, a Revolutionary soldier who had built here in 1787. The postmaster, a great-grandson of Kimberlin, was Dr. Ashley S. Johnson, who had already established a correspondence Bible college. He opened Johnson Bible College in 1893.

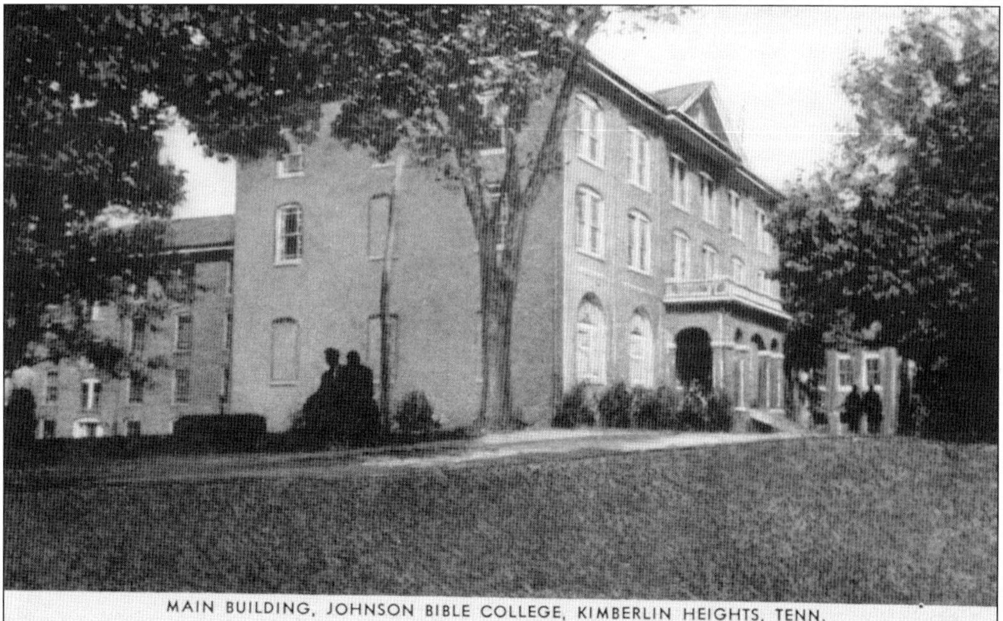

THE MAIN BUILDING, JOHNSON BIBLE COLLEGE, KIMBERLIN HEIGHTS. (Published by Eagle Post Card View Co., New York.) Dr. Ashley S. Johnson, founder of the college, lived with his family in the old Kimberlin home. His stated purpose for the college was to train ministers for the Christian church. He was president of the college until his death; he is buried on the grounds.

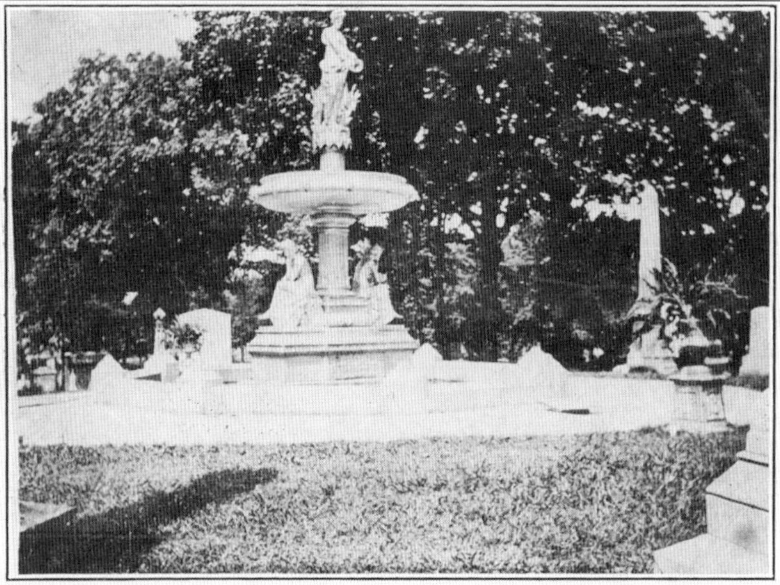

ALBERS' FOUNTAIN AND BROWNLOW MONUMENT, KNOXVILLE, TENN.
REESE & REED, PUBLISHERS, 1010

THE ALBERS FOUNDATION AND BROWNLOW MONUMENT, KNOXVILLE. (Published by Reese and Reed.) Andrew Jackson Albers (1844–1910) was a partner in the wholesale drug firm of Sanford, Chamberlain, and Albers. In 1890 he placed the Ella Albers Memorial Fountain in Old Gray Cemetery in memory of his wife. The cast-iron superstructure was removed during the scrap metal drive of World War II. The firm name later became Albers Drug Co. and exists today.

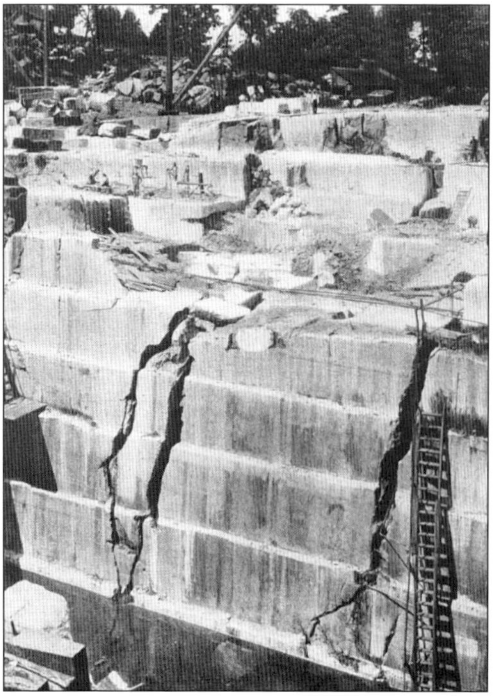

THE GREY EAGLE MARBLE QUARRY. (Published by International Post Card Co; card sent 1907.) Marble is one of Tennessee's most notable natural resources, along with coal and timber. The marble industry began to develop around the turn of the century, when several quarries began operations. The Grey Eagle Quarry here presents a typical scene. From this location about 20 varieties of marble in several colors have been taken.

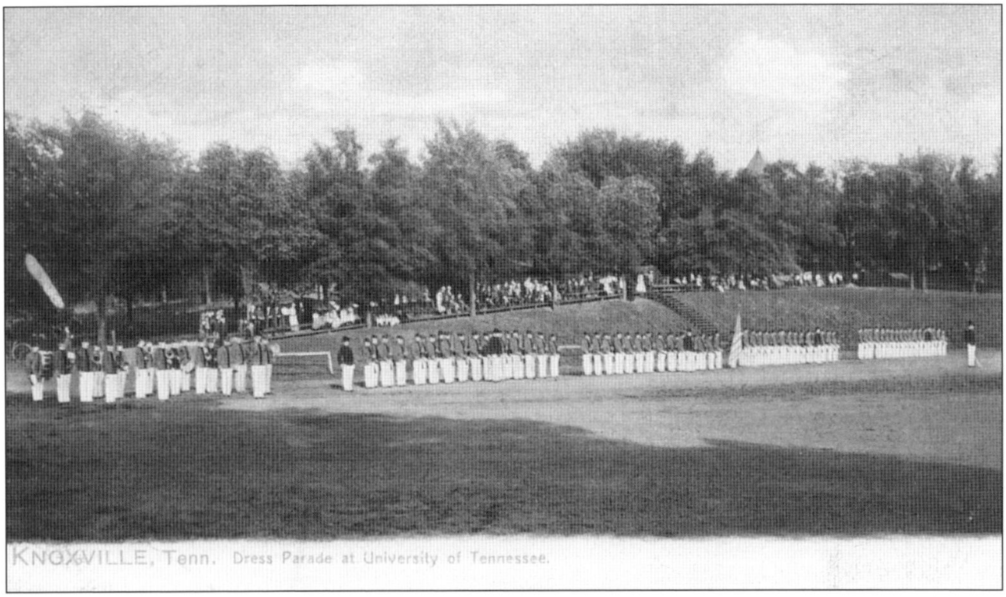

DRESS PARADE AT THE UNIVERSITY OF TENNESSEE. (Published by Raphael Tuck and Sons, London; series 2465.) The parade ground at the top of "the Hill" was in daily use between 1866 and 1917, for the University of Tennessee required military training of male students. The cadets on dress parade were a splendid sight, as seen here. This card was published about 1907.

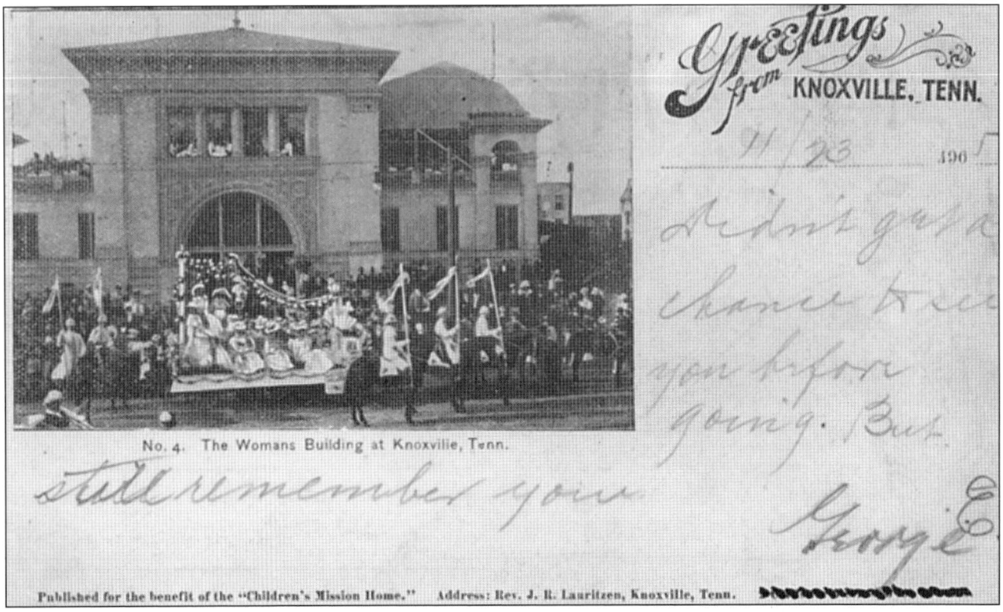

GREETINGS FROM KNOXVILLE, WOMAN'S BUILDING. (Published by Reverend Lauritzen; card sent 1905.) A rare card shows the Woman's Building (which perished in a fire in 1906) on Main Avenue as the locale of a parade or other festivity in an earlier year. Another of Reverend Lauritzen's cards, it was "published for the benefit of the Children's Mission Home."

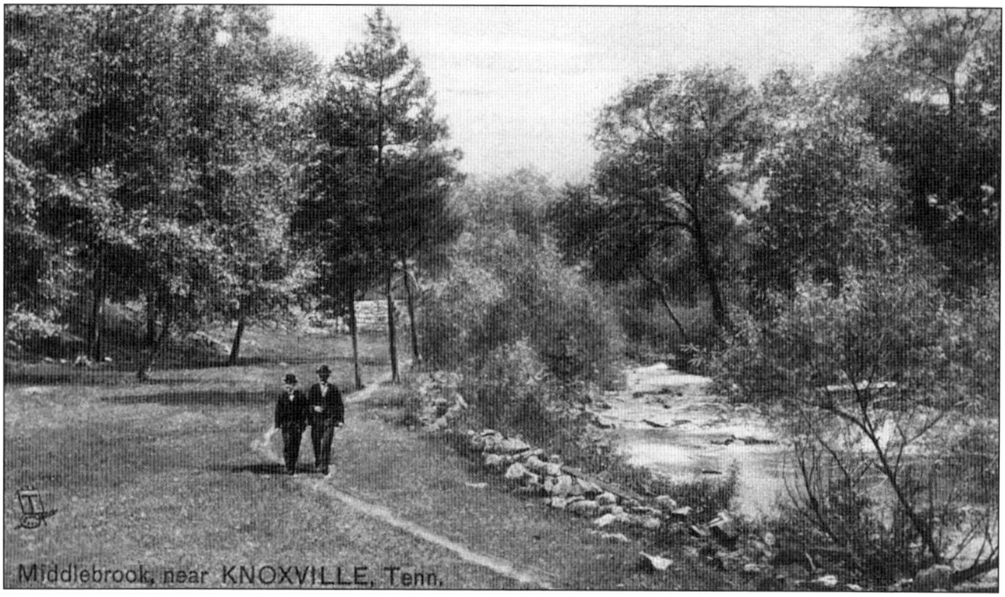

MIDDLEBROOK, NEAR KNOXVILLE. (Published by Raphael Tuck and Sons, London; card sent *c.* 1910.) In the early 1900s Middlebrook was a scenic farming area in the Bearden community of west Knoxville, where Gibson Morgan Hazen had built a country home in 1845. "Middlebrook," the house, not visible here, is regarded as one of Knoxville's historic treasures. Until 1886 Hazen and his partner Marcus D. Bearden operated a paper factory at the end of Papermill Road.

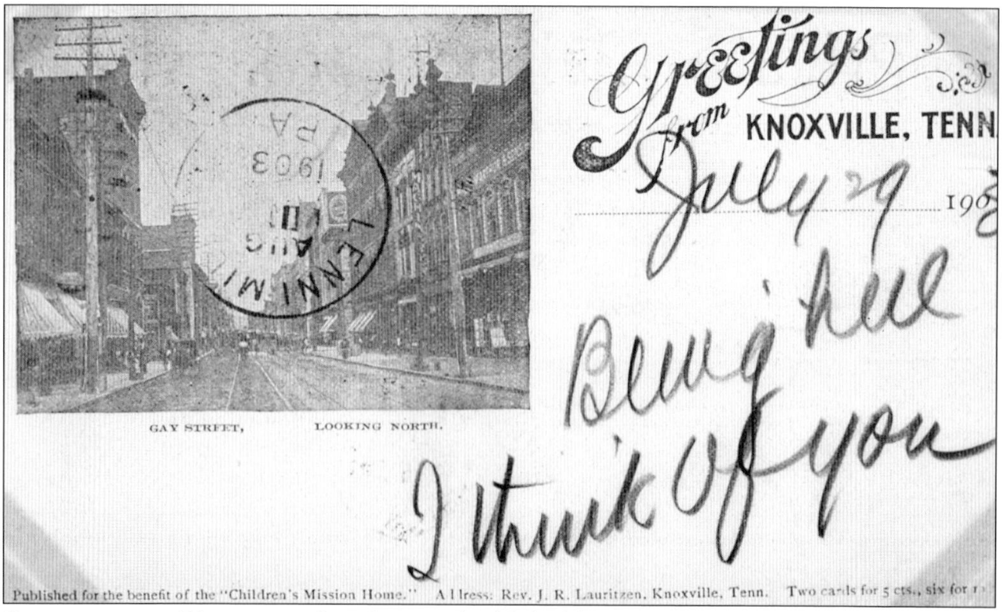

GREETINGS FROM KNOXVILLE, GAY STREET. (Published by Reverend Lauritzen; card sent 1903.) This very early postcard boldly inscribed in 1903 is another typical Lauritzen postcard published for the benefit of the Children's Mission Home.

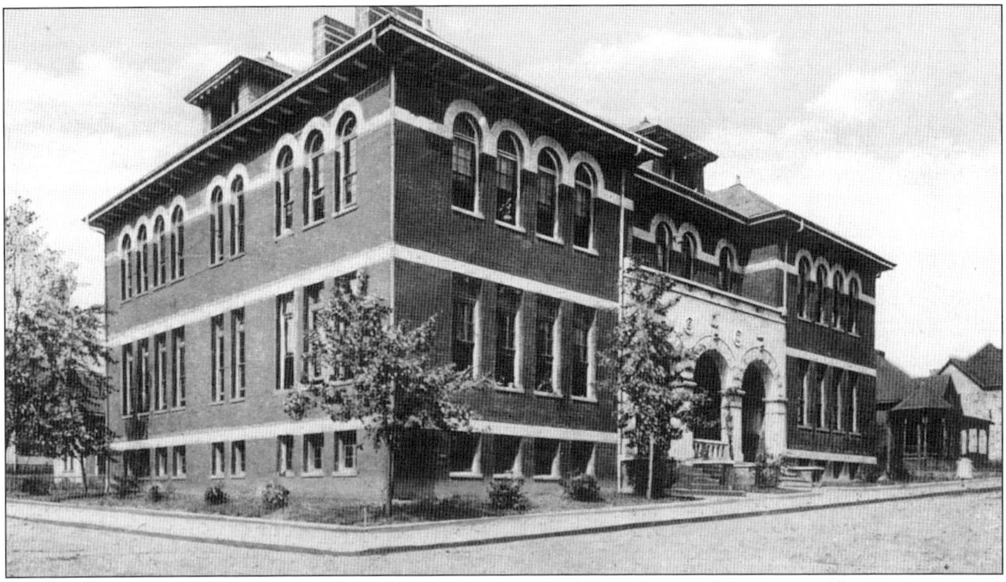

The J.H. McCallie School. (Published by Chapman Drug Co., Knoxville.) The elementary school building at the corner of Lovenia and Gratz Streets was named for J.H. McCallie, superintendent of Knoxville schools from 1897 to 1901. McCallie campaigned for the building of new schools to ease the crowding; he also added Latin and commercial courses to the high school curriculum. The building, long in run-down condition, has been destroyed. Its former site is now a grassy plot.

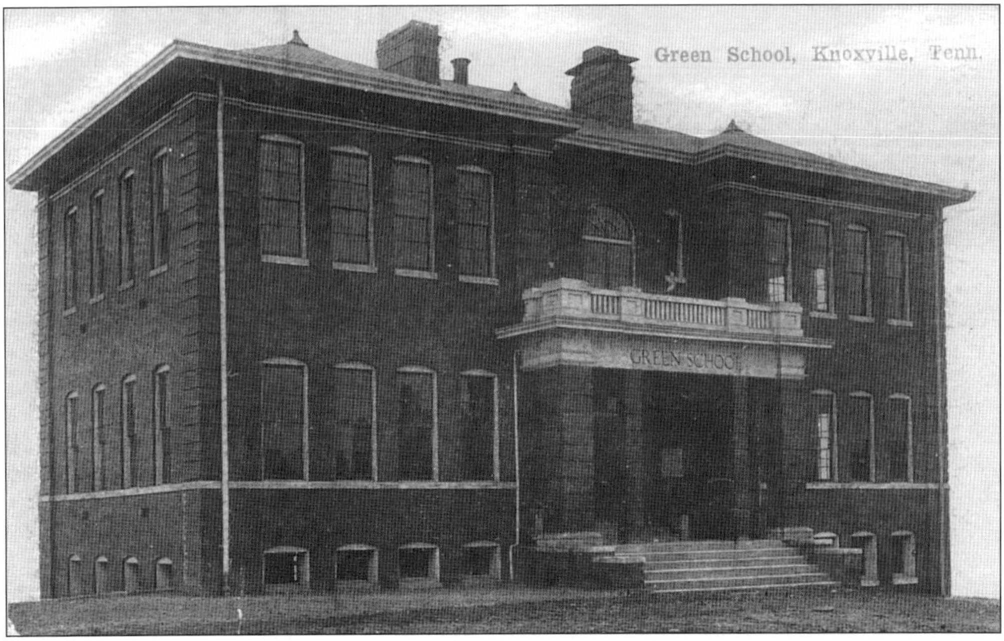

The Green School, Knoxville. (Published by Gredig and Lynn, Architects.) Built on Payne Avenue in 1909, the Green School was named for Dr. Henry Morgan Green (1877–1939), a local black physician who distinguished himself as president of the National Medical Association. The school was enlarged in 1915 and called Colored High School. When Austin High School was built in 1927, the Green School was restored to its former use and name.

Bibliography

Booker, Robert J. *200 Years of Black Culture in Knoxville, Tennessee: 1791–1991*. Virginia Beach, VA: Donning Company, 1993.

Brandau, Roberta Seawell, ed. *History of Homes and Gardens of Tennessee*. Nashville: Parthenon Press, 1936.

Creekmore, Betsey B. *Knoxville*. Knoxville: University of Tennessee Press, 1967.

———. *Knox County: A History in Pictures*. Norfolk, VA: Donning Company, 1988.

Deaderick, Lucille. *Heart of the Valley: A History of Knoxville, Tennessee*. Knoxville: East Tennessee Historical Society, 1976.

Goodman, W.M., ed. *The First Exposition of Conservation and Its Builders*. Knoxville: Knoxville Lithographing Co., 1914.

Hicks, Nannie Lee. *The John Adair Section of Knox County, Tennessee*. Knoxville: Nocturne Garden Club, 1968.

Isenhour, Judith Clayton. *Knoxville: A Pictorial History*. Norfolk, VA: Donning Company, 1978.

Johnson, Mayme Hart. *A Treasury of Tennessee Churches*. Brentwood, TN: JM Productions (JMP), 1986.

Manning, Russ, and Sandra Jamieson. *Historic Knoxville and Knox County: A Walking and Touring Guide*. Norris, TN: Laurel Place, 1990.

MacArthur, William J. Jr. *Knoxville: The Crossroads of the New South*. Knoxville: East Tennessee Historical Society, 1982.

McNabb, John Ross. *Tradition, Innovation, and Romantic Images: The Architecture of Historic Knoxville*. Knoxville: University of Tennessee Press, 1991.

Montgomery, James Riley, Stanley J. Folmsbee, and Lee Seifert Greene. *To Foster Knowledge: A History of the University of Tennessee, 1794–1970*. Knoxville: University of Tennessee Press, 1984.

Patrick, James. *Architecture in Tennessee, 1768–1897*. Knoxville: University of Tennessee Press, 1981.

Ross, William Cary. *A Scrapbook for My Grandchildren*. New York: G.P. Putnam's Sons, 1941.

Rothrock, Mary U., ed. *The French Broad–Holston Country: A History of Knox County, Tennessee*. Knoxville: East Tennessee Historical Society, 1946.

St. John's Lutheran Church. "History of St. John's Lutheran Church." n.p., n.d.

Tennessee Historical Commission. *Tennessee Historical Landmarks*. 7th ed., 1980.